BORDER

'A brilliant and hugely satisfying book' Philip Marsden

'Hums with the mystery, superstition, and terrible beauty of a place crushed between man-made borders but also defiantly announcing its sacred otherness. I can't stop thinking about it' Frances Stonor Saunders

'Riveting, beautifully written' *TLS*

'An exceptional book' *New Statesman*

'A timely and important book, and I can't recommend it highly enough' *Big Issue*

'Magical, brilliant and original' Pico Iyer

'Lyrical and gorgeous' *Literary Review*

'[A] timely and moving book' *Country Life*

'A magical book' *Scottish Legal News*

'Remarkable… [Kassabova] comes to it with a poet's sensibility and a journalist's curiosity. A wonderful, luminous combination' *New Internationalist*

'Extraordinary' *Geographical Magazine*

'This beautiful, tragic and universal new book may just be the most important you read in this year of Brexit' *Skinny*

'[Kassabova] writes exquisite prose, dripping with scorn for the politicians whose bone-headed rules and careless greed despoil the land and ruin the lives of those who still live there' Edward Lucas, *1843 Magazine*

BORDER

A Journey to the Edge of Europe

KAPKA KASSABOVA

GRANTA

Granta Publications, 12 Addison Avenue, London W11 4QR

First published in Great Britain by Granta Books, 2017

This paperback edition published in 2018

A CIP catalogue record is available from the British Library

5 7 9 8 6

ISBN 978 1 78378 320 5 (paperback)
ISBN 978 1 78378 319 9 (ebook)

www.grantabooks.com

Typeset in Bembo by Patty Rennie
Printed and bound by CPI Group (UK) Ltd, Croydon, CR0 4YY

People forget we are only guests on this earth, that we come on to it naked and depart with empty hands.

Esma Redžepova, Gypsy singer

CONTENTS

PART FOUR: STARRY STRANDJA

PREFACE

This book tells the human story of the last border of Europe. It is where Bulgaria, Greece, and Turkey converge and diverge, borders being what they are. It is also where something like Europe begins and something else ends which isn't quite Asia.

This is roughly the geography of it, but the map will only take you so far before you find yourself in the ancestral forest that teems with shadows and lives out of time. That is where I ended up going anyway. It may be that all borderlands hum with the frequencies of the unconscious; after all, borders are where the fabric is thin. However, this border region hums with an especially siren-like tone, and distinguishes itself for three reasons. One, because of unfinished business from the Cold War; two, because it is one of Europe's great wildernesses; three, because it has been a continental confluence ever since there have been continents.

My generation in Eastern Europe came of age just as the Berlin Wall came down. This border shadowed my Bulgarian childhood during the last era of 'Socialism with a human face', as the unfortunate slogan had it. So it was natural that a journey along the boundary quickly became fairly involving for me. Once near a border, it is impossible not to be involved, not to want to exorcise or transgress something. Just by being there, the border is an invitation. Come on, it whispers, step across this line. If you dare. To step across the line, in sunshine or under cover of night, is fear and hope rolled into one. And somewhere waits a ferryman whose face can't be seen. People die crossing borders, and sometimes just being near them. The lucky ones are reborn on the other side.

An actively policed border is always aggressive: it is where power suddenly acquires a body, if not a human face, and an ideology. One obvious ideology that concerns borders is nationalist: the border is there to divide one nation-state from another. But a more insidious ideology is centralist in practice: the belief that the centre of power can issue orders from a distance with impunity, and sacrifice the periphery; that what is out of mainstream sight is out of memory. And border zones are always the periphery, always out of mainstream sight.

Oddly, it was living in a borderless country that spurred me on this border journey. I live in rural Scotland, which counts as a sort of periphery if your centre is 'the central belt' of Edinburgh and Glasgow, and even more of a periphery if your centre is London. Scotland has traditionally been a land of diversity and liberty, of islands and eccentricities. But in Scotland, the era of the corporate bureaucrat with a human face has dawned, and every day another centralist rule clamps down on remote communities, another forest comes down to make space for quarries, wind farms that don't seem to turn, giant pylons that seem to conduct no electricity. Wastelands of subsidised profit appear where once there was quirky wilderness. Watching the roughshod levelling of the Scottish Highlands, I became curious about my native Balkan peripheries. I wanted to know what was happening there, twenty-five years after I had left.

If we divide political borders into soft and hard, the border of this book has half a century of Cold War hardness: Bulgaria to the north versus Greece and Turkey to the south marked the cut-off line between the Warsaw Pact countries of the Soviet bloc and NATO member states in the Western sphere of influence. In short, it was

Europe's southernmost Iron Curtain, a forested Berlin Wall darkened by the armies of three countries. It was deadly, and it remains prickly with dread to this day.

Now the Greek–Bulgarian border is softened by shared membership of the European Union. The Turkish–Bulgarian and Turkish–Greek borders have lost their old hardness but acquired a new one: its symptom is the new wire walls erected to stem the human flow from the Middle East. I happened to be there just as the flow was becoming a haemorrhage. Global movement and global barricading, new internationalism and old nationalisms – this is the systemic sickness at the heart of our world, and it has spread from one periphery to another, because nowhere is remote any more. Until you get lost in the forest, that is.

But the initial emotional impulse behind my journey was simple: I wanted to see the forbidden places of my childhood, the once-militarised border villages and towns, rivers and forests that had been out of bounds for two generations. I went with my revolt, that we had been chained like unloved dogs for so long behind the Iron Curtain. And with my curiosity, to meet the people of a terra incognita. When Herodotus wrote, in the fifth century BC, 'With Europe… no one has ever determined whether or not there is sea either to the east or to the north of it,' he could have been speaking about this part of the continent in the early twenty-first century. As I set out, I shared the collective ignorance about these regions not only with other fellow Europeans further away, but also with the urban elites of the three countries of this border. In the minds of those who don't live or visit there, this border is another country, a bit like the past, where they do things differently.

Whenever you come to speak of the Balkans, the weary old trope of the bridge is unavoidable, but nowhere is it more observably true than in the south-east Balkans, the everyday gateway between what we are used to calling East and West.

Paradoxically, this remains a hidden fold of the global matrix. Some of the realms I crossed are beautiful enough to give you a heart attack, but only botanists and ornithologists visit there, smugglers and poachers, the heroic, and the lost. Then there are the locals.

History is written by the victors, they say, but it seems to me that history is written above all by those who weren't there, which may be the same thing. I had a hunger: to look into the faces of those who *are* there, hear their stories, eat with them, learn new words. What does it take to dwell in a borderland so infused with ancient and modern myth, so psychically magnetised? None of us can escape boundaries: between self and other, intention and action, dreaming and waking, living and dying. Perhaps the people of the border can tell us something about liminal spaces.

The journey I describe here is circular, and follows the contours of natural realms within the border zone. I started on the Black Sea, at the edge of the enigmatic Strandja ranges where Mediterranean and Balkan currents meet; descended west into the border plains of Thrace with its corridors of traffic and trade; entered the passes of the Rhodope Mountains where every peak is legend and every village is not what it seems; and ended on the mirror side of the beginning – Strandja and the Black Sea.

With a few exceptions, names have been changed, and I have occasionally compounded topographic or biographic details in the interest of individual privacy and narrative economy. The natural wealth of the region deserves more space, but my focus was the human story. In the human story, borders are ubiquitous – visible and invisible, soft and hard – but the ancient wilderness that precedes them is finite. It is perhaps because this border is *still* a wilderness that I remain present with its people and ghosts.

Kapka Kassabova
The Highlands of Scotland

border

According to the *Oxford English Dictionary*:

1. a line separating two countries;
2. a band or strip, especially a decorative one, around the edge of something.

MOUNTAIN OF MADNESS, I

This moment came halfway through the journey. High in the Rhodope Mountains of the Greek–Bulgarian border, a serpentine road climbed the river gorge and where the road ended at the top, there was a last phantom village with gouged windows and a waterless stone fountain. Nobody lived there any more. Beyond the road and the village – the oak forests of no-man's-land. We think we'll go through life without knowing the uncanny except in films, but in that village, I had experienced something that struck terror in my heart. I still don't know if it was 'real', but the feelings accompanying it are inside my body to this day.

I had come to this forgotten fold of the mountains looking for something, and I'd spiralled into this. Maybe *this* was what I'd been looking for. Either way, I now found myself running down this canyon of scratchy forest full of boar and cliffs, twenty kilometres empty of humans, the pitiless sun hammering my head like a judgement for some distant crime.

Up among the peaks was a clifftop actually called the Judgement, a place from which bodies have been dropped into the chasm of time that lay between the first human sacrifices of the Thracians and the last years of the Cold War. But I was running in the opposite direction – downhill to the nearest inhabited village, which was far away, and so was everything else I understood.

The sense that this wasn't personal, that it wasn't only *my* terror, was, in retrospect, correct. I was picking up the frequencies of events that the mountain held. They were not natural, but border frequencies, the frequencies of a forest scratched with the initials of those who had been young and desperate in the twentieth century. I had come for their stories, but was I up to the task?

People had told me that things and people disappear here, but nothing really goes away. I felt that now, like a presence at my back. Though it was high noon, the mountain of Orpheus had turned dark. I reached an offshoot of the river and stopped to drink. The icy water burnt my throat. I knew that the source of the Mesta–Nestos River was up across the border in the highest range on the Balkan peninsula, and that its course ran over 234 kilometres before it met the Aegean – but what have facts ever done for the needy? This, here, wasn't a normal river. On the other side of the border was an abysmal cave with a thundering waterfall called the Devil's Gorge. It's where Orpheus went into the Underworld, they say. Nothing that goes in ever comes out, including the last speleologists who disappeared there in the 1970s, a man and a woman. Even Orpheus, the only creature to re-emerge from that chthonic realm, was eventually torn asunder by the raving maenads, his head thrown into the Hebrus, which runs for 480 kilometres before it becomes the Aegean. His crime? He had switched allegiances at the end of his life and crossed two dangerous boundaries: from his old mentor and god of nocturnal mysteries Dionysus to the Sun God Apollo; and from loving women to loving men. Trespassing boundaries isn't safe even for gods, let alone mortals.

Further downstream I came upon a woman and two men loading a small boat with loaves of bread. Dozens of loaves of bread. They had long hair and faces that were glad about something. My terror dissolved into enchantment. They invited me to cross the river with them. And there, on the other side…

But that's for later.

What is a border, when dictionary definitions fail? It is something you carry inside you without knowing, until you come to a place like this. You call into the chasm where one side is sunny, the other in darkness, and the echo multiplies your wish, distorts your voice, takes it away to a distant land where you might have been once.

PART ONE

STARRY STRANDJA

You too will run away, said the shepherd.
And if I stay?
If you stay… I give you a month. Then see that oak tree?
That's where you'll hang yourself.

Georgi Markov, *The Women of Warsaw*

via pontica

On land, it was once a Roman route that connected the Danube with the Bosphorus. In the sky, it is still a migratory route for birds. Via Pontica takes its name from the Black Sea, once called Pontus Euxinus, the hospitable sea. Though before the Miletian Greeks colonised it, it was known as Pontus Axinus, the *in*hospitable sea, because it was treacherous to navigate and its edges were populated by pirates and barbarians (read non-Greeks). Ovid spent time in exile on the west coast of this sea, penning his *Tristia* and feeling sorry for himself among the Getae, a Thracian tribe of barbarians (read non-Romans):

> *Here on the freezing Euxinus shores I stay;*
> *Axinus his name, the wiser ancients say.*

Poor Ovid, too dignified to enjoy himself. Since his time, barbarians and civilisations have come and gone, some have stayed, but one Pontic thing hasn't changed. If you come to the south-west beaches of the Black Sea where Bulgaria and Turkey share an invisible border in the water, where ships glide between the Bosphorus and Odessa, you can still see the sky eclipsed by fifty thousand storks heading to Africa on a single September day.

But it was still summer then.

RED RIVIERA

Summer 1984, the southern beaches of Bulgaria. All the birds had arrived, and so had the holidaymakers: the ones who looked like us, and the exotic ones with their fair plumage, bright beach towels, and air of permissiveness. The only thing that darkened the hot sky was the scavenging gulls which attacked the little plastic trays of salty fried sprat that everybody crunched on.

I looked up from the sandy pages of my book written by the excitingly American writer Jack London whose character in *Martin Eden* drowns himself because becoming a successful writer was devoid of moral meaning in the capitalist world. My favourite book of his was *The Call of the Wild*, adventure gone wrong – but what adventure! I yearned for adventure of almost any kind. If you started swimming at this beach and kept going south, like my father, who would disappear in the sea for hours, past the shoals of giant jellyfish, past the camping ground and the beach famed for nudists and bohemian types, not tame families like us, you ended up in Turkey.

Although Turkey was on the same side of the Black Sea, it was on the other side of the border, and things that included the word border, *granitza* – even the sound of it was barbed, like the gra-gra of the seagulls – were best avoided, even I knew that. For example, to go abroad was to go 'beyond the border', which was like beyond the pale, a place from which there was no return. In fact, those who went abroad and didn't return were called non-returnees. They were condemned in absentia and their families made to suffer in their place. The only such person I knew was my piano teacher's husband, whom I'd never met – because he was beyond the pale. He was one of the hundreds of Bulgarian musicians who went abroad for concerts and became non-returnees. The price they paid was the risk of never seeing home again.

As it slowly dawned on you why the border was there (so that people like us couldn't leave), you developed a permanent border-like feeling inside you, like indigestion. I was ten years old that summer, old enough to be in the throes of passion. The object of my lust was an older blond boy on holiday with his parents. We had come from Sofia, they had come from Berlin, and for two weeks of delicious torment, we spied on each other from our beach towels, joined by the whiff of Nivea cream and pre-pubescent longing. But the lack of experience showed, and when I found myself in the ice-cream queue with him standing behind me, tall and golden like an Apollo, I forgot every word of Russian – our common language – I'd learnt at school. When his family left, I cried for a day. We were so clearly meant for each other.

What neither of us could know was that the beach was awake with spying eyes. They were to be found in their greatest concentration and glamour at the legendary International Youth Centre nearby where, for thirty years, the gilded youth of the Eastern bloc came to party and strut in beauty contests, Neptune fests, and music evenings on the beach. These were no ordinary beaches. This was the red Riviera, the shop window of the communist bloc, in the avuncular words of Khrushchev, who was confident that the 'Bulgarians' friendship for us is particularly ardent'. Here, East and West Germans, Norwegians, Swedes, Hungarians, Poles, and Czechoslovaks came to play on the Golden Sands and Sunny Beach resorts that had sprung up in the 1960s and quickly become the biggest-grossing industry for the State. Because this was totalitarian tourism, and everything here belonged to the State, even the sand. We were staying in an illegally rented single room in a local's house – illegal because only State hotels could do legal business. Our sleepy seaside town was named Michurin after the Russian biologist who revolutionised crops. Michurin with its Mediterranean climate was the site of a kooky agronomical experiment, Soviet-style, in which scientists tried to grow eucalyptus and rubber trees, tea and mandarins. True, this fertile land was already producing walnuts and almonds, figs and vines, but the point was to prove that Mature Socialism could control everything, from the course of history to the behaviour of micro-organisms.

This was a place where every second barman was in the service of the Bulgarian State Security, while a specially trained 'operational group' of KGB, Czech and Stasi agents, disguised as holidaymakers, kept an eye on the hedonists. The East Germans were known among locals as 'the sandals', because it was in their sandals and beach clothes that they would sneak away from the beach at night, and into the dark forest of the gra-gra granitza, whose name was Strandja.

Those who didn't go for the forest went for the coast, in diving suits, with inflatable beach dinghies and mattresses, paddling south towards Turkey, which seemed so close, until they were swept out to sea. On the other side of the tideless Black Sea – with its 90 per cent anoxic water below the oxygenated top layer – was the Soviet Union.

I missed my German crush, unaware that my longing was replicated by other bodies on the beach in search of mates – for one-night stands, for trade, for exchange, for marriage. For a way to cross the border. Since its beginnings in the 1960s, the red Riviera had been a human market where the highest bid was not for love, but for freedom. And the highest price you could pay was your life. Many did.

It was a long walk from the beach to the Turkish border, and that walk passed through Strandja's forested hills that cast a midnight shadow over the sunny resorts. All that we knew about Strandja was that it was full of rivers, rhododendrons, and reptiles, and that its villages were home to a fire rite where people walked on embers. Confusingly, the practice of that rite was banned by the State – except in official places like the International Youth Centre, where the fire-walkers were State-approved, and so were the dancing bears on chains that they brought in to amuse the visitors; they were official bears. And in order to visit Strandja, you needed an official permit from the Ministry of Internal Affairs, called an *otkrit list*. In other words, you couldn't visit.

'Why can't we go to Strandja?' I asked when the German boy was gone and the ice cream had lost its taste.

'We have no business there,' my father said.

'The forest is full of soldiers,' my mother said.

There was a wall of electrified barbed wire, as long as the border. Those who entered the forest could read the warning sign meant for them in the two main languages of desperation:

внимание гранична зона!

ACHTUNG GRENZZONE!

But if you had walked far enough to read this sign, through days and nights in the reptilian forest, why would you turn back?

If innocence is the sense that the world is a safe and fair place, that summer I began to lose mine. Why couldn't we follow the German family to Berlin? Why couldn't we – or the German family for that matter – go to Turkey, just down the coast? Why did a German man have to fly over the border in a hot-air balloon, as the apocryphal story went, unless it was actually true? Because we were living in an open-air prison. A feeling of melancholy revolt began to germinate.

Six years later, 'the sandals' didn't have to come all this way to escape because the Berlin Wall fell. Our family crossed the border – though not *that* one, but some other imaginary border over the Pacific, on the way to a new life in New Zealand, a place defined by beaches of a different kind.

It was summer again when I arrived, thirty years later.

At Burgas airport, vineyards lined the landing strip and the air smelled of petrol and imminent sex. I had flown from Edinburgh with a holiday airline, the plane full of tattooed men and women loud with laughter and make-up. I stepped down onto Bulgarian soil in the company of damp, excited Russians, young Scandinavians pustular with hormones, pale-fleshed families from other northern latitudes. From this peppery port city, the consumer tourists of Europe were packed off like canned meat to the pulsing resorts of Golden Sands and Sunny Beach. My red Riviera had become a happy inferno of global capitalism.

I rented a car and drove past the multicoloured salt lakes of the Gulf of Burgas. The strangled calls of pelicans, cormorants and kingfishers, the smell of ripening figs, of dusty, lusting, Nivea cream summer, the cranes of the port, and the giant ships like motionless cities. Here began the dark hills of Strandja.

I took the quiet seaside road which I'd last seen thirty years ago from the back of the family Skoda. Before the road turned inland, I stopped in the last seaside town: sleepy Michurin of my childhood. But it had reverted to its old name of Tsarevo, and for a moment, I couldn't find it on the map because to me it is forever Michurin. The attempts to grow eucalyptus and rubber trees had long ended, and it was back to the native fig and vine, almond and walnut. Along the road into town, women and men in shorts sat on stools with hand-written signs: 'Rooms for rent'. In the days of the red Riviera, they could have been arrested as 'privateers'.

By the harbour, I ate a plate of fried sprat. Kids jumped in the water with cries and everything tasted like tears. But I was here for once-forbidden Strandja, not for the sea. I pulled myself together and drove on.

Strandja: you knew you'd entered it when traffic suddenly stopped and the forest engulfed you. The road became broken and muffled in jungle green, and the green was full of mossy lagoons and megalithic rock sanctuaries once used in Dionysian cults. The only traffic I saw was a Gypsy couple who squeezed past on a horse cart and smiled dazzlingly with gold teeth, as if all was well.

Four black horses without saddles ambled ahead and broke into a gallop when they heard the engine. They separated to let my car through and closed behind me like a silent film.

My destination was a border village inside a valley, where I planned to spend some time and explore the area. Thrown by the ambiguous road structure and bent road signs that pointed into the wilderness, I lost my way. When I stopped on the deserted road to open the car boot for a water bottle, I heard crackling twigs and went to investigate – always a bad idea. In the woods, I felt something approach me from all sides. Midge-like flies entered my nose and mouth and, running back to the car, I nearly trod on a knot of frisky adders. I drove on with clammy hands.

Naked vistas opened below the high road, like a slap that made you reel. Vertigos of velvet, a folded world, as if you had to take a plunge in order to emerge on the other side of an abyss.

strandja

The last mountain range of south-east Europe. Surface: 10,000 square kilometres. Age: three hundred million years. It begins at the Black Sea to the east and tapers out into the Thracian plains to the west. It was formed gradually by the colliding and parting of Eurasian plates whose last drastic result was the Bosphorus Strait. The river canyons of Strandja are shaped by the continuously sinking coast of the Black Sea. Though Strandja's highest peak is only 1,031 metres, you feel close to the stars here, too close. On the Turkish side they call the range Yildiz, the starry one.

Because Strandja missed the last ice age, its habitats preserve plants from the Tertiary age, providing a veritable open-air museum of relic species, including the original good old *Rhododendron ponticum*, planted in other parts of the world, but continuously in residence here since the Tertiary. Twenty-something species of reptiles breed in this ornithological, herpetic, and mammalian heaven where one thing is certain: although people are scarce, you're never alone in the forest.

Strandja still holds megalithic cult sites and other mysterious remnants of the ancient Thracians, who left unwritten traces of their existence. The few written traces they did leave were enigmatic, like this friendly stone inscription from the second century BC, in Greek: 'Stranger, you who come here, be well!' To the ancient Greeks, it was the Thracians who were the strangers – the 'new-comers, outermost of all', wrote Homer in the *Iliad*, if you can call newcomers tribes that were well established in these lands by 4000 BC. Though it wasn't until the middle of the second millennium BC that they became a cohesive ethnic population. Homer was the first to mention the Thracians, and wrote of their king Rhesus as his armies appeared alongside the Trojans in the Greek–Trojan War, with his snow-white horses 'in speed like the winds' and his chariots of gold and silver that 'beseemeth not that mortal men should wear but immortal gods'. We'll return to the gold.

Before the fourteenth century AD, when the Seljuk Turks rocked up, Strandja was dotted with a shifting Byzantine–Bulgar border, and somewhere in Strandja was Paroria, the monastery complex of the great hermit Gregory of Sinai. His influential quietist philosophy of Hesychasm pioneered a form of psychosomatic prayer akin to ecstatic meditation. But Paroria vanished without trace.

Traditionally the villagers of Strandja were Bulgarian- and Greek-speaking and lived from milling, logging, charcoal-making, and boat-building, but the mountain's two great riches were gold and livestock. In the Ottoman Empire (1300s–1900s), Strandja had special status: owned by the Sultan's family, it was almost exempt from taxes and there were no outside settlers. In fact, from antiquity until the Balkan Wars (1912–13), Strandja's population was very isolated. Today, the Bulgarian–Turkish border dissects the ranges. Counting those on both sides, only around eight thousand people live in Strandja.

About the gold. The Thracians, who were very fond of the stuff, mined it extensively in Strandja, and treasure hunters and archaeologists still dig up astonishing artefacts of pure gold. It was on these Pontic shores that in 4600 BC a body wearing humanity's first gold jewellery was placed in a necropolis (the Varna Necropolis). Ancient mines also reveal intense silver, copper, iron and marble extraction, especially following the Trojan War. Some say Strandja is a giant Swiss cheese of antique tunnels and sealed subterranean secrets.

Knowing these facts about Strandja felt like a good start – until I arrived in the Village in the Valley.

THE VILLAGE IN THE VALLEY

The Village in the Valley was the end of the road. You descended into it through a mixed forest that was the oldest protected reserve in the Balkans. The faces of deer appeared and disappeared in the green light, and woodpeckers tapped out messages in code.

I rented a two-storey house in the last lane, newly built by absentee owners. The two houses next door were abandoned, their gardens dense with wild fruit trees that shed golden pears into my courtyard. A tortoise crossed the lawn in the morning and recrossed it at dusk. The abandoned houses were three centuries old and wood-clad, with a curious removable tile in the roof for letting light in, or perhaps for spying on the neighbours.

Until the 1990s, two thousand souls had lived here; now it was down to two hundred. The school stood empty with its broken windows, and so did the bakery, the general store, the military blocks. The meanders of the river flooded twice a year, along with the village, and until the twentieth century, the people had preserved a tradition from ancient Egypt: they harvested the fertile residue of the swollen river with woven-twig contraptions attached to the walnut trees that lined the banks. The walnut trees were still there, heavy with bitter green fruit.

The village was named after the Greek merchant who founded it, because this had been a Greek-speaking village until the Balkan Wars, when millions lost a homeland or worse, and gained an empty house in a foreign country with the kitchen pots still warm. In the mirthless merry-go-round called 'exchange of populations', the Greek-speakers of villages near the Black Sea like this one had fled to the villages around Thessaloniki, and in their place arrived Bulgarian refugees from Turkey. Muslims from both countries were expelled to Turkey. This civilian catastrophe was just one refrain in the long threnody of the Ottoman Empire.

A stunning Orthodox church, once called Constantine and Elena after the local protector saints, punctuated the village skyline with its wooden bell tower. The icons had remained intact since the moment a hundred years ago when the Greeks had run, leaving an unintended gift for the Bulgarian arrivals. Soon afterwards, there was a church fire. The villagers watched until they heard human screams and then rushed into the flames, but there was nobody there; the icons were screaming.

Beyond my lane, there were only old drove roads and wooded hills all the way to Turkey. At night, jackals came to the edge of the village and howled, and the village dogs howled back in an infernal orchestra. Unable to sleep, I sat on my balcony and followed the yellow eyes at the edge of the forest. Hornets the size of sparrows invaded the house and I squashed them with Russian hardbacks from the shelves, because a hornet sting can kill you, people said. *War and Peace* proved ideal.

My nearest neighbour across the street was a very tall former basketball champion. He had lost his wife and his son, and spent the summers here, in the old family house, though his garden looked derelict like the rest. He lit up when he saw me:

'Have you fallen for Strandja too?'

He didn't wait for an answer.

'You'll see. Stay another week and you won't be able to leave. Or you'll leave and get sick. It's the way of the mountain.'

I laughed too soon.

The village square was remarkable for two things. One, a stone ring built into the ground where once a year at the *panagyr,* or village fair, a fire was lit and fire worshippers called *nestinari* trampled the embers, holding icons. Two, a café–bar which was the central gossip head-quarters. New arrivals were sighted here, including tourists headed for Istanbul whose sat-nav systems had brought them here because it was the shortest way to Turkey as the crow flies. People called this estab-lishment The Disco, because in the basement interior an iron pole was rammed into the ground that served as a dance floor, though I never saw anyone dance.

The owners were a local couple: a chatty fat man with small features called Blago, and slender Minka, a woman of few words. She put your order on the table with a blunt, fatalistic 'Enjoy.' Behind her grey eyes, she seemed to dream monolithic dreams, as if her face was carved from the hills, young yet ancient.

Blago sat smoking all day, his shaved head like a beacon. He told me how, in his childhood, which was also my childhood, when Greeks came to visit their ancestors' houses, the people's militia rounded up the kids afterwards and asked them: Did you take anything from the Greeks? The kids couldn't lie so the militia confiscated the chewing gum, the pens, the chocolates, and then shaved their heads.

'To teach us about taking from the capitalists,' Blago snorted. 'Don't look so appalled. It was normal. Like when they called us to the square whenever they caught sandals at the wire. We had to watch.'

Watch what?

'They roughed them up,' he said. 'I can still see them as if it were yesterday. Young. Handcuffed. In sandals. Sometimes bloodied from the dogs. I remember their dark clothes, to blend in with the forest. Here was the enemy, our cops said. And we believed it. 'Cause other-wise they wouldn't get into this awful mess, would they?'

Blago stubbed out his cigarette.

'Enjoy.' Minka put a salad before me and sat gazing at the hills.

Minka had witnessed what she called 'the fall and fall' of her pretty village. There were two reasons: the Cold War and the border, which amounted to the same thing.

In autumn 1944, the Red Army arrived and Bulgaria, until then convulsed by a homicidal alliance with Nazi Germany, was now convulsed by a suicidal coup d'état, complete with People's Courts that dished out death sentences with Soviet abandon. This had been an agrarian economy (the Agrarian Union was the largest political party, and around 70 per cent of people worked with the land), but once the Communist Party assumed absolute power, collectivisation began. Collectivisation was of course a euphemism for State theft, but those who pointed this out were killed, exiled, sent to labour camps or otherwise silenced. The Agrarian Union was outlawed along with the Social Democratic Workers' Party and every other party. Those who lost their land, which was everyone who had land, had two options: migrate to factories in the new five-year-plan towns, or continue working the land that was no longer theirs, to fulfil the unfulfillable quotas of the five-year plan that lasted forty-five years.

My great-grandfather was one of the country's modern vintners, and co-founder of Gamza, a thriving wine cooperative on the northern side of the Balkan range. Overnight he became 'enemy of the people', narrowly escaped execution, and was stripped of his pension; he spent his last decade sharing a tiny flat in Sofia with his daughter, who supported him, though he never lost the spark in his eye or his taste for wine. Oddly enough, despite this rapid and rabid industrialisation, the main export products remained the same: tobacco, and fruit and vegetables, all of which Bulgaria supplied to the Eastern bloc.

Eventually, industrialisation did produce the results that should have been the driver behind the revolution that wasn't one: out of this land-rich country emerged a society where rural and urban people were equally dispossessed.

'A bit ironic,' I said.

'That's history for you,' Blago grinned. 'All it does is manufacture ironies.'

'Living here is like a joke without a punchline,' Minka said.

Minka's family had always been in the village; like everybody else in the days of the Cold War, they weren't allowed to live or work elsewhere. But if you lived here, you also needed a special stamp from the Ministry of Internal Affairs, because this was the Border Zone.

'Indentured. Branded,' Minka said with an impassive face. 'Still, it was better in those days. Simply because there were people. And now?'

By the 1970s, industrialisation had been a success, in the sense that many giant structures had been erected, including dams like the one that flooded the antique city of Seuthopolis, the largest Thracian site ever excavated. Fair enough: communism was in a rush, it had no time for bourgeois things like the past or the environment. But with all this industrious activity going on, border villages and towns were drained of their lifeblood. In the late 1970s and early 1980s, the State tried to jump-start the local economy by opening copper mines and offering houses practically for free. But it was too little, too late.

Then, in the brutal freefall of 1990s post-communism, the free market overnight bulldozed the elderly structures of the planned economy. The border army got up and left. People emigrated en masse. Wilderness closed over the land as if after an apocalypse.

'There's no livelihood left,' Minka said. 'The only hope is eco-tourism.'

'But look at the roads,' Blago said.

The roads were so potholed, you had to lie in a dark room after each car ride.

Discarded in a corner of the mayor's garden was an old hand-painted sign:

LONG LIVE THE INTERNATIONAL UNION OF THE WORK-
ING CLASSES, OF ALL THE PROGRESSIVE FORCES UNITED
IN THE STRUGGLE AGAINST IMPERIALISM FOR PEACE,
DEMOCRACY, AND SOCIALISM!

A utopia that has gone wrong in exactly the ways in which it should have gone right deserves a minute of silence and a lot of reflection, and here it had gone even more wrong than elsewhere, which is why the locals had an insight into something usually experienced in war: collective heartbreak. There were no champagne socialists in the Village in the Valley, no anti-globalists, no anti-communists, no anti-capitalists. Just survivors. The women were old, the men were lonely, and the children were gone. Forgotten by justice, the survivors celebrated small successes, and life in the Village in the Valley was sweet and broken.

'I'm in charge of a dying village, a death foretold,' the mayor said. He had joined us at the outside tables for a coffee. 'As my great-aunt would say when the ember reading wasn't good, *cherna chernilka*, blackest of blackness. All I can do is make people's lives as good as possible, which isn't difficult – they're happy with so little.'

His great-aunt had been a fortune reader, but the mayor was a pragmatist. A car mechanic who'd spent his life in Burgas with grease up to his elbows, he went around in flip-flops and shorts, fixing everybody's cars for free. But even a pragmatist couldn't help having the odd dream, and he loved his village so much that he had built a playground for the absent children.

*

Morning and night, I was at The Disco watching eagles hang motionless over the hills, and waiting for some miracle to happen. Miracles felt as inevitable here as disasters. I spent afternoons browsing in the village library, where the literature published in my youth was alphabetically shelved, locked and unlocked by a librarian, even if only three other people used the library regularly: a gentle ninety-year-old former shepherd who told me confidentially that a life of books and hills is the only meaningful life; the beautiful Russian; and Nedko.

The beautiful Russian worked for the forestry marking trees and maintaining paths, with two others. One of them was a well-known bagpipe player, a chubby man of ruddy complexion who couldn't be separated from his bagpipe. He took it with him to work, and during lunch breaks he'd bring out his little hip flask of rakia, sit on a tree trunk and play the ancient, bitter-sweet melodies of Strandja.

'When the bagpipe opens its throat, we all forget our troubles,' the beautiful Russian said. 'And anyway, trees are much nicer company than humans.'

She was married to a once-brilliant mathematician, now a man who drank half a bottle of rakia by lunchtime. They were so broke that in thirty years she hadn't been back to Russia. One morning, she leaned over her coffee and whispered:

'Don't leave washing in your garden overnight.'

'Yes,' Nedko said. 'That's what my mother says too.'

Nedko was her friend. He was a handsome guy with blue eyes and a sun-baked face. Once a restaurant chef, he'd been forced into a decade of nursing ill parents. His thirties had gone, his mother was still bedridden, and although he clearly loved her very much, he had the haunted look of the dutiful. He lived in a house at the top of the village with an immense view of the wooded hills that filled you with a heavy happiness.

'There are women who roam the village at night and throw cursed water and graveyard soil on people's clothes. You put on your clothes and you're cursed,' he said.

'Don't laugh,' the beautiful Russian said. 'One day I found a black crucifix outside my door. In my ignorance, I picked it up. That was twenty years ago. I've had nothing but bad luck since. You never pick up a crucifix from the ground with your hands.'

'There are women here,' Nedko said, 'with the evil eye. They can't help it.'

'Who are they?' I glanced round, not laughing any more. Truth be told, one of the old women had looked at me in a way that made me go completely cold.

Nedko shook his head. 'You can't name them. But everybody knows.'

At another table sat S., a smooth retired émigré who had lived in Poland for thirty years, but who came to his parents' house every summer.

'I don't know why,' he said. 'I'm lonely like a cuckoo here.'

He drove a shiny Land Rover and boasted that he had as many children as grandchildren, as many cars as houses, and that from an early age, he'd been incredibly lucky with women. He'd grown up in the barracks behind the barbed wire with his border-guard father. He had seen it all with his child's eyes. For example, the German who used a metal detector to outwit the alarmed wire wall; the guards found out about him from the next German who tried it with less success.

The soldiers were bored witless, the émigré said, and amused themselves hunting wild pigs and turning them into sausages. And, big problem – the émigré shook his head – no women. Occasionally, a visit from a wife or a whore. He couldn't have lasted, he would have made a run for it.

'Come to think of it, I did, didn't I!' He laughed bitterly. 'Ran from the goddamned communists who poisoned everything with their gaze. The evil eye all right! No matter how much you enjoyed yourself. And I was incredibly lucky with women.'

I liked S. and wondered why his Polish wife never came with him.

One Sunday, there was a party at The Disco. A concrete landing had been poured in someone's house, a small success to celebrate. Minka was cooking in the basement and everybody sat around a long table outside.

The old mothers were chewing on chunks of pork, downing shots of rakia, and laughing with missing teeth. They had buried husbands and more; they could afford to laugh.

An accordionist sat in the middle; his nickname was Wee One although he wasn't wee, he was normal-sized. Next to him was his son, a guy with chiselled cheeks and cagey eyes, who kept to himself. Unlike Big Stamen, whose person was so big it burst out of his flip-flops, his laughter like a gunshot in my ear. His smile was full of appetite, like a friendly young cannibal's. The table, the beer glass, this village – everything was too small for him. During the week he oper-ated a logging machine in the forest, as befits a giant. Like everyone here, Big Stamen was the descendant of refugees from villages across the border in Turkey where the abandoned family houses crumbled through the seasons.

'Hey Wee One,' someone said to the accordionist, 'what's your favourite song?'

'"Communism Is Gone"!' Stamen boomed, and everyone laughed – except a couple of people who missed the old days because the new days were so bad.

'No,' the Wee One said, 'my favourite is this one.'

And he played a song about a shepherd who has a secret but can only tell it to the hills. Wee One was once a pig herder, and before he lost his farm and became an employee of state forestry, his voice had carried over the hills all day.

'I still sing, every night, oh yeah!' he said. 'Because I drink, and I can't drink without singing.'

Every time he opened the old German accordion and the veins in his neck strained and he sang in his emphysema voice, I feared it could be his last song. Everyone drank heavily. Everyone except D., who sat at the far end and drank Fanta. D. was forty, with a gentle, slow way about him. He had been a chef in seaside resorts until one night in the village he'd gone into a drunk rage and battered a man to pulp. Not long out of jail, he had recently set up a beehive and that summer had his first harvest of Manov honey, a valuable variety that bees collect from the oak forest. Before I left, he gave me a honeycomb full of treacly black honey. He didn't touch the honey himself, as if penance barred him from too much pleasure.

The next song request was from a young cop. He patrolled the towns and resorts of the southern Black Sea. 'What's the work like?' I asked him.

'Nuts in summer,' he said, 'and quiet in winter. Mostly drunks. The British are the worst drunks. Their women are like enraged elephants.'

The Bulgarian police, in an echo of the old days, worked alongside German police patrols along this last outpost of Europe, because it was the terminus for all manner of wanted international fugitives, smugglers, desperados.

'They come here to hide,' he said, pointing to the dark hills rising on all sides. 'And look at it. It's perfect!'

He would soon pick up his gun and drive through the forest to Tsarevo for his night patrol. But for now, he was drumming along on a giant goatskin drum, and his batons were two broken car aerials.

Someone requested a folk ballad called 'Nine Years', which told the story of a man in love with a woman who casts a spell over every man crazy enough to live with her. After nine years, the men waste away and die. The protagonist's mother begs him not to go to her. 'But what are nine years, Mother?' he says. 'I have already wasted an entire life without her!'

Some of the men had girlfriends in other towns, some were divorced, and some had no one. The women were either widowed or married, like Minka and the beautiful Russian. 'Nine Years' was a slow burner and the mood changed, became oppressive with regret, as if everybody's losses came crowding in. The hills darkened with storm clouds.

Ivan stirred in the corner and reached for his rifle. He was the youngest here, a border guard with a completely vacant face. When the final chord drew to an end, he walked across the empty square with purpose. Dread seized my throat, and then he lifted the rifle into position, pointed at the gathering storm, and fired one, two, three, four, five times. The empty cartridges fell into the concrete fire ring.

He came back and propped the rifle against the wall.

'That's better,' he said and sat down.

'I need a lot more emptying to feel better, but now's not the time,' Stamen quipped, and the tension dissipated. The accordionist wiped his face with a hanky. I was sure my eardrums would never be the same again.

'It's the bachelor life does our heads in,' Stamen said, pushing a plate of pork before me. 'Eat up. What we need is women, nice ones who can sing. Why don't you stay?'

'Or at least come once a year, like me,' the Polish émigré said.

'All these big empty houses,' the beautiful Russian said. 'Crying out for people.'

'Our church hasn't seen a wedding in twenty years,' Stamen's mother said.

Then the skies opened and curtains of rain slapped down on the empty square. The table dispersed. I went home and collected my washing from the line before night fell. I didn't believe in the evil eye, but just to be on the safe side.

When the rain stopped, I sat on the balcony waiting for the jackals to come out of the mist, and the thought of having to leave this village, as everybody did sooner or later, pierced me with such regret that I could have howled.

agiasma

Greek word for curative holy spring. Springs were once cult places for the Thracians, whose worship of the Mother Goddess was embodied in the womb-like sanctuaries and moist cave slits of Strandja, where the rays of the Sun God and son and lover of the goddess were received.

Thousands of years later, the human relationship with *agiasma*s endures, perhaps because the agiasma is a mediator between the material and magical realms, between the night of winter and incubation (Chaos) and the sun of summer and rebirth (Cosmos).

From May onwards, the water starts flowing freely. The agiasmas have opened, people say. You come to an agiasma to wash your face and conscience, be cured of ailments and curses, and greet the new season. Hang a strip of your clothing on a nearby tree and your sickness will stay behind, or a little bit of your sorrow. The trees are so heavy with fabric that in winter, when the springs retreat into themselves, the grumpy authorities come to clean up the mess.

One morning, I was taken to a place deep in the border forest. It was called Big Agiasma.

EVERYTHING BEGINS
WITH A SPRING

It was from The Disco that the journey to Big Agiasma began. I joined the convoy that crept along the canyon to a place off the map. That place was a clearing in the border forest criss-crossed by hunting tracks and drove roads. Past the disused, snake-infested border barracks where the smooth Polish émigré had spent his boyhood and where a ghostly slogan decorated the broken-tiled entrance:

ON THE NATIONAL BORDER, NATIONAL ORDER

I travelled in a Soviet-era minivan with women from the village. The driver did his best on the dug-out road but we still jumped up and down on the hard seats until the remaining teeth in the collective mouth rattled. The women carried icons propped on their laps, like children, 'dressed' in lace and red fabric, but when I peeked underneath, I was startled by the human faces with expressive eyes.

'Some of these are very old,' said a woman with thick, man-like features. The oldest icons dated three centuries back. The women looked after them as if they were orphans.

'That's why we only take them out of the church on the day of Constantine and Elena,' said a woman called Despina. She lived in my street and had a lush garden and a bedridden husband.

'How are you enjoying our village, dear?' said another woman who always chewed gum. I liked her; she had an open face that said *Shit happens*. 'The cherries are coming. You don't get cherries like this in the city.'

'Maybe they have cherries in Scotland,' Despina said.

'No, in Scotland they have whisky,' corrected the woman with the chewing gum, and she winked at me. 'And the men wear tartan skirts. Right?'

There was a chuckle. As a sign that I was with the in-crowd, they gave me an icon to hold on my lap. I avoided looking at the woman with the scary blue irises who said nothing, and who may or may not have had the evil eye.

'We don't have many visitors, dear,' said another woman, once a cook at the school canteen. 'You should've seen the village before.'

'The school, the library,' said Despina. 'The orchards, the fields, the herds. Thousands of cattle heads. Our village was wealthy.'

'Let bygones be bygones,' the woman with the chewing gum said.

'A few years ago, we went to Meliki,' the man-faced woman said, 'to visit the Greeks. Lovely people.'

'Lovely people,' everybody agreed. The Greeks in Meliki were descendants of those who had left the icons behind a hundred years ago. They still practised the fire-walking ritual that was called *anastenaria* in Greek, *nestinarstvo* in Bulgarian.

'We've been to Turkish Strandja too,' the woman with the chewing gum said, 'to our old villages. To see Mum and Dad's house. But there isn't nobody living there any more. Just ruins.'

'Empty villages,' the man-faced woman said. She was a street sweeper and people called her The Ear because she had phenomenal hearing and could eavesdrop on a whispered conversation streets away, inside houses, perhaps even inside people's heads. I saw her every day with her broom, sweeping invisible dust from the empty square, tuned in to some frequency across the hills. I tried not to have thoughts when I passed her but she always squinted at me hard, and I shuddered.

The van finally came to a stop. In the clearing, the people were gathering.

The clearing was known as The Homeland, a real feat of metonymy. It had seen gatherings of fire worshippers, musicians, revellers, mystic seers, and ordinary drunks for hundreds of years, and quite possibly thousands, until the late 1940s when the cult of nature was interrupted by the cult of Stalin. My generation had grown up in the last blink of that interruption.

Cauldrons of lamb soup were bubbling on fires and the women from the van set about stirring the broth. There were five wooden platforms called *odarche*, one platform for each of the five fire-worshipping villages along the border. Empty, they looked like execution stands. Now people were coming up to them in small processions from the river and placing icons on the stands. It looked like a scene from *The Wicker Man*. Instead of a prayer, the icon-holders did a ritualistic circular dance on the spot with small steps and hand gestures. The whiff of paganism was unmistakable under the burning incense of Orthodoxy.

To the sound of a bagpipe and drum, or *tupan*, I joined the small procession down to the river, where the women, without any water touching them, undressed the icons and washed them, then dressed them again and placed them on the platforms.

The wooden tables, like the platforms, were fixtures and this whole place was a permanent set-up for parties. The orgiastic vibes were already in the air at midday. It felt as if the ritual of the icons held a meaning beyond faith, revelry, or culture – there was something else here that was being re-enacted. I sensed it but couldn't name it; it was something to do with the border.

There were visiting Greeks who had brought their own icons, and a group of Greek women at the river were bending down. This had been their ancestors' Homeland and their grandparents were buried in the Village in the Valley. So the Homeland was also a site for a special brand of tourism: ancestral tourism.

I headed up the hilly track to the Big Agiasma that had just opened – which was a big deal because once the Big Agiasma opened, so did all the springs of Strandja. A girl came up to me and touched my shoulder. She was dressed in white, like a nymph.

'Hello,' she said, 'I'm Iglika.' Iglika means primrose. 'What's your name?'

I stopped in my tracks. Her skin was a golden galaxy, her hair a river of wheat. She belonged in a song. I felt a superstitious worry; how can you go through life like this without someone giving you the evil eye? I told her my name. She laughed with pearly teeth.

'Your name is Waterdrop!' she said and took my hand in her cold palm. 'You have an affinity with water. I think we're quite similar. You know, I studied at Manchester University for two years. But I can't live in Manchester. Nobody can live in Manchester. I came back.'

She talked all the way to the Big Agiasma, bubbling like a spring, but when our turn came in the line of people, she fluttered away. Iglika was from a village called Crossing because it's near one of the few existing crossings over the 147-kilometre-long Veleka River that erupts in a Turkish hill and carves out canyons through Strandja before it joins the Black Sea without a thought about borders. Rivers *are* borders in the mythical mind – that's why the icons were being 'washed' here.

I didn't see Iglika again that day. The people from my Village in the Valley welcomed me to their table. The lamb soup was poured into bowls and passed round; it was the *kurban*, cooked from the lamb slaughtered early that morning. Kurban (from the Arabic *qurban*) means the sacrificial killing of an animal, sometimes to the sound of drum and bagpipe, that still accompanies major celebrations in rural Greece and Bulgaria, both Christian and Muslim, though I had never seen a kurban until now. In the old days, each fire-worshipping village had its own sacrificial knife, axe, and tree stump. Those were gone, but what remained were the little chapels or *konaks*, on the fringe of fire-worshipping villages, usually built on top of a spring where the icons were blessed and incensed before being taken to processions like these.

'There is a church in the Strandja village of Zabernovo, built on top of a spring and an antique cult site,' someone said behind me with perfect timing. The woman had ash-blonde hair, a tobaccoey complexion and secretive eyes. She sat apart from the tables, at the base of a giant oak, as if she had always been there. Her name was Marina.

The church in that village, she went on, contained a well where the original mythical act of wrestling took place. Even now, if you go to the well at the right moment in the seasonal cycle, and know how to see it, a man and a black ox come out of the well at nightfall and wrestle until dawn. There is no winner. At first cock's crow, they go back into the well.

Marina was an ethnographer, and after thirty years in Burgas she had returned to Strandja and her native border town to look after aged parents. She didn't ask what I was doing there; she had a way of reading people.

High above us, the oak forest swayed soundlessly and the sky was young with summer. There were children and octogenarians, alcoholics and ethnographers. You could tell the incomers like me – we looked inhibited. The locals had wild faces, faces that aren't seen in cities. Men were pouring potent home-brewed beverages. Someone stood guarding the icons on each platform.

'Theophany,' Marina said. 'The belief that icons are human mani-festations of gods and so mediators between the mortal and the divine.'

I asked her why the Big Agiasma is called big. It looked quite small to me.

'We mustn't take things literally.' Marina's face shook into a smile, and she told me the following story.

In antiquity, a divine stag came each springtime and cleared the spring with his horns until the water began to flow. Then he offered himself voluntarily for slaughter as the sacrificial kurban. He did this every year. Which is why you never shoot a stag in this forest, just in case it's the divine one, the gold-horned one who, from the Bronze Age onwards, runs towards the sun of the new season and whose earthly embodiment is fire, Marina said.

Though it seemed to me that these days the forest belongs to the various hunting mafias who shoot whatever they like.

'This is how the Big Agiasma opened,' she concluded. 'And because of that, it's here that the fire worshippers of each generation first tune in with the fire. Opening, undressing, bathing, dressing, moving in a circle anticlockwise, these are rites that have been with us for a long time.'

But what was the connection with fire?

'It's obvious,' Marina said. 'Today is the fire festival of Saints Constantine and Elena. They are just a variation of the double cult of the Earth Goddess and her son and lover the Sun God. Representations of the Dionysian–Apollonian duality at the heart of fire worship. The solar and the chthonic come together. Briefly. They can only come together briefly.'

Stags were hunters and hunted. Mothers and sons were lovers.

'That's how the metaphorical mind works.' Marina smiled with nicotine teeth. Of course what I really wanted to know was when we would see the fire-walkers.

'Fire is a nocturnal mystery,' Marina said.

'Does that mean we have to wait all day?' But suddenly Marina was gone. Like a tree spirit.

'The embers of the kurban traditionally become the stomping ground,' someone at my table said. It was an odd-looking young man who sat without drinking. He was pallid and bug-eyed; the overall impression was of someone with reptilian-cold skin. This was one of the local nestinari.

Then the band arrived – a man with a huge drum, the chubby bagpipe player, a Gypsy accordionist with melancholy Egyptian features, and a young singer with a face like a sunflower. His arrival brought something new, as if a door opened and a stream of light rushed in. His whole body beamed. The bagpipe approached down the path with a single quavering note, the sound of time itself, archaic, not of the conscious mind. The primal beat of the tupan set the rhythm, then the accordionist picked up the sorrowful melody, and sunflower-face opened his throat.

A fever gripped the crowd. As if the forest clearing became suspended with all of us in it, each figure captured with drink in hand, reclining on the grass, peering into the river as into a mirror.

'A true *nestinar* always has another gift,' Marina said. She was back at the roots of her tree. 'Either song or prophecy.'

At the time of World War I, she said, in the nearby village of Urgari there was a great nestinarka called Zlata. She prophesied, with cruel accuracy, which of the young men of her village wouldn't return. Other nestinari could see the future in a lump of coal, and somehow, the future was always bad news here. The visiting Greek women today were the grandchildren of those old *anastenarides* who, just before the Balkan Wars, went onto the fire, and saw it all with their second sight: war, exile, the lost houses, animals, and children, the long, plundered road to Greece.

'Why,' they wailed and covered themselves in ash, 'why sow fields, bear babies, build houses? *Vuh vuh vuh*, blackest of blackness!'

The abandoned houses next to my rented house had belonged to them, and they knew they'd never see them again even before they lost them. In the mass exodus of people across the new border after the Balkan Wars, some families lost babies and children in the forest. Paramilitary bands of every stripe attacked refugees of every creed, and the young weren't spared. It was a typical Balkan predicament: a war that was more terrible for the civilians than for the combatants, and whose aftermath hums in the background, still.

'Fire and water,' Marina said. 'It's collective therapy. Without it, people would go mad.' She went on: 'Fire and water. Purifying but destructive. Which is why those who go into the fire have to channel something.'

'Channel what?'

'Suffering,' Marina said and stubbed out her cigarette on a tree root. 'We all know suffering. But to come through it, come through fire and water and allow the rest of us to do it too – that's why the passion for fire isn't passed down in the family. Because it's knowledge from elsewhere.'

Since the beginning of the fire cult – which may have been as far back as antiquity – fire worshippers and their communities came to the Big Agiasma to attune themselves to the new season with its fire-sun, water-life, and forest-home. The first known anastenarides–nestinari came from the Greek- and Bulgarian-speaking villages of Strandja. In Ottoman times, this was known as *kyor kaz*, the blind district. Why here? No one knows, and the two heartland villages of fire worship – Madjura (population: 0), Pirgopulo (population: 0) – no longer exist on any map, their houses burnt during an uprising against the Ottomans in the early twentieth century, their names like border ghosts, only invoked in memory. Today, they would have been in Turkey.

They were typically women of reproductive age or older, and come May or June, a kind of passionate fit would seize them, a rush of desire for fire. Nothing else would do. Field work, children, and small-town decency were forgotten. They would go stone cold and shivery, their eyes would turn, they would let their hair down, tear their clothes, and rush to the fire with moans of lament and passion. *Vuh vuh vuh.*

The earliest written records of Strandja fire worship date only from the 1800s, but there is a school of research that traces it back to our old friends the Thracians. True, the Thracian elite and their king–priests and queen–priestesses practised the solar rituals of Orphism, while the plebs practised the chthonic ecstasies of Dionysian rites. But whether the Thracologists are right or being a little fanciful, one thing is clear: Christianity is a fig leaf for a primal spiritual practice. Typically, the rapture of the fire began with one woman or man, and infected the community over the day and night of the festival. Local priests often took a discreet part in the fire festivities, though to this day, the Orthodox Church condemns it as witchcraft – not surprisingly, since the Orthodox Church has never been known for its liberalism. In fact, the Greek Orthodox Church put an anathema on the practice so fierce that Greek anastenarides had to tweak their instruments and swap the animal-skin *gaida* (bagpipe) for the less animalistic *lyra* (fiddle).

The oral stories of great fire-walkers echo the nature of the worship: it is about seeking a balance between the human world and the spirit world. Zlata would go stone cold just before the festival. She'd hug the red-hot stove and hold embers in her fists to warm herself. Once, out of embarrassment, her husband prevented her from going on the fire. Instantly, she was felled by a stroke and paralysed. But then she heard the beat of the tupan like the beat of blood, threw her blanket away, and rose from her bed. Like a sleepwalker, she walked to the fire and entered it. The following season, the husband found himself moaning *Vuh vuh vuh* and running to the fire. He too had been seized. The revenge of Saints Constantine and Elena perhaps? In any case, Zlata and her husband became a duo, and health and good fortune were restored. Briefly. Then he died, leaving her with six kids.

Another fire-walker, called Kerka, went onto the fire while heavily pregnant with her sixth child. She fell onto the embers in a fit of rapture, belly-down. The girl child survived, and Kerka even prophesied her future: you will marry twice and bear a child at forty-eight. Nobody believed it but it happened exactly so. The daughter Kostadinka is an old woman now, and lives alone in a coastal Strandja village, in such poverty that visitors know to bring a kilo of flour and a bottle of oil. Why? Because she likes to make a bread offering for the local *konak,* or chapel. It's the only konak with a bed in it, and not just any bed. Once, Kostadinka fell and wounded her leg. It became infected and eventually gangrene set in, but she was so poor, she couldn't afford a visit to the doctor. One night, in a fever, she saw her dead mother walk into the house, and Kostadinka cried: Mother, I'm dying. Of course you're dying, Kerka said, you're not taking care of yourself. Now here's what to do. Bake a loaf of bread, take it to the chapel as an offering, and sleep there. Kostadinka followed the instructions. The morning after, her wound began to heal.

But there are no great nestinari any more in Strandja. It's a dying art, I kept hearing. The chubby bagpipe player was the son of one of the last ones. The repeated spells of persecution, first by the Church and then by the Communist State, have stamped out the female communion with fire. The State had its own approved faux nestinari who performed for tourists in the kitschy seaside resorts of the red Riviera (sometimes with bears on chains), but the real thing was criminalised.

Marina sighed. 'They arrested the forest. Still, in the last four thousand years the cult of fire hasn't died. There is hope yet.'

The forest was closing in with its bubbling agiasmas, its coils of

music, the faces leaning in, the sap rising in our bodies. I felt trapped
in a dream – good or bad, I didn't know. Marina smiled enigmatically.

'You've felt it,' she said. 'The energy is very concentrated here.
You have to be ready to receive it. Otherwise it makes you ill. There
are places like this in Strandja. If you stick around, they'll find you.'

'I am sticking around,' I said. Marina looked at me without making
eye contact, a disconcerting trick of hers.

'Beware,' she said. 'Strandja isn't for everyone. It's a mountain that
doesn't let you in.'

Everybody looked stoned. The forest was like an opiate.

'And doesn't let you out,' Marina added.

It suddenly struck me why it was important to come to this forest.
It had nothing to do with Saints Constantine and Elena.

Behind the faces of the old women, their children and grandchildren far away in foreign countries, cold and hot wars waged, political
regimes and armies swept away, only the human-faced icons still in
their laps, I saw why. This was a story untold – but it was sung, danced,
purged in fire and water every year. When the Ottoman Empire was
slowly dismembered and the Balkan Wars ripped people from the
land, they were forced to cross this border under pain of death. Then
for half a century, they were prohibited from crossing it under pain
of death. That's why it was important to come here, so close to the
border in space yet so far away from it in time.

In the afternoon, the icon team piled into the Soviet van and
headed back to the village, with the dressed icons on their laps.

'They need to rest,' the woman with the chewing gum said and
winked at me as she left.

When night fell, a man raked the embers and the drum and bagpipe
struck up their ritual fire-walking tunes. Three, one for each stage of
the rite. The first was called 'Departure', and with it, the band and
the fire-walkers circled the embers three times, anticlockwise. To

this yearning, lustful beat, the kind of music that makes you feel as if you belong in the forest, the chthonic phase began. The second tune, 'Possession', accompanied the nestinari into the fire. The two reptilian men and two Greek women stepped on the embers, each with an icon's face pressed to their chest. The four trampled the embers and passed each other without eye contact or crossing each other's way. It wasn't about the people connecting with each other, it was about them connecting with the fire, helped along by the icon.

Several things distinguish the Strandja nestinari from other traditional fire-walkers, Marina whispered. The trampling of the embers until they are ash. The additional gifts they have. And most of all: in the old days, the physical communion with fire was the culmination of a year-round ritual calendar that featured different avatars of the two primal elements: fire-sun-God and cave-night-Goddess.

It was like being inside the collective unconscious. The two Greek women came from a village where the rite is best preserved, but only practised in a closed initiated society where outsiders aren't admitted, and it was this protectionism that has saved Greek anastenaria in its authentic form. The heat of the embers lapped at the onlookers. My hair was about to combust. I can't remember tune three, the one called 'In the Fire'.

Ecstasy: to be taken out of yourself. Ecstasy has been collectively experienced in these forests since the time of Dionysian revelries. But that's only one kind of ecstasy. Some historians believe that ancient Thrace is too far to go in search of the first spark. A local researcher speculates that the Hesychast monks of Paroria could have been the original anastenarides. After all, there are similarities: the intense meditation, the change in body temperature, the dissolving of the ego and the communion with a divine energy. There are also the gestures: just as the Hesychast monks practised a rocking meditation, so there was a custom here (lost in the demographic chaos of the Balkan Wars)

where the anastenarides rocked and banged their heads with icons of
the Virgin Mary. Finally, the material symbols: in old nestinar icons,
Saint Marina walks on a fire-red ground as snakes come out of her
skirts, and the Virgin Mary is dressed in red. Red like the 'dress' of the
icons today, red like the mantles of Saints Constantine and Elena. The
monks of Paroria were scattered by the soldiers of Islam in the 1350s,
but could they have left this secret legacy to the civilian population?

'Sssss,' one of the Greek women on the embers hissed, snake-like.

Bewildered, I looked at Marina, but her ember-lit face was turned
up at the night sky. The hissing was in honour of Saint Marina, I was
told later, the patron saint of snakes and fire.

'Look out for the ball of fire,' Marina said. 'Sometimes it appears,
around this time of year.'

The mysterious ball of fire sighted by Strandja people, which may
be a flying dragon. I looked up at the spectral sky and saw galaxies
moving in.

A few days later, on an errand to the village of Crossing, which looked
down its own precipitous river valley, I saw Iglika with one of the pale
nestinari. They were at her grandmother's house on a vine-shaded
afternoon. Untouched by the sun, they looked like twins from some
milky latitude, on a brief visit to earth.

The fire-walker greeted me with a formal smile. I asked how he
felt.

'Charged,' he said from a distance. 'The fire charges me up.'

When I greeted Iglika, she didn't remember our meeting by the
Big Agiasma, perhaps not even the gathering itself. Her eyes were
completely empty. And when I held her cold palm in a formal handshake, I too was seized by doubt.

cheshma

From the Turkish *çeşme*. The pan-Balkan roadside drinking fountain where you tie your horse, fill your goatskin with water, slice a watermelon, drop your rubbish in the vicinity of the public bin. Sometimes a plaque marks the resting place of a local hero, or remembers a person somebody loved. An everyday cousin of the agiasma, the *cheshma* is hospitality without a host, the Balkans without borders. The water is good and you want to linger, tickled by butterflies.

But if you linger, things happen. I had stopped at a roadside cheshma at the edge of a sleepy hamlet. When I turned, the man was already there.

A MAN OF LEISURE

He was tanned, and moved as if the road belonged to him.

'Just came to see what's up,' he smiled urbanely. He was so well turned out, so unlike the locals, it was difficult to age him. 'I saw you from the house.'

He looked me up and down. We had reached my car.

'Care to join us for a coffee?' He saw the doubt on my face. 'Orange juice? We're just over there.'

He pointed to the palatial house half-hidden by a wall that I had passed before, marvelling at the fine example of gangster-baroque, not the kind of house you expect to see in these ghostly villages. Later, when I described the encounter to a local from 'my' village, he said, 'Ah yes, the one with the wife who throws out the rubbish, butt naked.'

I parked outside the hacienda-style wall and entered with misgivings. The swimming pool in the courtyard was dotted with plaster statues of exotic fauna.

'My wife is Austrian, a retired anaesthetist,' he said ambiguously and went inside the house to get refreshments.

His wife was slouched on a chaise longue in a bikini. She smiled with eyes like slits. Her hair was white blonde and her skin mahogany brown.

'Our dogs,' she said, and told me the names of the two German

Shepherds. They were the breed once trained to hunt people, lovable mascots of border life during communism.

'I take the dogs when I go hunting,' my host said, emerging with a glass of juice for me, whisky for him, and nothing for the wife. 'But I don't kill. I have everything already. I don't need to kill as well.'

'Sit down, relax.' The wife gestured at a chair next to hers. I sat down stiffly.

'Do you know anyone who will buy this house?' the man said. 'It's up for sale.'

I asked why they were selling it.

'Why, why. We're moving to Spain. We've had enough of here. We built our dream house, all we want is the good life, but every time I leave the house, I see nothing but Gypsies.'

'Gypsies.' His wife shook her head, a gash of a smile across her horsey face. 'We have to keep the gates locked at all times.'

'The gypsification of this country has reached epidemic proportions. You must have noticed,' the man said glumly and looked at me over his whisky for agreement, then changed tack. 'Are you alone? What are you doing in this wilderness?'

The closed gate in the wall was electrically operated, with a code.

'Looking for stories about the border,' I said. He looked at me sharply.

'What about the border?'

'You know,' I said. He did. He went inside the house and brought back a sheet of paper.

'Let me show you, because there are things you don't know, my lovely,' he said, and began to draw. 'This here is the Rezovo River. It's where the East Germans used to cross the most. They thought, it's only a forest, it's not like Berlin. Piece of cake. But they had another think coming. Because the decoy wire was here... and the real one was here.' He drew the double barbed wire.

'When those smarty-pants didn't make it to the other side, their relatives or friends or whoever was waiting there knew... And then, back in Berlin, they'd get two years. Some didn't make it out of jail alive. But first, they'd put them through the works. They had a special department for that. And after a few days, they sang like nightingales.'

Behind a curl of smoke, his wife smiled her vague ironic smile.

'How do you know all this?' I asked.

'Because back in the day, I worked at the Cultural Centre in Berlin. I had a passport to all of Europe, though I never abused it. Of course I served as a courier, between East and West Berlin. But I've been a man of leisure for a while.'

'What kind of courier?' Though I already knew.

'Oh, letters, things in envelopes.' He winked. 'Nothing sinister.'

He had been on the payroll of State Security. The Cultural Centre in Berlin was a decoy behind which the real 'cultural' work was done – spying, smuggling, and siphoning state funds.

'I can see you're naive. Things were not so black and white,' he went on with sudden passion. 'There were no innocents, only opportunists. Asking for it, they were, trying to outsmart the system. But the system was smarter. You think the locals were innocent? Ha! Take a local shepherd, a simple soul. The kind of person a young fugitive who's starving, freezing, and lost in the forest can trust when the shepherd says, "You stay here, I'll bring you food." Then he goes and tells the border patrols. Handcuffs, and *auf wiedersehen*. And the shepherd was given a watch. A Soviet watch. That's what these friendly locals were like.'

A Soviet watch for a human life.

'See that tower over there?' He pointed to the transmission aerial on top of the nearest hill. 'That was used by the State for eavesdropping. In the rest of the country, they blocked out transmission waves, but here on the border, they tuned in and listened.'

His wife had closed her eyes and was concentrating on her sunbathing.

'The Communist State and its protégés took billions. They robbed the country blind. Carried out antiques and fortunes in briefcases. And you know why many of the same people have stayed in power to this day? Because they are professionals. They couldn't be beaten.'

'And you?' I said. 'What about you?'

'Me?' He raised his hands in neutrality. 'I stayed abroad.' He nodded at his wife. 'I only came back a couple of years ago. To live the good life. But it's not possible.'

'The Gypsies,' his wife said. 'I hate these Gypsies.'

'Not just them. It's everyone. Are you alone? You must stay away from Balkan men. They are really bad.'

'Yes,' his wife said, opening a flirty eye. 'Balkan men, very bad.'

She took off her bikini top and for a horrible moment I thought they would invite me for a threesome. Her breasts were tanned like the rest of her.

'Sexist, racist, backward, chauvinistic,' he said. Then he turned to me. 'Who is paying you for this? Someone must be paying you.'

'I am a writer,' I said. 'Nobody pays me for anything, unfortunately.'

He scoffed cynically and shook his head.

'In the good old days, we had methods for the likes of you,' he said.

'What do you mean, the likes of me?' I already understood *methods*.

'Progressive types,' he said. 'Who go around asking questions. It's a shame. In many ways, those were the golden days.'

It was time to thank them for the juice. I reached for the sheet with his drawing.

'Let me give you my number,' he said, 'in case you think of someone who might buy the house.'

He took the sheet from me, tore off a corner and scribbled something on it, then ripped up the rest into small pieces and piled them in a heap on the glass table.

His watch wasn't Soviet but Swiss.

'Come again,' his wife smiled. I wondered how much she understood or cared, but now wasn't the time.

He walked me through the electrified gate to the car, and when I was sitting behind the wheel, he leaned into the open window and said casually:

'Don't go round digging up old graves, my lovely. Nobody's interested.'

'I'm interested,' I said.

He banged the roof of the car in farewell.

The only people I saw on the way out of the village were two crumpled men who sat on a collapsed bench, dressed in those faded blue workers' ensembles that the State used to issue people 'for free', as prisons do for their inmates. If I were to touch them, I might just find that some inner mechanism had stopped twenty-five years ago.

I went back to the cheshma and emptied my bottle with a shaky hand. I held it again under the spout for a long time, letting it overflow, before I looked at the torn corner where he had written his number.

But there was no number, just a message that said: 'You only have one life.'

The number of 'missing' foreign tourists between 1961 and 1989, cited in various sources as being recorded in the archives of the Bulgarian Interior Ministry. I don't know if this is the true number, but I do know that not a single soldier or politician has been indicted. Many of those 415 were buried in unmarked graves by the soldiers who had shot them. They were Germans, Poles, Czechs, Hungarians, Chechens, and other citizens of the Soviet Union, usually young couples, solo travellers, or pairs of friends. Their reasons for taking this desperate step were diverse: social entrapment, family disputes, troubled love, shirking military service, wanting to be reunited with family or lovers in the West. Bulgaria had a deceptively friendly reputation for its 'green border', much easier to cross than the Berlin Wall. The most frequent victims of this border, however, were the Bulgarians; over the course of the Cold War, hundreds were shot, sometimes women and children. Hundreds escaped too.

Among other nationalities, the greatest numbers were from the GDR. The attempts made by East Germans to cross this last border between the Warsaw Pact (Bulgaria) and NATO (Turkey and Greece) number around 4,000. Of those, 95 per cent were arrested by Bulgarian border guards and served prison sentences. One of them was a young DJ from Leipzig called Thomas who was mauled by dogs and shot in the leg in 1981. The army took him to the Burgas hospital, where his leg was amputated before he was repatriated. Thirty years later, he travelled back to stand once again in the spot by the wire where his body and his life had changed for ever, and meet the nurse who had looked after him in Burgas.

The Germans were bureaucratically a special case: the two brotherly governments signed an agreement 'to prevent the escape into the West by citizens of the German Democratic Republic across the border of the People's Republic of Bulgaria, detain law-breakers, and hand them over to the respective organs of power', and in the late 1960s – it has been alleged – the Stasi went one better: it set up a fund, via its embassy in Sofia, to reward Bulgarian soldiers who killed errant German citizens. There were other perks: medals for 'exceptional services', extra leave, and sometimes even holidays in the GDR.

One of the last victims of this border was a 19-year-old from Leipzig called Michael who was executed by a 20 year-old guard with a point-blank shot to the cheek, and bled to death a hundred metres from Greek territory. It was in July 1989, four months before the fall of the Berlin Wall. His divorced parents travelled to Sofia to see his body, and his mother spent the rest of her short life trying to indict the guard. Michael had spent his whole adolescence planning his escape from his foretold future. He had taken all his savings with him: 790 marks and a gold coin.

WIRE IN THE HEART

The house was an ordinary, run-down village affair with a low stone fence, rubber galoshes in the doorway, and cardboard in place of a broken window. The garden whispered with roses and small early apples that fill your mouth with bitterness when you bite into them. Home-made plum brandy fermented in hundred-litre tubs by the outdoor tap. The woody smell of the bulbous sweet bull's heart tomatoes hit me from the gate when I reached in to open it.

Here lived an old man I wanted to see because through the 1960s, 70s, and 80s he had been a corporal in the 7th division of the border army.

Don't go, locals warned me, he's not right in the head. Nobody talks to him, he has no friends, there's ill fate hanging over him, ever since he did those things.

Inside the gate was a human-sized monolithic stone memorial to a border guard who had been, in the favourite phrase of Balkan self-pity, 'savagely murdered by the Turks' in 1948. This was his father, and later an airbrushed story of a hero emerged, though he had been no hero but a spy betrayed by fellow spies and kidnapped to Istanbul. It was a brain-scrambling story of double-agent machinations that involved the Bulgarian, Soviet, and Turkish counter-intelligence, and left the impression that the savage murder was committed not by 'the Turks' but by the MGB, successor of the mass-murderous NKVD and progenitor of the KGB.

Pinned to the gate was a commemorative notice, showing the portrait of a smiling young man in an army uniform. His name was Nasko and he had died in 1986. Something about his intelligent hazel eyes broke my heart in a second. It was the hope.

I found the old man in the chicken coop behind the house, chasing hens with an empty wheelbarrow. He was powerfully built with a hollow chest, in head-to-toe camouflage and army boots with the laces undone. When he saw me, he stopped swearing at the hens and dropped the wheelbarrow.

'What is it?' He came up to me and stared with a menacing blue eye. In the place where the other eye would have been, the skin was sewn up flat. I took a step back. He was unshaven and smelled sour, of sweat and last night's booze.

'I'm visiting the village,' I said, and added, 'Sorry about your wife.'

His wife had died the previous week. For a moment, I thought he was going to push me down the steps with a stream of obscenities. But he said, 'Sit,' and pulled up a plastic chair for me, and another one for him. He asked my name and where I was from, and then we fell silent. His huge gnarled hands were restless in his lap. I imagined them wringing a hen's neck. But he picked a blue plum from a low branch and handed it to me.

'What happened to your eye?' I asked in a hoarse voice and put the plum in my lap.

'An infection,' he said. 'And last week the old lady died. Everything's gone. I don't know why, but my life hasn't worked out.'

Then he said: 'I had a son. Nasko.'

His jaw began to tremble and from his single eye came sudden tears.

'A bright boy, a good boy. He was going to be an officer. In radio communication. He was our hope.'

'What happened?'

'An accident, they said. His commanding officer got him to dyna-mite a quarry. To get stones for some general's villa. In the middle of the night. A fuse hit a stray stone. Stone shard cut him in half.'

Soldier 'accidents' were so common until 1990 that his death was not investigated, and anyway, soldiers' lives were as expendable as those of the fugitives they were obliged to hunt down.

'My boy, gone in a second. Because some general wanted a villa.'

The tears were now pouring through the eyeless socket too.

'Then in 1989, the world turned upside down. Bundle of money I'd saved turned to dust overnight. And Nasko was gone.'

I stayed all morning, hoping for an admission, a hint, a resolution of some sort. Through his tears, he darted an alarmed eye at me:

'Eh? I can't hear.'

Repeatedly, he couldn't hear *that* question.

'My life hasn't worked out,' he repeated.

He cheered up when I asked about the rest of his family. His daughter's son was in the border police.

'What do you make of that?' I said.

He turned to me, puzzled, as if I'd spoken in a foreign language.

'He's a good boy,' he said.

'Four generations of border guards,' I insisted.

'Yes,' he smiled vaguely, and I saw doubt on his face.

Here is what I'd heard, in hushed tones from locals. Here, where facts and deeds had been so final, rumour remained the preferred currency.

He had executed a couple of Czechs or maybe Poles, people said. Because they were the enemy, because this made barrack life easier: no need to fill in forms. They buried them in the forest, in shallow graves.

He had poured gasoline and set alight two young ethnic Turks, people said. Because they were trying to cross the border, because they were 'the Turks', because he could.

He had seen a soldier from his division make a run for it, people said, as those on compulsory border duty sometimes did, and shot him in the back. Because traitors deserved to die, because he could not bear to see a man break free.

Accounts were contradictory, however. Perhaps these crimes were not his, or not only his. Perhaps over time he had become a convenient repository of other people's darkness.

At one point, I noticed I was crying too. Some things are beyond repair, and that's what tears are for. In his blue steely eye, there glinted the animal cunning of survival that in humans is the need to be liked, to be right, so that you can live with yourself. He changed, people said, he withdrew into himself, became deranged, and then his son died. That's what people said, quietly, with a mixture of pity, repulsion, and shame.

Men like him, honest fanatics, Frankensteinian monsters of the totalitarian machine, were cursed to carry the Iron Curtain in their hearts, so that men of leisure could sip whisky and reminisce about the golden days.

'You going already?' he said, startled, as if waking from a dream. 'I didn't offer you anything. I'm getting forgetful. Come again. Take some plums, here.'

He shuffled to the plum tree and started picking the fruit feverishly, with a trembling hand, piling them in the cradle of his arm, piling them until the plums started falling to the concrete ground with a bruising thud.

klyon (1961–1990)

The pet name Bulgarian border soldiers gave the electrified, alarmed wall of barbed wire that ran through the forest and sealed off the country from its neighbours. The official name was *Saorajenieto*, The Installation, and The Installation was ostensibly there to stop enemies from infiltrating. But if you look at the top of the wire, parts of which still stand, you see that it points to the real enemy: inwards.

In that twilight zone the soldiers lived, counted the months and sometimes years till their promised leave, and sometimes died by their own hand or the hand of a comrade gone berserk. Their only company consisted of the pet dogs trained to console some and hunt others. There were two types of border guards: career soldiers like the one-eyed man, and those nineteen-year-olds on compulsory two-year military service who had drawn the border lot. Border duty was the most dreaded service because the colonels in charge of the Border Forces were notorious for being, in the words of a former soldier, 'daemons in human disguise'. Another former guard said to me: 'When you have no contact with the outside world, they can make you believe anything.' With its well-oiled feudal barbarity, life behind The Installation was a perfect microcosm of totalitarian society.

★

The strip of land that ran alongside The Installation was known as the Furrow of Death. Even a bird's footprint could be seen in its carefully tended soil.

THE TOMB OF BASTET

There were stories I'd heard about this place over the years, and now I'd come to see it with my own eyes. It was so close to the border that a message popped up on my phone: 'Turkcell Welcomes You to Turkey'.

To get there you needed a guide with an off-road vehicle. The guide was called Niki, and young Niki was short but broad of shoulder; he wasn't yet thirty but had gone grey. He drove an iconic Soviet-style van affectionately called UAZ-ka by those who own one. UAZ-kas are made in the Ulyanovsk Automobile Plant in Russia, the model unchanged since the 1940s, and in this vehicle Niki took visitors from the last border town along the short road to Turkey, and into the forest.

We saw no traffic, except, suddenly, a pair of unshaven men with rucksacks who looked the way you do when you've walked across Turkey. They were human shadows. I caught their eye as we passed them. They made no gesture.

Stop! I said to Niki. Perhaps we could offer them something? But Niki drove past them and made a phone call on his mobile. 'Two guys on the road just before the turn-off to the Big Site,' he recited. And that was it.

'They want to give themselves in,' he said, clocking my expression. 'That's why they're walking along the road and not hiding in the forest. At least the guys on patrol will come and give them a lift to the police station, save them walking.'

'But,' I said.

'I see guys like this every day now. I can't get involved.'

'But don't you feel something?'

'Sure,' he said, and turned off the road, up a rough track. 'But I can't stop the war in Syria, can I.'

I took his point, even if it didn't change the fact that we had not stopped to offer anything to two men who needed everything. This was a year when refugees still came across the border in twos, rather than in hundreds and thousands.

We drove through the open, rusted portal of the *klyon*.

'This portal was locked until last year,' Niki said. 'You had to have a key.'

Where did you get the key?

'You didn't. You had to come with a local guide who did.'

They kept it locked for twenty-five years after the end of the Cold War!

Niki, who *was* twenty-five, couldn't see what I was so worked up about. To him, the klyon was just a museum exhibit from the mythical era of communism when this whole area, including the pretty border town, had been known as Border Zone Number One. But there was apparently another reason why this stretch of the klyon was locked for so long.

The following story I'd heard begins in 1981 behind the klyon and goes back to an unspecified time in ancient Egypt. It's impossible to separate the truth from the conspiracy theories; the only certain facts are the deaths.

In 1981, a sapper from a local unit of the border army was called in to a top-secret meeting with archaeologists from the Department of Cultural Heritage. When a mere mortal was issued with an invitation of this kind, he started to sweat because he knew it wasn't an invitation. He was to take part in a classified expedition to a remote hill of Strandja, behind the klyon.

The area was topographically known as the Big Site because several layers of ancient habitation had been found in the vicinity: a circular Thracian cult complex called Mishkova Niva, complete with sacrificial altar and shrine inscribed by Orphic priests; a tumulus necropolis; a Romanised Thracian fort; a Roman holiday villa; and a network of antique copper mines. From the top of the 700-metre-high hill you could look down at the sprawling green hills of Turkey.

And if you looked up at the hill from below, they said it was shaped – more than most pyramid-shaped hills – like an Egyptian pyramid. The only people who came here were soldiers on border duty and Cold War archaeologists. This had kept the ruins in decent condition. But the treasure hunters of the last twenty-five years have depredated the necropolis, and somehow managed to raze an entire Roman tower to the ground. Niki and I stood looking at the sun-shaped necropolis. In the daytime, the place emanated its own high-pitched energy.

'It's not surprising,' I said to Niki, 'that bloody treasure hunters reign supreme. They're following a well-trodden path.'

Niki smiled with polite indifference.

In the early 1980s, the communist barons set up a Department of Treasure Hunting within the Bulgarian Academy of Sciences; citizens were encouraged to report sites where antiques might be found. Ministers, deputy ministers, and high-powered officials initiated classified archaeological digs, then briskly removed the archaeologists from the dig, and after the treasures were extracted and carried out, never to be documented, itemised, or seen again by mortal eyes, the sites were blown up. It is said – but then what isn't, in this story? – that priceless treasures were found: the fourteenth-century gold treasures of the last Bulgar tsar, Ivan Shishman, and of Lysimachus, who succeeded Alexander the Great. Nothing could stop the over-lords from the Central Committee of the Communist Party – some of whom couldn't even spell the word 'archaeology' – from plundering the country. Antiques were sold on the international black market, and the hard currency was shuttled in diplomatic bags, with the help of cadres like our man of leisure. The hub of antique smuggling from east to west was Vienna. With the proceeds, the comrades sent their wives and mistresses to shop in Paris, while they holed up in their hunting lodges and seaside residences to drink whisky and whore it. The golden days. The 'golden days' are unforgettably portrayed in Georgi Markov's *The Truth That Killed*, for which Markov was indeed killed by a secret agent on Waterloo Bridge, three years before his executioner's daughter, Lyudmila Zhivkova, issued the order to begin work here at the Big Site. Am I ranting?

Niki shrugged, hands in pockets.

'It's all before my time. I'm just a guide.'

Lyudmila Zhivkova was then the country's most powerful woman: Minister of Culture, daughter of the Head of State and General Sec-retary of the Communist Party Todor Zhivkov, and visible evidence that the first totalitarian dynasty of Eastern Europe was in action. Zhivkova, however, seemed not to be your average dictator's daugh-ter. She appeared to challenge the philistinism of her father's cronies by embracing a life of eccentricity. In the late 1970s, she began to con-struct a cult around the mega-projects she initiated. One of these was the Children of the World Assembly of Peace which brought thou-sands of children to my home city of Sofia. There, we were to gather at a gigantic concrete complex outside the city that represented each country through its national bell. It was called 'Bells of Peace', and we sang the specially composed songs during our school visit there to meet the children of the world. But I never spoke to the children of the world – we only tolled their national bells, politely, in a queue, because it was clear even to an eight-year-old that the event was not staged for us but for Zhivkova and her entourage who waved from public platforms with gestures reminiscent of the Roman emperors' sign for execution, then disappeared into tinted-window limousines. Although the glint of megalomania was indistinguishable from the messianic aura, there was *something* about her – perhaps the simple fact that she was a woman in power, and she dared raise a different voice of madness among the zombie chorus of brown suits. Her speeches and writings were high-pitched and utterly incomprehensible.

Lyudmila had an obsession with antiquities. An old treasure hunter who worked with archaeologists at the time tells the following story. One day when she was in her early thirties, Lyudmila arrived at the excavation of a major treasure inside a Thracian tomb. The archae-ologists had found a stunning gold wreath of a priestess–princess (Thracian royalty had priestly status and performed rituals). When Lyudmila saw the dazzling wreath, she picked it up and went to put it on her head. The team rushed to stop her: Don't, it's a bad omen, you can't tinker with objects in tombs! Of course she put the wreath on her head anyway. Soon after, she suffered a near-fatal car crash which damaged her head and she took to wearing white turbans. The old treasure hunter never saw that gold wreath again.

Lyudmila was a creation of her era, the offspring of a drooling feudal gerontocracy that sucked the lifeblood of the nation to ensure eternal life for themselves. She did not, in the end, challenge anything – she was simply the next Draculian organism. The workers who built her pharaonic monuments in record time were put to unpaid weekend labour in order to fulfil the five-year plan in one year; they were treated as a slave force.

But she was also a manifestation of a kink in the collective psyche. Decades of dialectic materialism rammed down people's throats had to produce a compensation mechanism, and in a way she embodied the spiritual void at the heart of absolute power. Anything can happen in a void. Soviet dogma had failed to replace the undercurrent of mysticism that runs through the Bulgarian psyche. People had lived close to the land for millennia, and a few decades of Soviet social engineering had made them scared and suspicious, but the land's mysteries were still there. They spoke to those who could tune in. Lyudmila wanted to tune in.

They say it all started with a map. A treasure hunter who may or may not have been called Mustafa turned up one day at the house of the clairvoyant known as Vanga, asking to be admitted. The most famous seer in Eastern Europe, Vanga channelled news from the past and the future. People travelled from Moscow and Belgrade to see her, in her town at the foot of vapour-veiled hills full of hot springs by the Greek border. Here is Vanga's story.

Born in 1911 in the Macedonian town of Strumica, Evangelia 'Vanga' Gushterova was picked up by a freak tornado and her eyes were damaged by dust. An eye operation in Belgrade failed to restore her sight and by the age of thirteen she was blind, orphaned, and bone-poor. But in the midst of this, Vanga began to communicate with an invisible world, acquire knowledge of medicinal plants, and have prophetic dreams. One night in 1941, the night before the Axis powers invaded her town, she had a visitation from a divine horseman who spoke to her and instructed her to remain on this earth for as long as possible. Her mission was to help people. The next day, she was lit up from within, started speaking in voices, and described events from the past and the future. She didn't sleep 'for a year', her sister said – she could not stop channelling. It was the beginning of her life as an oracle and healer, and people from all over came to her with their sorrows, including her husband-to-be, who came to ask her about the killers of his brother. Though she knew who they were, and predicted their downfall, she didn't reveal their identity to him. Never take revenge, she advised him, because it bounces back on your descendants. Her moral advice was always to be kind, to spare others, because nothing goes away. A human destiny could not be changed, all she could do was watch the 'film' of someone's life, and report. Despite this determinism, Vanga gave people guidance and consolation at a time when psychotherapy was considered too bourgeois.

When the Soviets arrived in 1945, she narrowly escaped execution as a subversive agent. For years, she remained ideologically awkward – a witch, an anachronism, an enemy of the people, an affront to Marxism–Leninism. The government jailed her, intimidated her, tried to shut her up. But she couldn't be bought, sold, or silenced. And there was another problem: she was too popular, not only with ordinary people, but with the political elite. They grew to secretly depend on her – maybe there was something beyond dialectical materialism after all? – so in a stroke of creative thinking, in 1967 they put her on the State payroll of the newly established Institute of Suggestology. She became an official seer, complete with a chauffeur, and a handy source of income for the entrepreneurial Communist State, which then pocketed the generous fees paid by her visitors. Once in a while, the dictator Zhivkov himself, or one of his ministers, would send a tinted-window limousine to bring her to their residences on the outskirts of Sofia. And who was especially close to her? Lyudmila Zhivkova, of course. So much so that Vanga's niece was appointed to the Ministry of Culture. Vanga's niece, busybodyish in her exalted role as the clairvoyant's 'daughter', as she called herself, was always around, listening, recording.

I grew up with rumours of Vanga, and we knew people who had been to see her, but even though she kept her common touch she had become the property of the elite. By the 1980s, you had to be someone or know someone to see her, and my parents didn't, they were ordinary scientists. Her house was bugged by State Security agents – to listen in to her visitors from Tito's Yugoslavia – and she knew it and laughed it away because it was one of the in-jokes of twilight totalitarianism.

Which is why Mustafa the treasure hunter must have been sweating when he turned up with his yellowed map and could he please see Vanga to help him with the map, because there was great treasure buried within it, but he couldn't decipher the hieroglyphics.

Vanga didn't like treasure hunters but she let Mustafa in. With her sewn-up eyes, she perceived the map's message. And the message was spectacular but terrifying. Mustafa was relieved of his map and sent packing.

The place marked on the map was in Strandja, Vanga told her niece, she knew exactly where the hill was. Inside it was no treasure, but a black granite sarcophagus inscribed in an ancient script and carrying a message to humanity from past millennia. Those who had participated in the expedition that brought the sarcophagus over the water from Egypt to Thrace were slaughtered on the spot so that the rivers of blood would wash away all memory of it. But humanity is not ready for the message contained within, Vanga warned. Tamper with it at your cost.

Naturally, the next thing was that Vanga's niece, who studied Egyptology, took the map to the experts. Soon enough, word reached the turbaned one and her entourage. Deciphering the symbols proved impossible, but what proved possible, as Lyudmila snapped into fatal action, was to visit the place Vanga had described in some detail, and prepare to excavate. And that's what the first team did: in the spring of 1981 they came to the Big Site, where I now stood with Niki.

We were looking up at a vertical rock face, and underneath it – a cave full of stagnant water. You'd have to dive in and swim under water to enter the cave. I had asked Marina along but she didn't like coming here because of what the expedition had done to the hill.

'You don't break in, the land must let you in,' she said. Marina knew treasure hunters who had appropriated antiquities and suffered personal misfortunes, usually involving death.

There were five or maybe six of them in the excavation team: the head of Cultural Heritage, a historian called Mutafchiev who was close to Zhivkova; Vanga's omnipresent niece; the head miner of Strandja Ore Mining Company; a journalist; a numismatist; a driver. In this tale of increasing mystery, there are no reliable narrators, but what is half-certain is that they camped here the night of 4 May (according to Vanga's niece, but not according to others), and just before dawn, they waited for the rays of 'the sun and the moon' to appear together, just as Vanga had instructed *against*. Then they fled.

'Have you been here at night?' I asked Niki. He looked at me.

'You'd have to pay me a lot of money to spend the night here.'

'Do you know people who have?'

'I know all sorts of people.' He looked away. 'Sometimes there's a gathering of mediums and astrologers who sleep here. They say the energy is prohibitive.'

What Vanga's niece and Mutafchiev reported to have seen has been described by others since, but with variations. The lunar–solar rays drew circles upon the rock face, then a triangle, then (said Vanga's niece) a spectral projection appeared, 'like on a television screen lit up from within the rock', of two figures: an old man with a beard, holding a round object in his palm, and a younger man or woman, in a high conical pharaonic hat. They were three-dimensional, as if coming out of the rock to approach the company, who were in a state of paralysis until the vision subsided. Then they got the hell out of there. The projection didn't appear on subsequent visits.

Lyudmila's wishes were law, and a reconfigured team arrived at the site next: Mutafchiev was in charge, and this time there was an army reinforcement, including the local sapper, who had sworn not to talk. He still hasn't.

They dug their way into the hill and discovered Thracian and Roman-era mining galleries, as you would in many Strandja hills.

In the aftermath, locals said that tons of soil were shifted and the stuff they found was loaded onto army trucks and taken away – but nobody said what was inside the trucks. Others say that there was an Austrian-registration car present at the excavation – because of the Vienna black-market connection. Yet others say the KGB was keeping tabs on the project, and its interest in the area went back to the late 1940s when a Soviet team might have excavated the mines. Which explains, some say, the 1949 issues of the *Pravda* newspaper found inside. A local cart driver at the port of Burgas testified that the Soviet team had loaded up ancient statues – only half-bodied, from the waist up, he said!

A conspiracy tale wouldn't be complete without the Nazis. During World War II, two German units were stationed here, with the main objective of spying via radio transmission lines, the same ones later used by the communists. One of their posts happened to be here, at the top of the Big Site. The Nazis' taste for the occult leads some to conclude that their real objective was to rummage inside the ancient mines – which explains, some say, the German detritus found inside the mines. One of the Germans died in a freak accident here, run over by a truck driven by his friend while they were building bunkers in the forest. His tombstone is nearby, Niki said, but he refused to take me there.

Vanga's niece claimed, unconvincingly, to have burnt the original map. A bit late for that, Vanga might have pointed out, but then she knew it was pointless to stop people marching towards destruction. She had tried it many times, most painfully during World War II with her brother, whose death at twenty-three she predicted, and begged him not to join the resistance; still he went back to their native Macedonia, where he was captured and executed by the Nazis on the day of his twenty-third birthday.

For reasons of her own, Lyudmila Zhivkova had previously visited holy lamas, who told her that an ancient sarcophagus was buried within Bulgarian territory. Which is why she and Mutafchiev were hoping to find no less than the Egyptian cat-headed divinity Bastet.

Bastet – daughter of the Sun God Ra, protector of femininity, engenderer of light and joy, principle of life. Bastet – who would hold the cosmological key to human civilisation in her cat-paws. If Lyudmila could uncover Bastet, the two of them would unite and rule not just a small Soviet satellite, not just the Children of the World, not just ancient Egypt, but – well, the whole Cosmos.

Here is the official version of what was found in the ancient mines before the expedition was terminated. Niki listed the items for me: black granite, though no sarcophagus; artefacts from the first century AD; antique agricultural tools; an old railway used to transport ore in wagons; Nazi boreholes; Soviet and Bulgarian newspapers from *circa* 1950; Roman pottery; medieval oil lamps. Then people started ailing and dying.

Lyudmila was the first to go. Already her esoterics infuriated the KGB and therefore also the KGB-oriented wing of her own State Security apparatus (as opposed to the pro-Western wing, the two of which waged their own discreet Cold War), who viewed her as an apostatic figure. It is no surprise that her sudden death in July 1981, a few days before her thirty-ninth birthday, became the subject of KGB-related conspiracy theories, ensuring that in addition to being a messiah she was also a potential martyr. But she was probably the victim of a brain aneurysm due to complications from the earlier car accident. She died in her bath just as the secret excavation was making inroads.

Soon after the grandiose state funeral, the team drove back to the site, with the blessing of the Minister of Mineral Resources, who was sympathetic to the project. But no sooner had the team arrived than the local Party secretary who was looking after them came running to tell them that the minister had just died. Meanwhile, the soldiers brought in to do the work began to develop a paralysis in their extremities, their eyes became infected, and it is said that two of them died soon after they were released from duty.

In any case, there seemed to be radiation of sorts on the site, some kind of energy field to stop intruders from penetrating the deeper levels of the mines. Later someone told me to wash my sandals of any earth that might stick to them. Just in case. As Mutafchiev had pointed out early on, nothing grows on one side of the Big Site, not even grass. But the ground there looked a bit rocky to me anyway.

Next, the architect who designed the terracing of the mine excavation apparently crashed his car and went into a coma. With Zhivkova gone, her enemies in the KGB wing of State Security began a brisk purge of her entourage. Mutafchiev was put on trial and sentenced to fifteen years – ostensibly for State-fund embezzlement, but since embezzlement was the chief activity of the entire Party elite, the real reasons for his removal remain classified to this day, though logic points towards power games within the politburo.

Mutafchiev had been the brains behind the expedition and remained obsessed with the Big Site for the rest of his prison-shortened life. He'd had a recurring dream in which he saw his own body with steam coming off it, and an eagle circling above. Apparently, a similar dream was reported by the team who worked in the Tutankhamun tomb before they sickened.

State Security special forces blew up the entrance, sealing the mines off. And as if blowing it up, flooding it, and keeping it behind the klyon wasn't enough, State Security special forces patrolled the area until 1989. Some locals say there was an additional 'live fence' of thousands of vipers specially bred for this purpose by Uzbeks along the southern Black Sea, under something called decree number 56. Why Uzbeks? Why vipers? Did decree number 56 read: 'Let us fulfil the five-year snake plan in one year'?

The roads to madness are many. It is hard to identify *one* strand of this story as the kookiest, but the Uzbek-bred vipers are hard to beat.

The young sapper who had signed his life away survived. The numismatist was removed from the dig early on. The head miner went on working for the Ore Mining Company until it closed down in the 1990s and emptied Marina's pretty border town of its people.

And what of Mustafa the treasure hunter? Described by Vanga's niece as a nervous man clutching a crumpled map, he was the first victim – not of Bastet, but of Zhivkova's State Security agents, who apparently 'interrogated' him so savagely that he later died of internal injuries. However, this is impossible to confirm, and none of the witnesses or commentators mention him by name; Bastet was more real to them than Mustafa.

Zhivkova's treasure-hunting team were after no less than celestial secrets, but beneath their feet lay fresh bones. The border forest contains unmarked collective graves from the 1950s, when those who protested against their land being nationalised were simply brought here and shot.

When I asked him about this, Niki said he didn't like *to rummage in the past*. He knew where they were, but his friends called them 'bandit graves'.

'Because if you're shot and buried in the forest, what else are you?'

I checked, but he wasn't joking. According to this logic, if he were to shoot me and bury me on the spot now, it would be my fault.

Many of those in 'bandit graves' were in fact part of a nationwide resistance movement in the first decade and a half of Soviet terror. They called themselves *Goryani* or Woodlanders, because the outlaw takes to the hills, and they were cousins of the Forest Brothers in the Baltic states. Their revolt was not ideological but visceral; they were mostly young country folk, peasants who witnessed the confiscation of ancestral lands, the ritual humiliation of their families, and the destruction of their communities. One *Goryanin* who served two sentences in a labour camp breaking stones simply said: 'It was the soul of the people that was being devastated. That's what we revolted against.' He served two sentences because when the first was up, he was asked to publicly denounce the Goryani; he refused. Unknown numbers of Goryani were tried, executed, or sent to labour camps, their families exiled and written into the black book of the State.

But Niki didn't know this because it is still absent from history lessons and public discourse. The Goryani were one of the largest, longest-sustained resistance movement against Soviet state terror in Eastern Europe, but their mouths are full of earth.

I walked back to the rusted portal, with Niki driving slowly behind me. I was too scared to expose my back, though I also felt uncomfortable about Niki now. It was nothing specific, just a sense that he wasn't what he appeared to be. For one bleak moment, I thought he was leading me round and round in circles for some reason of his own. Because the forest roads behind the klyon did go round in circles. They led nowhere. They were the internal roads of the Furrow of Death, trodden only by border guards and fugitives, then and now.

Vanga's niece escaped illness, accidents, and opprobrium and in the 1990s wrote a best-selling memoir of Vanga.

Mutafchiev did eight years in jail, and although he emerged with his health broken, he hadn't wasted his time inside: he began work on *Homo Sapiens on Homo Sapiens*, a brain-scrambling 'study' redolent of Zhivkova's messianic exultation that blends astronomy, ancient history, and a nervous breakdown. He called the map a rebus, and went on to decode its symbols, creating an astonishing reconstructed diagram of a Cepheid-star galaxy that shows how the layout of the 'hermetically sealed', 'three-tiered' tomb at the Big Site is a mirror image of a key part of that galaxy. Among the symbols he decoded were a cat-headed Bastet representing the Mother Goddess; a two-headed turtle representing the Earth; and a flock of birds representing the intergalactic beings who travelled to the Earth and left us the legacy of ancient sites like this. Our task was to decode them. Those who had accompanied the sarcophagus from Egypt had not been slaughtered, but had settled in these parts, to guard the tomb (in Vanga's vision, they wore masks, like mummers). In which case, some of Strandja's people are their descendants. There were marks on the rock face that served as coded instructions to the chambers within that were blocked off by huge man-made slabs.

To recap: inside the Big Site is an intergalactic portal left to us by the creators of the 'real' Egyptian pyramids (the suggestion is that there are also fake ones) and of other megalithic sites in the Middle East and in Strandja, once called Haemimont, writes Mutafchiev, rather vaguely for a historian. The Big Site contains a message from our most ancient ancestors, many light years away from the Earth, which also explains the nature of the solar vision the team had witnessed. The sarcophagus and its message were sealed in a chamber that, upon opening, would release an unknown radiation. I picture that man, fallen from the height of power all the way to the damp floor of a prison cell, skinny, riddled with cancer, wearing thick glasses, drawing diagrams of galaxies so that he wouldn't have to look inside himself.

What strikes me about this tale, apart from its contents, is its complete lack of form. Deliberately misleading, the accounts of

Mutafchiev and the niece differ on key points: dates, the figures they saw on the rock face, and the fruits of the excavation. This happened in 1981, but it has acquired the twilight aura of ancient history many times removed from us. In one conspiracy theory, Zhivkova had secret communication with the British on the subject of satellite images of the Big Site that showed a huge man-made hollow inside the hill. Because it wasn't just the Russians, the Nazis, the communists, and our ancient extraterrestrial ancestors who were interested in the Big Site, it was also MI5.

Vanga's niece claimed that all they found inside was a large pit, but it is only a matter of time before its mysteries are unearthed. More sober commentators speculate that the team found unspectacular gold deposits and sold them in the West for hard currency. Or maybe what they found was nothing. A void onto which all of this was projected with the feverishness of the demented collective unconscious.

In *The Myth of the Eternal Return*, Mircea Eliade suggested that prehistoric cultures are based on a cosmology where earthly reality is mirrored in some celestial dimension, and human actions are given meaning only in a projected divine pattern. That is why the archaic concept of time is not linear and historical, but circular and based on endlessly repeated patterns. It's what fire worship, agiasma worship, and all mystic and spiritual practice are about. The brains behind the communist expedition had simply tuned in to vibrations of a prehistoric nature.

Vanga too apparently received her visions from an entity she called 'the others', and the others lived in another galaxy, from where human civilisation came. After all, her niece reminds us, Vanga identified three types of time – big time, time, and times. The Big Site deals in big time. Perhaps Vanga was onto something when she 'read' the map: not as fact but as metaphor.

★

On the way back, we passed the border barracks. Two bored guards stood on the empty road, rifles over their shoulders. They waved us down, for company.

'What's up?' Niki said.

'Nothing,' one of them said, biting into a pastry.

'Where were the two refugees from?' I asked from the passenger seat.

'Egypt,' one said. The other shook his head and sighed. I looked at them, two uniformed guys in an off-kilter world. If they swapped clothes with the two Egyptians, would anyone notice and would it matter, in the world of big time?

Later, I was told that behind the casual front, Niki was a passionate treasure hunter. That he knew every stone in the forest, every scrap of human and animal remains. That he had seen unspeakable things with other treasure hunters, which explained the grey hair.

There are rumours of a new team reopening the flooded mines, and Niki may be among the first to glimpse whatever is there. I wish him luck.

cold water

The name of the last cheshma before the stretch of no-man's-forest. Locals call it *Kreynero*, a distortion of the Greek for cold water, *kryo nero*. It sits along an old drove road to Turkey, just outside the Village in the Valley, and its stone basin still bears a faint Soviet star carved and dated 1971. The Kreynero water lives up to its name: it is cold, tasty, and heavy as iron. No matter how much you drink, you can't be sated. And no matter where you come from, they say if you drink from it three times, you'll keep returning to this valley that lies between Bulgaria and Turkey, though it feels like neither. It feels like a place without a country.

You'll keep returning even if you don't know why.

PILGRIMS

One evening, when mist had risen from the river, chill and clammy on the skin like a ghost, a Belgian guy arrived in the Village in the Valley. He wore a filthy leather hat over his sunburn, and had walked twenty kilometres to get here. I was sitting in the mosquito lights of The Disco with a plate of fried liver. I was the only customer. He put down his pack and ordered a beer.

'Where are the people?' he asked.

I shrugged. I'd seen the beaten-up old four-wheel-drives vanish in the fog: it was a good night for hunting boar.

Minka put his beer down in front of him.

'Enjoy,' she said with finality and sat at her table gazing at the fog.

'Why are you walking such a long way?' I asked the Belgian.

'*Je ne sais pas*,' he shrugged, exhausted and happy–sad.

But he did know. He was compiling an inventory of mountain plants in the region – thirty thousand so far, he said. To be close to the plants, you have to walk. Last year, he had done the Balkan range. This year, Strandja. Next year, the Rhodopes.

'I'm a gardener,' he said. 'Do you know where I can stay for the night?'

He looked towards the end of the village where the river followed a winding path to no-man's-land, marked by Kreynero, and after that

– only large tortoises travelling onwards and little chapels with subterranean agiasmas that bubbled up suddenly.

'Can I go that way?' he asked.

That way's the border, I said.

He looked surprised. 'Which country is over there?'

Turkey, I said, and he looked mystified. He didn't think in terms of countries, he thought in terms of ecosystems. I drove him to the steep street where Ivo the herbalist lived. He was busy laying out slices of courgettes on the kitchen table to air-dry them.

Ivo had a heroic white moustache and had run a business in medicinal herbs until catastrophe struck: a lorry carrying a consignment of plants was caught in a flood on the Danube. He had no insurance and bankruptcy forced him to retire here, to the holiday house that he had bought twenty-five years ago when his daughter had been wasting away in the city from a bronchial disease. It was to do with the plants and the altitude here, there was *something* about Strandja that healed, Ivo said. His daughter recovered and went on her way, but Ivo stayed.

In Ivo's garden grew aubergines heavy as grenades. And he made a special healing ointment that fixed everything from deep cuts to sore backs, from psoriasis to alopecia. The recipe was a secret because he hoped to patent it and finally make a bit of money.

'Very good in risottos,' he said, meaning the courgettes. 'Who is the boy?'

A complicated exchange followed in German, French, Russian, Flemish, and English. Out of those, the two gardeners didn't have a single language in common, but they didn't need to – here were all the plants they shared, fresh and dried, on muslin and in jars, hanging in bunches and growing audibly in the black soil of the night.

Across from the herbalist were the Irish Belgians. They were building two houses for a Dutch owner. Every summer, they came: the pater familias, the wife, four blond sons, and assorted friends with tattoos. They came down to the village in the evenings to buy beer by the crate.

How can you take ten years to build two houses? locals muttered. You'd think they were building Versailles. But their custom at The Disco was most welcome.

'Enjoy,' Minka said as she put down mugs of frothy beer in front of the multiple Belgians. The Irishman was an entrepreneur. He had a factory producing billiard tables ('where I make my money'), a consultancy business for foreigners buying real estate in Bulgaria and Romania ('poor buggers'), and he wanted to buy a Soviet-era factory on the coast ('a nightmare'). The sons were in their thirties, a lost look about them, the gold of their youth beginning to fade. Their father, meanwhile, had forgotten to age.

But why come all the way here to build a house, among the derelict army buildings and rusty Soviet trucks, on top of that forgotten hill?

The Belgian Irishman shrugged.

'Because it's beautiful. Besides,' he said in his Belgian–Irish English, 'once you lose your roots, it doesn't really matter where you go, does it.' He looked at me with momentary interest. 'And what are *you* doing here?'

I shrugged. It's precisely when you have lost your roots that everywhere you go matters hugely. But he had moved on with his sons. Two years later, they would stop coming, leaving the Dutchman's houses unfinished on the hill. Perhaps they had only drunk from Kreynero once.

One afternoon I was sitting at my usual table at The Disco with a cherry juice imported from Turkey via Germany – although the derelict gardens here were raining cherries – when a flock of cyclists arrived in the square. They were Spanish.

'Not Spanish,' the man who sat at the next table corrected me, 'Basque.'

His leg was bandaged. 'I sprained it,' he said in Spanish, 'and now I can't cycle. I have to sit with the driver and watch the others.'

He wasn't bitter about it, but his buggy eyes were restless, looking for something to alight on. While the others unpacked their bikes from the white van under the instructions of their guide, he ordered a cherry juice.

'You live in Scotland?' He lit up. 'Scotland must win independence. Because then we Basques can follow.'

It was the summer of the Scottish independence referendum.

'I would even become a terrorist and join ETA, if necessary, because they are heroes. Spanish colonialism must die. English colonialism too. Down with imperialism!'

'Enjoy,' Minka put the juice in front of him.

I changed the subject.

'Why do I cycle? Because that's how you stay close to the landscape,' he said. 'Smell it, touch it. I've cycled all over Europe – France, Spain, Italy, Croatia. But Bulgaria is the most extraordinary.'

'Really?'

'Oh yeah, because it's wild, man. And wilderness is dying. Once it's gone, it won't come back.'

'I hear the Basque country is beautiful too,' I said, trying not to mention Spain.

'You know, it's not about beauty. Roots are about something else. I always know, wherever I go, that I am Basque.'

He got up and limped to the van while his friends zoomed off on their bikes, down the chipped road to Kreynero, with cries of delight. Before he climbed into the driver's cabin, he waved and shouted in Spanish:

'Greetings to the Scottish people from the Basque!'

I waved back on behalf of the Scottish people, trying not to wave on behalf of the English people too, or the Welsh – and should I even think of Northern Ireland?

Another stranger sat at the far table, with a camera. He had arrived quietly, making himself invisible. There was no car – he had hitched a ride with someone. He was in his forties and had an emotional face that gladdened and saddened easily. We started chatting.

His name was Nevzat and he was Turkish, from a mountain village just across the border.

'Enjoy.' Minka put a salad before him.

'I'm not *Turkish* Turkish,' Nevzat said in fluent but heavily accented Bulgarian.

His grandparents, ethnic Bulgarian Muslims, were exiled from the Rhodope Mountains after the Balkan Wars. In fact, he had just visited his grandparents' village for the first time; he'd toured for three weeks with his camera, with a group of other Turkish photographers with similar backgrounds. How was it? I asked.

His face looked at once glad and sad. 'It was good,' he said.

I sensed a big story but let him eat his salad.

How is Strandja on the other side? I asked after a while. He shrugged.

'Like here but different. Come and visit us. It's just over there.' He pointed at the impassable hills. Two years later, we met again on the other side.

And five days later, the Belgian herbalist was still there. He had been to Kreynero and drunk from it three times. His big book was full of notes on the herbs he had been collecting. There are 1,760 endemic wild plants in Strandja, he said, and though most of them aren't medicinal, they're definitely poisonous. It's easy to get confused, he said with excitement, and eat the wrong one.

'I don't know what it is,' he said, his eyes sparkling over a triple

shot of golden 'Sunny Beach' brandy, under the mosquito lights of
The Disco, 'but I can't leave. Every day, I say I must leave tomorrow.
Vous avez quel age, quarante ans?'

He rose and came to sit at my table, brandy in hand.

'I'm thirty,' he said. '*Quel dommage*. I'm too young for you, am I?'

You're not too young, it's that I don't fancy you. But I smiled
from the height of my great age instead and said:

'So, where are you off to next?'

'*Je ne sais pas,*' he shrugged, happy-sad, like a true pilgrim.

The next morning I saw him from The Disco, up the steep road,
his pack blocking the sun, and it was only then that one of the hunters
sat down with a coffee and said to me:

'Now, don't be upset but…'

And the hunter told me how the night the Belgian arrived in the
foggy forest, he had mistaken the dark moving bulk for a boar, and
had he not glimpsed the rim of a hat, he would have shot him.

atonement

This is how you defang a viper, said the border guard. You drop the viper in a plastic bag. You make a cigarette burn in your army-issue jacket and let the viper's head out of the bag. Hold it firmly. The viper is drawn to the smoke, and the moment it sinks its teeth into the burnt fabric, you yank it back. The fangs remain in the fabric. It's a way to pass the time on patrol.

But you could also kill it. Because for every viper you kill, you atone for forty sins, so the saying goes. And from May onwards, the forest twitches with vipers.

ONE HUNDRED AND TWENTY SINS

Along the broken forest road between the Black Sea and the Turkish border, the car radio flickered between stations: syrupy Turkish pop ballads gave way to the summer edition of Radio Tsarevo which served the news in Bulgarian, English, and Russian. The odd village plunged out of sight as soon as you glimpsed it. The only thing on the road was the occasional booth marked Border Police. Inside the booth were two border guards. I pulled over.

'Nah. There's nothing to tell, it's a life like any other,' shrugged the older guard. 'The shifts are long, no dogs any more, things have changed since the old days. This used to be the most dreaded army service, and now—'

'Now it's not army any more, but police,' said the younger one.

He kept his arms crossed and appraised me with cagey eyes. He had familiar chiselled cheeks, but I couldn't place him.

'I'm retiring,' the older one said. 'Gonna fish all day. You know the spring of Saint Marina?'

'Things used to be quiet, but it's been busy since the Syrian war,' said the young guard.

'Saint Marina, protector of snakes. You go to her to heal yourself,' said the old guard.

'All sorts come across now,' said the young guard. 'Some are even armed.'

'I remember the fugitives from the old days. Every single face,' said the old guard. 'They ran the other way, south. We arrested so many. Two German guys in their twenties. I remember the night. We surrounded them, eighty of us with dogs and just two of them. Their trousers were in shreds from the wire. The searchlights were on them. And they stood there, I'll never forget it. Because they looked defiant. Even though their lives were over. I opened a passport. His girlfriend's photo. But what can you do? Fate. They had signed their own sentences.'

'Last week, we found a pregnant woman,' the young guard said. 'Her husband had grenade wounds. Syrians.'

'One guy, Klaus Hoffmann,' said the old guard, '1986. I see him like it was yesterday. Forty-five-year-old radiologist from East Germany. I remember spelling his name on the form. Handsome, smart. He deserved better.'

'Some destroy their identity papers and give themselves up,' the young guard said.

'Fate,' the old guard said. 'Everybody who passed through the arrest room was recorded in those thick green logbooks. Which have now gone missing. I'm retiring next year. Gonna take my memories with me.'

'They're starving, exhausted, there's no point hiding,' the young guard said. 'They give themselves up and we do the paperwork and they end up in the refugee camp.'

'One time,' the old guard said, 'late 70s, me and my mate found a rucksack in the forest, stuffed with US dollars. We found the footprints but never caught him. Thousands of dollars. So what did we do, dutiful soldiers of the People's Republic? Took the rucksack to the boss. Thinking he'd reward us for our honesty. Hah!' He opened a packet of chocolate biscuits and offered me some.

'The patrol up the road found this woman in the forest,' said the young guard. 'Left behind by the rest of the group. She'd frozen to death.'

'The hardest time was the late 80s,' said the old guard, 'when our Turks started leaving 'cause of the name-changing campaign. Remember?'

I did. The younger guard didn't, he was too young. The younger guard looked at his watch and said:

'You learn one thing in this job. People survive things you can't imagine.'

'Summer 1989,' said the older guard. 'This road was black with cars, carts, buses, taxis. Three hundred thousand people emigrating to Turkey. Some came back. I remember one woman. She'd been raped by soldiers on both sides.'

'The other week, two Palestinians popped up in the forest,' said the young guard. 'Wouldn't talk for days. People crack up when they're given food, but those two had eaten plums and weren't hungry. It was the cigarettes that did it, on the third day. They inhaled like Hoovers. And they broke down. The story came out.'

What was the story?

He looked at me with mistrust and I recognised him. Of course – he was the accordionist's son, from the Sunday party! How a uniform and a gun changed a man.

'Well,' he said and his face didn't move, 'I recognised you. It's my job.'

The old guard started telling another story, but the young one interrupted:

'Let's run a check on you,' he said and went inside the booth. 'We have an identity-verifying system that can look you up. You can see how it works.'

'Oh leave it,' said the old guard, embarrassed.

But the young guard was new school, scrupulous. He picked up the radiophone. He gave my name to a woman at the other end and as we waited in the sudden silence, an old chill crept in. The chill of being found out, hunted down, a searchlight shone on you. A border chill.

The old guard wanted an audience. The young guard didn't; he had turned the tables on me. Then the calm female voice came back with my details, adding:

'No criminal convictions.'

'That's you verified,' said the young guard and went off to nap in a forest hut behind the booth.

'Oh well,' said the old guard apologetically, 'a job's a job.'

A car with a Sofia registration plate pulled over. A man with glasses got out. They were looking for the cave of Saint Marina and the older guard gave them directions.

'And keep clear of the vipers!' he banged on the roof of the car.

'A little crippled girl in the back,' he said when he came back. 'Fate. But they might be in luck. One time I went fishing in the river by Saint Marina. Had a heavy heart, the way you do sometimes. I slipped and fell in the river, ripped my hand on a sharp rock. Ripped it right into the palm. Blood everywhere. What happens next? I wash my hand in the Saint Marina spring, and the wound closes up. Bloody hell, like nothing's been there! Nobody believed me.'

'That's nice,' I said.

'Nice my foot,' he said, 'because listen what happens next. I go back the following week and what do I see? A knot of snakes by my feet. Bloody hell, I took a stone and crushed their heads. Three snakes it was. You kill one viper and that's forty sins taken care of.'

'That's one hundred and twenty sins,' I said.

'But here's the catch,' he said. 'Saint Marina is the protector saint of snakes. You mustn't touch the snakes at her spring. They might be, you know, something else. What devil got me to kill those snakes after the miracle with the hand?'

He undid the top button of his uniform. The tarmac was melting under our feet.

'When you visit, keep away from the vipers. 'Cause one thing is sure, by Saint Marina. We sign our own sentence.'

And he reached out and pressed a packet of melting chocolate biscuits into my shoulder bag, suddenly keen to end our conversation.

I couldn't get Klaus Hoffmann out of my head – because of all the victims of the border I had heard about, he alone had been named by a border guard. When I contacted the expert on German fugitives, he did find a Klaus Hoffmann in his files. But several things didn't match. The Klaus Hoffmann of the files was younger, and he wasn't a radiologist. The year was different too. After his arrest, he had spent several months in a Bulgarian jail, followed by a long sentence in the hospital section of Hohenschönhausen, Berlin's Stasi prison. Most mismatched of all was the following detail: the Klaus Hoffmann in the files had been shot and beaten by the soldiers before they had entered his name in one of those green logbooks that have gone missing.

Were there two Klaus Hoffmanns? Or was the remembered Klaus Hoffmann a fictionalised creation of my border guard, an amelioration of reality for everyone: Klaus Hoffmann, the guard, and me?

I had waved as I drove away, and the older guard had waved back, holding his arm up in the air longer than usual, a strangely final gesture. Perhaps he was afraid that if I stayed, he might get carried away and make a confession so awful, so intractable that once it was uttered, it would become the only reality there is. And who would want to live in such a terrible world?

sozialistische persönlichkeit

Socialist personality in German. In East Germany and the rest of the Soviet bloc, a prescribed set of attitudes and behaviours that confirmed you as politically correct. In theory, the socialist personality was a repository of moral rectitude and 'class consciousness'. In practice, it was an embodiment of that long-suffering creature *Homo sovieticus*, and effectively meant not having a face, a name, or a destiny, unless it was the right one.

One day when the forest of Strandja was beginning to stifle me, I drove to the last lagoon before the red Turkish flag, to swim and find peace. Instead, I found the source of a story about how one German broke the most basic rule of socialist personality: the border rule. And what happened after.

RIDING THE IRON CURTAIN

The coast was rugged with cliffs, and you heard the boom of breaking waves before you saw them below, the sound of eternity. In the distance, a naked child ran across a spit of sand so golden against a sea so blue that it looked digitally retouched.

To get here, you started at a pretty handcrafted noticeboard which told you that you are at the estuary of the Veleka River, and that the path entails several ecosystems – river, sea, forest – with sand lily, wild fig, thirty-two types of river fish, the last white Pontic dunes along this coast, and the endangered monk seal. Something on the back of the board caught your eye: a sentence in German, handwritten in ball-point pen:

'Here on 21.9.1971 two men began their Calvary.'

A rare memento of a special brand of tourism: the tourism of exorcism. Someone had returned forty years after the fact to write this, but hadn't signed his name. Who was he?

By a stroke of luck, I was able to trace him through contacts, and in the winter, I went to meet him in a quiet Berlin neighbourhood. His name was Felix S. and he was an artist.

In his leather coat and peaked cap with 'Deutschland' on it, Felix S. looked like an old biker. His gaze was distracted and there was a dishevelment about him, as if he had lost something and couldn't remember what it was, but his handshake was firm. We climbed the cold stairs to his studio in one of those tower-like Berlin buildings with courtyards like dark wells. The damp was inside the walls and the carpets were full of cigarette ash and old sorrows.

His wife was here too, a tall woman called Renée, Amazonian in a long raincoat, her face beautifully lined. We sat inside the freezing kitchen next to Felix's studio – him and me at a small table piled with papers, and Renée huddled in her coat on a hard chair in the corner. The thin cigar in her fingers kept going out. She didn't want to assume a central position because this was his story.

Even stooped as he was, weighed down by the grey November sky, Felix was an impressive, big-chested man with strong teeth and feline eyes that gazed inwards to a place that didn't include others, and only looked at you from time to time, surprised you were still there. On every surface were metallic ashtrays of the old-fashioned kind where you press and the butt sinks out of sight, until a compost of butts emerges and you have to clean it. The walls were plastered with sketches and collages. A canvas of a naked woman with sprawled legs dominated one wall.

'The twenty-first of September 1971. A stormy, pitch-black night. All we could hear were the waves crashing below,' he began without preamble. 'We walked for a few hours along the clifftop and when we reached the estuary, we started singing because we thought we'd reached the other side. We thought: Freedom, at last! Even Dominik sang.'

Dominik was his friend and they were both eighteen years old. They were using a map, but it was a GDR-bought map, made especially for those like them, interested in borders, and GDR-manufactured maps of Warsaw Pact countries featured deliberately false borders.

When they turned, there were two soldiers with Kalashnikovs trained on them.

How many seconds did it take for the two soldiers to decide not to gun down the 'sandals'? Some soldiers were instructed to shoot at the fugitives first and *then* fire a 'warning' shot in the air. In any case, these two soldiers fired the warning shot instead. More soldiers came, with dogs. Dominik was beaten and kicked to the ground, and just as Felix was wondering if his friend was dead, they got to him.

'What had you planned for yourself, once you crossed?' I asked him.

'I had no plan. I just wanted to taste freedom. To come and go as I pleased. I would have completed my degree or done a degree in philosophy. But first of all, I wanted to go to Paris.'

His smile was kind, indulgent of the young man's dream, not tainted by what happened to that dream.

Felix had grown up near Erfurt, the capital of Thuringia, in a politically bipolar family. His father came from an Austrian hotelier dynasty.

'As conservative as it gets. Then the Nazis came. My grandfather disagreed with them and refused to let his son join the army. It was only because of the family name that he got my father a job at a posh resort, as a barman. The Nazi elite went there. Then misfortune struck.'

His father's boss was gay. The Nazis arrested both men because they were friends. It was on the train that was taking them away that a mistress of Goebbels, an actress from the misnamed beau monde, spotted the S. son sitting next to the other young man, both in handcuffs.

'"What on earth are you doing here, *mein schatz*?" kind of thing.' Felix coughed. 'She saved his life. He would have hanged with his friend.'

Soon after, his grandfather was in a bistro. Still reeling with relief after his son's release, he couldn't resist telling a joke about Hitler.

'His health wasn't good and he didn't survive the beatings. He died in jail.'

Felix was born nine years later in what had become East Germany, to a mother who had an impeccable communist pedigree – her father had been the founder of the local Communist Party – and a bourgeois father. What was that like?

'Constant bloody conflict! My father was openly against the regime. He didn't vote and voting was compulsory. He had five Stasi agents who shadowed him everywhere.'

Five! But wasn't it sufficient credibility that his grandfather was killed by the Nazis? He laughed and the cigarette ash fell on the unopened mail on the table.

'The family had gone down as enemies of the people. Still, I was on my mother's side. My communist grandfather was an influence, but it was also what they taught us at school. I was trained to agree so I agreed. Then, around the age of sixteen–seventeen, it was time to choose my higher education. And that's when I began to disagree.'

He paused and heard my unspoken question.

'Because one by one, all avenues that had looked open began to close. My dream was to do skydiving. For that, I had to join the Gesellschaft für Sport und Technik, a special division of the armed forces. At first, they told me that because of my solid record as a young communist, I would be accepted.'

But it didn't work out. He was rejected by the army for being the son and grandson of enemies of the people. Then he thought of becoming a sailor. The merchant navy in Rostock granted him an interview, but just before he was due to take up his new post, two Stasi officers came and explained that he was barred from joining the merchant navy too, due to being under suspicion.

Suspicion of what? Felix asked. Of intending to escape from the GDR through maritime means, they said.

'That was the beginning of the end. I was seventeen. I felt like a caged animal. Whichever way I turned, they cornered me. Then they started inviting me "to talk". Either you're with us or you're against us, they said. Either you work for us and make a brilliant career or we'll waste your life in a factory somewhere. I started making statements in public about the Stasi, comparing them to the Nazis.'

He agrees it is surprising that he wasn't arrested for such reckless statements, but there was a reason. His uncle worked for the Stasi. It can't be proven, but later, when he was in a Black Sea jail and a Stasi officer interrogated him, the uncle connection must have provided a lifeline.

'So this caged animal went to Erfurt to study the only thing still open to him. Gastronomy, the family trade. I didn't give a stuff about gastronomy. But Erfurt opened my eyes. For the first time, I was mixing with artists, musicians, writers. I wasn't from an artistic family but I'd been drawing since the age of ten.'

In Felix's studio was a stack of portraits: Hitler as a child, then as a young man, then as the man he became. Felix's art had two main subjects: oppression and the body, one as a subset of the other, because in his work the body is oppressed.

'In Erfurt, I became radicalised against the system. The system that specialised in preventing you. Preventing you full stop.'

I had felt the same at sixteen, in that same system. I'd felt old before I was young. In a liberal democracy, Felix would have been a run-of-the mill anarchist, a regular angry young man, and his rebellion would have run its course. But not in East Germany of 1971.

'We tried to organise a jazz festival in Erfurt.'

Was that allowed?

'No!' he cried in exasperation. His cigarette had gone out. 'Of course it wasn't! After that, I decided to leave. I had a girlfriend. We loved each other. Tried to talk her into coming with me to the Bulgarian sea coast, but—'

He waved vaguely. She'd been too scared.

'Dominik was calm and disciplined, not chaotic like me. We were diametrically opposed. We studied gastronomy together, we worked as waiters-in-training. He was scared but he wanted to get away too. So we hatched a plan.'

Later, the Stasi would force Dominik to sign a statement under duress that Felix had corrupted him and persuaded him to 'sabotage' the German Democratic Republic. Dominik was so mortified to have signed that statement that in forty years he has only seen Felix once.

'We planned it carefully. Nobody knew except my brother. The idea came from all the family holidays we'd had in Bulgaria. You couldn't go over the Berlin Wall, but we'd heard that in Bulgaria it was easy. There was no wall, just a bit of barbed wire in the forest.'

The two teenagers went to Bulgaria and became part of the tourism of escape. Once in Burgas, they took a bus to the last sizeable town on the coast.

'We tried to blend in,' he smiled. 'We chatted to locals in Russian and found rooms. In the morning, we were off to the border.'

When Felix came round from the beating, he found that his and Dominik's hands were tied with rope. A long walk began in the darkness, along the clifftop, and the soldiers rammed their rifle barrels into their sides.

'Like cattle.'

Then they came to a stop and pushed Felix onto his knees. It was the highest point above the sea, on the edge of the cliff, where you heard the booming of waves before you saw them.

One of the soldiers put the barrel of his handgun to Felix's head and Felix heard a finger release the catch.

'In that moment, I knew it was all over.'

The soldier pulled the trigger and the gun jumped against Felix's head.

But there was no sound.

'That moment is burnt into my brain.'

At the barracks, they were pushed into a room with portraits of Lenin, Marx, Engels.

'And Stalin!'

Then, to their amazement, an urbane German-speaking officer walked in, the first in a linguistic line that would lead all the way to the Stasi interrogator later. He looked shocked by their youth and their bloodied state, and although he believed them when they said they weren't American spies, despite the American chewing gum in their pockets, that they just wanted to quit the communist bloc because they couldn't take it any more, he couldn't do a great deal for them except let them sleep on the floor. The next day, the urbane officer took them to someone's villa in the Strandja hills, in a sedan with tinted windows.

'There was a swimming pool. They gave us nice food. I thought, maybe they'll just let us go, they can see we're okay. Why invite us to this villa otherwise?'

Maybe it was done out of cruelty, or perhaps the German-speaker was really trying to give them a final moment of pleasure before the lights went out for them. Because afterwards, they were taken to the port city of Burgas and separated. Felix was locked in a dark muddy cell with a steel door. He couldn't stand up. One other man was there with him; he spoke English, but Felix didn't, so in a mix of Russian and German the man conveyed his conviction that they were both going to die, but especially him because, unlike Felix, no one was going to bail him out. He was Bulgarian and he knew that the closer you got to the border, the less your life was worth.

Felix spent three weeks in the steel box with his companion. The only food brought to them was halva, the crumbly Turkish sweet made from sugar, sesame seeds, and vanilla.

'I still love halva,' Felix smiled.

'He loves it too much!' Renée stirred in her corner. 'He always had a sweet tooth, but at one point he was buying half a kilo of halva at the Turkish shops in West Berlin and eating the whole thing in one sitting!'

Felix grinned like a naughty boy and pointed at the large collage on the wall above him. When I looked closer, I saw that it was made of hundreds of sticky medical bracelets from his trips to the hospital over the years.

'There's no diabetes in their family,' Renée added. 'It's stress. It had to come out somehow. When we first got together in 1980, I wondered how he could be so unaggressive after all that had happened. Then one day I went to his flat and saw, on the door of the bathroom, this drawing of a headless woman with a Kalashnikov. I understood that it was all coming out in his art.'

When they finally dragged him out of the cell, the light blinded him. There was a fat man sitting behind a desk. He was German and spoke with a Saxon accent.

'So,' he said. 'You wanted to fuck Turkish women. Tough luck. And how come you're covered in piss and shit and your hair's so long?'

Because I don't have water or soap or scissors, said Felix.

'Cut it with a spoon then,' the Stasi officer sneered. 'And if you manage to keep yourself alive, you might even see your beloved GDR again. Though sadly,' he concluded, 'you'll never get to fuck Turkish women.'

The officer never introduced himself by name. Felix thought he identified him thirty years later, from photographs of Stasi officers working abroad, as Peter Pfütze. By 1989 Pfütze was very high in the Stasi, answerable directly to the one man in East Germany who had a Roman emperor's power over life and death – Erich Mielke, chief of the Stasi. East Germans joked grimly that their country was in the hands of two Erichs (the other one was Erich Honecker, leader of the GDR). In his memoir of his service for the Stasi, Pfütze didn't mention any interrogation rooms or political prisoners. Instead, he recalled leisurely summers at Golden Sands, so leisurely that Erich Mielke himself, sunbathing with his wife on a politburo-only beach, looked up from his beach towel and sent Pfütze straight to the changing cabins to strip to his trunks before he reported again. The Stasi had their own chartered planes that took them to 'special operations' such as the surveillance of the Black Sea coast.

By 1989, there were around 91,000 full-time Stasi agents. That's not hard to understand – the payoff was tremendous. What's harder to grasp is that alongside them worked 189,000 unofficial collaborators, most of whom received no reward – except the power to hurt others. Three thousand of the Stasi agents were West Germans, though Pfütze was an Easterner. He may or may not have been the one who signalled to the two soldiers standing by to take Felix away to have his head shaved with a razor, afterwards the blood dripping from his head all the way down the corridor.

'I was pretty apathetic by then,' he said, 'as if the blood wasn't mine.'

'He did a series of art performances last week, in Erfurt,' Renée said from her corner. 'The first one is "The Hair Cut".'

'But I don't use my own head,' Felix said, 'because I don't want to feel like a victim again. I use a mannequin and have her head shaved instead. By someone else. Because I don't want to be an executioner either.'

In the second part of that performance, Felix shoots a model of Pfütze in the head. That he does himself.

'Yes. And it's a nice feeling,' he grinned. 'But it's only art. And it's only revenge. It doesn't change the fact that I still haven't met him since that day.'

'No,' Renée shook her head. She was from West Germany.

I wonder why he would want to meet the Saxon again.

The third part of the performance is an actor reading Peter Pfütze's memoir in which the likes of Felix are described as 'criminal elements'.

'Why?' Felix replied at last. 'Because until we are able to sit at the same table, me and him, the two Germanies won't be truly united.'

'Yeah.' Renée puffed cigar smoke into the freezing room. She had barely moved. In the fading light, she looked carved out of stone. 'We want to think it's over. But it isn't.'

Felix was one of the lucky ones. Three years before his arrest, three Bulgarian friends tried to cross into Greece. Young Todor had gifted his motorbike to his brother. It was April, the birds were singing. Grigor, Todor, and Ilcho were smart and enterprising and, like the young guards who shot them and buried them on the spot, they had their lives before them. When the three men's families asked for the bodies, they were told to go home and stop asking questions.

The reason there was no serious crime in the communist bloc was because serious crime, like everything else of note, was the exclusive right of the State.

A few years after Felix and Dominik's ordeal, two families in East Germany were visited by officials and informed that their children, Brigitte and Klaus, had died in an accident while on holiday in Bulgaria. Road and drowning accidents were exceedingly common among Eastern bloc tourists in Bulgaria – you'd think those tourists would learn to drive and swim. In fact, the couple had been shot.

Out in no-man's-land, Klaus had pulled out a hunting knife in self-defence but was shredded in seconds by gunfire, and Brigitte's

Russian didn't help because it was four in the morning and the corporal in charge had been on his feet all night and was tired and fed up, he explained later to a local forestry worker, so he *liquidated* her on the spot. 'Liquidate' was the word used throughout the Soviet world for approved murder. Something strange happened next: the corporal kept firing, until one hundred and forty Kalashnikov bullets had been emptied into the couple.

One hundred and forty bullets for two people. As if he'd wanted to kill not just the present, but the future too. I wonder whether his soldiers were infected by his rage, or whether they stood by, fearful they might be next. In the Stasi files marked 'operative information', Brigitte and Klaus were tidied away as GDR citizens who died abroad in the *sozialistischen Ausland*, a categorisation that fulfilled an agreement between the two countries: the remains of East Germans killed along the Bulgarian border were returned to the Stasi as accident victims. Though Klaus and Brigitte were first buried in Sofia, at the insistence of her mother, they were later transferred to the GDR, in sealed zinc coffins, like the fallen Russian soldiers in Afghanistan – so that no one would know how they had really died.

It was the summer of 1975. I was one and a half years old, on my first Nivea-scented Black Sea holiday. My father was away doing army service, like everybody's father, though he'd had the luck not to draw the border lot. My mother had the same hairstyle and was the same age as Brigitte, twenty-seven.

In Felix's studio, the daylight declined and the shadows on our faces deepened.

'He was educated, and a nice man.' Felix was still on the subject of his cellmate. 'Must have been a former high-ranking person who fell from grace. He begged me to remember him when I got out, and tell the foreign secret services about him. That was his only hope, he said.'

Felix's body shrank at the memory.

'But then I forgot his name. I even forgot I'd shared that box with him.'

'One day in the 90s,' Renée said, 'we took a boat trip on the lake in West Berlin. And suddenly, out of nowhere, he started crying. He'd remembered the man in the Burgas cell. All I could do was hand him tissues.'

Ten years ago, Felix made a steel box the size of the one he'd shared with that man. On top of it, he planted a bed of roses.

'The door is sealed,' he said, 'so that no one will have to experience what we did, not even for a moment.'

He wrote to the Bulgarian government, requesting permission to install his box in front of Burgas Prison. The government did not reply.

'It's still too early.' Renée shook her head. 'Forty years isn't long enough.'

The detention building where Felix and his nameless companion were held has been demolished.

The guard who emptied his Kalashnikov into Brigitte and Klaus died later. He had been decorated.

Peter Pfütze is a published author; perhaps he goes to literary festivals.

Why this politeness? Why isn't forty years long enough?

Felix and Dominik were flown from Burgas to Berlin in handcuffs, at the back of the aircraft, among returning German tourists. At Berlin Airport, they were loaded onto a van that said 'Refrigerated Fish'. The Stasi had a fleet of those vehicles; sometimes it was 'Fish', sometimes 'Baked Goods', but the passengers were always the same – political detainees on their way to some awful place.

'The strange thing is,' Felix said, 'in Andreasstrasse jail I had a toothbrush. There was a flush toilet and the food was so good that prisoners and guards ate the same. At Christmas, there were bananas! Was I in the West already? No. Because after the initial euphoria, it was worse than Burgas. Total silence. Nobody spoke.'

He was held in solitary confinement for weeks.

'I felt not so much pain as annihilation. Like they had made me cease to exist.'

The only company was the resident spider inside his cell. He talked to the spider. Sometimes at night, in the toilet, tapping from the women's cells below travelled up the pipes – but what were they trying to communicate? Perhaps he was imagining it. Perhaps he had finally gone insane.

The first thing someone said to him was when a guard came with a bucket and rag and took him to the cell opposite his. 'Clean this,' the guard said. Inside the cell was a pool of fresh blood. The person inside had just opened an artery with a plastic knife and been taken away. But there had been no sound.

When he first arrived at Andreasstrasse, there were folded grey blankets, and as the guards took him to the showers, he started screaming.

'I thought they were going to gas me,' he said. 'You see, I get the Bulgarian soldiers with their drunken animal violence. But this – this systematic, sober destruction of human souls that the Stasi practised, and the Nazis before them – it's something else.'

'Death by bureaucracy,' Renée said from her corner. 'It is part of the German psyche. It has been with us for a long time. We don't like it but it's there.'

Eventually, he figured out the tapping. One tap was A, two was B, three was C, and so on.

'It took ages to tap out a sentence. But I got the message. It had been passed on from my mother. She'd come to visit but they didn't let her see me.'

Looking at Felix, I saw a man almost childish in his self-absorption and stubbornness, but I liked him immensely.

What followed were the interrogations. They took him from his cell in the small hours – the Stasi did that with political prisoners, to disorient them.

'I was elated. Finally, human contact! The interrogator was this young guy, and I couldn't stop talking. I told him about what happened at the border, how the Stasi officer treated me, how this should all be documented and known. But he wasn't interested. He wanted to know who my friends were. They wanted names.'

Felix was interrogated many times, always in the middle of the night. More Stasi staff came, sometimes there were four of them in the room.

'I said, Torture me if you like, I won't give you any names.'

The next time Felix saw Dominik was at their trial.

'Not a trial, a farce. Our parents weren't allowed to attend. They had to sit outside. I wanted to speak, but the judge kept interrupting me. Shut up! Shut up! We don't have to listen to you.'

Felix was charged with being the leader of a 'subversive group', group meaning more than one person, and got one year and seven months. Dominik got the same minus two months. It was a light sentence. What about a lawyer?

'There was a lawyer. Our parents had hired a lawyer but the outcome was decided already.'

Six months after the trial, the lawyer jumped out of a high-rise.

I stared at Felix and Renée. This detail seemed too horrible to be a detail.

'I think it had little to do with our trial. It was general despair. He was a good man, and how can a good man be a lawyer in a dictatorship?'

The next stop was Cottbus Prison, which specialised in political prisoners. Among his fellow cellmates were a mathematician guilty of political jokes, a disgraced spy, and a musician who had spoken about the health impact on its workers of the Soviet–East German uranium factory Wismut.

'The food was so terrible that we staged what now I'd call performance art, but it was really us prisoners throwing food at each other.'

Once a week, the prisoners were ushered into compulsory lectures by a philosophy professor. The prisoners called this 'irradiation by red light' because the subject was always the same.

'Marxismus–Leninismus,' Felix grinned gleefully. 'And how to develop sozialistische Persönlichkeit! Very good if you suffer from insomnia, sends you straight to sleep. But here's the thing: I knew my philosophy. I had read everything up to and including Trotsky. I started arguing with the professor over certain nuances. So they banned me from attending the lectures! No, I said, I insist.'

I laughed at the hilarity on his face as he recounted this, but Renée didn't. She was so emotionally involved that she seemed to have no distance from the events of his life, especially those that preceded her.

Felix was bought – literally – by West Germany, where a human rights lawyer named Dr Vogel specialised in cases like his. By 1989, between 30,000 and 40,000 East Germans were bought out of Stasi jails for hard currency and given West German residence. Felix gladly surrendered his GDR citizenship. But before he could be a free man again, he was sent to a transit camp in the West. There, he was taken to a room where a charming American sat with his feet up, smoking a cigarette. In perfect German, he explained that they had to double-check some things about his account of events.

'But you already know everything! I protested. Still, the charming man said, there are certain things. Like the topography of the Bulgarian–Turkish border.'

As soon as the CIA agent left, the MI5 agent arrived. Then came the French with an offer to join the Foreign Legion.

'By the time the West German secret services arrived, I was fed up. I said, Enough already! I want my life back!'

He got his life back, or some version of it, but there was a twist.

'Remember the shithouse tapping code?' He leaned over to offer me a light for the roll-up he had made for me. 'The message was, my girlfriend was expecting a child. She was pregnant when I left with Dominik but she didn't know it.'

Felix's daughter was born while he was in prison. He saw her when mother and child were allowed to join him in West Berlin. She was one and a half.

'We loved each other. We lived as a family for a couple of years.'

He trailed off. By then, Felix had joined an evangelical community that took in stray souls, and he even enrolled as a seminarian.

He didn't do things by half. And he took what comfort he could find.

'West Berlin was hell. It was nothing like what I'd imagined. I was used to a nanny state where all your needs were taken care of.'

Even the ones you didn't have, such as staying put.

'Exactly. They took care of you full stop. Someone was always watching you. Not in the West. Nobody gave a shit. And the shops, the lights, the crowds. I went into shock. Paris felt just as far away.'

One day, there was a knock on the door of their flat.

'This gorgeous woman, about thirty, in plain clothes. I instantly knew what she was. I invited her in. She said they knew all about my desire to do parachuting. And she made me an indecent offer. Needless to say, I refused her!'

Renée raised her eyebrows and smiled for the first time. That was the last time he was courted by the secret services.

Felix had managed to keep madness and sadness at bay through a continuous gesture of artistic creation. This is how he had travelled across the last forty years that are my lifetime, the time it took for me to come to this cold Berlin studio with a box of halva, not the best present for a diabetic in retrospect, though he looked delighted with it.

And what about Dominik?

'I saw him once more, in Munich. There was an aura of sadness about him.'

I wonder if Dominik had thought the same of Felix. Felix shrugged.

'I need to see him again. After all these decades. I'm only an artist, my domain is the soul. I can't explain why, I just know I'm going to go to Munich and look for him.'

In the year of his father's death, 1988, Felix performed a symbolic act with some friends in West Berlin, which they called 'Riding the Wall'. His father had joked that one day, the wall might fall.

'But it was a joke,' Renée said. 'Nobody really believed it.'

Felix hadn't been allowed to attend his father's funeral in East Berlin. They had stopped him at Checkpoint Charlie and turned him back.

'So instead of attending his funeral, I did this thing, in his honour. The ladder was too short, so a couple of friends hoisted me to the top of the wall.'

It was a euphoric feeling, even if he could only stay for thirty seconds.

'I was so close to the soldier on the East side, I could look into his eyes. And the barrel of his gun. Then it was 1989 and the whole nation followed.'

The whole nation minus Brigitte and Klaus and all the others who hadn't made it.

I had Dominik's number but didn't call. He had been hounded enough; his story was written in his silence.

Felix showed me the canvases and collages in his studio. There was a series of fantastical nudes.

'A different model for each,' Renée said. 'One was his mother.' She clocked my surprise and smiled as if to say, Isn't life stranger than fiction?

This cheered me up – to think that his mother, a woman who had given her best to her country and got the worst in return, had survived to pose naked for her son. We went down the cavernous stairs. It was only now that Renée mentioned her excruciating toothache. She had not wanted to rush things by saying anything before.

'When we went back to that beach together,' she said, 'I worried about how he would take it. And he worried about how I would take it.'

They had gone climbing the cliffs, in search of the spot where Felix had the gun put to his head. They couldn't find it and Felix became agitated, but Renée persisted.

'I knew that was the place,' she said. 'It was important for him to spend some time there, alone.'

'Where this implausible thing happened to me. Because some people didn't believe me.' Felix stopped and looked at me under his Deutschland baseball cap which on most heads would look silly but on him was poignant.

'They didn't believe this could happen. And in those months in solitary, with the spider, I had moments when I doubted it myself. That doubt was the greatest terror, greater than the Stasi. Greater than jail, starvation, and exile.'

Felix and Renée had found the border barracks where he and Dominik had slept on the night of their arrest. They looked into the window. The portraits were gone. At the long table, a lone border guard was eating soup. They wanted to go in but didn't.

'He was young,' Renée said. 'What could we say to him?'

Out in the dingy street, I thanked Renée and said I'd been nervous about our meeting.

'Me too,' she said and we hugged. Felix smiled like a man who knows his name means luck. I watched them walk away in their bohemian jackets in the murk of the Berlin winter, hand in hand, young lovers when seen from the back.

The following summer, I went back to the lagoon. Felix's message was painted over and only the information about sand lilies remained, about the endangered monk seal and the fig trees. I could hear the boom of breaking waves before I reached the clifftop.

'Do you sometimes wonder,' I'd asked Felix, 'how your life would have panned out if you hadn't taken that step? Do you have regrets?'

'No,' he'd said. And I believed him.

The eighteen-year-old had come to a threshold and done what any eighteen-year-old should do in order to be young before being old. He was light, and he took that step for those who were heavy. For our mothers and fathers whose age Klaus and Brigitte would be now. For the naked child down on the beach, whose future is unknown and who runs across the picture, shiny with Nivea cream, shouting something. Though there is no sound.

zmey

In Slavic folk mythology, a shape-shifting dragon that embodies protection and possession. In Strandja, the *zmey*'s natural dwelling is caves. It travels across space and time as a ball of fire and can manifest in a male or female form. Each village once had its own zmey, who looked after harvests and other seasonal affairs. But the other side of dragon protection is dragon desire. If a zmey sets eyes on you, your heart sickens and you are compelled to follow it to its cave, which is another way of saying the Underworld.

BALL OF FIRE

The weeks went by in the Village in the Valley, and I felt dark and heavy like the plums in the abandoned gardens. The sizzle of insects intensified with the fragrant decay of summer. I didn't even have the motivation to take myself to the beach any more. My sense of impasse was mixed with languor, as if I was waiting for something to split open and reveal itself. Petrified at the bottom of the valley as if by a spell, all I wanted was to sit at The Disco, eat goat's yogurt out of a jar, and gaze at the hills with Minka. I was undergoing some kind of change, and I felt helpless against it. The car hadn't been used for so many days, I'd lost count. Several times, I put off my departure.

A few days before I was due to leave again, the river burst its banks. Each year it was the same. The river lashed out like a beast, then withdrew, leaving a hinterland of mud and debris. Nobody complained, though everybody knew the cause – the truckloads of the logging mafia who slaughtered forests without replanting, and the construction company which extracted sand six metres into the riverbed. The result: a derailed and polluted river and a change in microclimate, both aggravating floods. The locals were up against a Hydra of legalised crime. Instead of help, there were bribes and threats.

In the aftermath, people waded thigh-high in the water to clean up. I joined in. It was a dirty, upsetting task, and at some point I shouted, 'Something must be done!'

'It's because you don't live here,' Blago snorted. 'You still believe in justice.'

When the sun was high in the sky, three of the women sat on a bench in their rubber galoshes and knitted socks, and Despina said:

'Once, a caravan heading for Istanbul crossed the river hereabouts. It carried tax in silver and gold. All of a sudden, the river rose in a big wave. Every man and horse was drowned. Later, the village folk came out and what did they find? Huge treasure washed up on the banks. Ever since, when the river floods, we keep an eye out.'

'But the river ain't chucking out gold and silver,' the woman with the chewing gum said and winked at me. 'Only mud.'

The youngest woman was The Ear. She was looking at the hot cloudless sky with her squinty eyes.

'It's coming,' she said. 'It always comes after a still spell.'

'What's that?' I said, not knowing which eye to follow.

'The ball of fire,' The Ear said.

There were four of us. I felt like the surplus harpy. In local folklore, the daemons called *orisnitsi* (from *oris*, fate) are always three women: young, middle-aged, and old. The eldest has the last word. They come to you when you're born and decide on the shape of your life. You will be as rich or poor as they like, and die when they say so. For you, it's life and death, but for them it's just a game.

The other two nodded in agreement.

'Aye, it passes every year,' said Despina. 'In the direction of Kreynero fountain.'

'Must've slept through it,' the woman with the chewing gum said. 'Like I slept through the river treasure.'

'My mother saw it,' Despina said. 'She was pregnant and ploughing the field when she saw it. A ball of fire, except it wasn't no ball, it was a flying zmey. Big snake, I tell you, with a tail like a comet. It passed

over, scorched the earth. When she came round, her hair was singed
and the earth was full of golden scales.'

'In the olden days, folk say it hit the ground and turned into a
human. That's why, when you see it flying overhead, you keep quiet,'
The Ear said. 'Or the zmey takes your speech.'

'You'll be lucky if it's just your speech. It could well take *you*.'
Despina winked. 'For his bride.'

'But only if you're young and pretty,' the woman with the chewing
gum said. 'You're safe, I'm telling you now.'

Despina chuckled.

'You know Ruska's Cave?' she said. 'A dragon lived there who fell
in love with Ruska and took her for his bride. Popular spot for infer-
tile couples.'

'They had a sprog,' the woman with the chewing gum said.

'Aye, a dragon and a human can have offspring, but it dies. Because
it's against nature,' Despina said. 'Anyway, when my mother came
round, she went into labour. Dragged herself home, and sent me for
the doctor.'

But it was the late 1940s and the doctor was under arrest for helping
someone cross the border.

'So she gave birth the only way she could. He was a good man, the
doctor, but they shot him anyway. God almighty, the number of good
people they shot...'

The Ear was eavesdropping on the conversation of two men across
the square.

'What are they saying?' I asked her.

One of her eyes looked at me with mistrust.

'Must get on with it.' She picked up her long-handled broom. 'But
mark my word, it's coming.'

★

The nocturnal sighting of fireballs and fire discs was so common in Strandja that people accepted it as a law of nature. A local historian told me that his grandfather had spotted fire discs over the border river many times in his lifetime. Always over the river. A local from a distinguished family, Mr N., told me how in the 1990s his young son, a keen fisherman, had been freaked out by something one evening when he'd gone to check the nets on the river. Mr N. ran to his help and saw them: two flaming objects hovering above the river. Father and son stood until the objects moved away over the forest. Mr N. could understand why some would be sceptical.

'There was a guy in the Village in the Valley who laughed at this,' he continued. 'He was an engineer with a university degree, he said, not a superstitious peasant. One evening, we were sitting in his garden under the vine.'

There had been three of them: the doubting engineer, Mr N., and a woman neighbour. Then suddenly, there were five.

'Two men appeared between us at the table. Dressed like us, normal folk. Do you know these guys? Nope. So we asked them: Who the hell are you?'

At this, the two visitors had simply looked at each other and laughed soundlessly – they were like twins, or reflections of each other. Then they'd risen above the table and drifted towards the river, like mist.

'And no, we weren't drunk.' Mr N. smiled. 'This is a spiritual mountain. Some things you can't explain, and maybe just as well.'

He had a point. It is when we have an explanation for everything that we begin to feel reduced, plundered. And the people of Strandja had been plundered in every way except this. No one could take *this* from them.

One night, I was sitting at The Disco with the beautiful Russian and her husband who had been a mathematician.

'I only saw it once, in the 1980s,' he said. He was relatively undrunk this evening. 'After they closed up the mine by the river.'

The mine had revealed unexpected deposits of uranium and had been closed after two months.

'I had gone fishing,' he said. 'I saw them over the mine entrance. Flaming discs. They formed different shapes – stars, concentric circles. Like they were trying to show me something.'

So what were these objects? He shrugged and smiled with blackened teeth.

'There is a theory that extraterrestrials have been visiting Strandja since before human civilisation. I am not saying I buy it. But I'm not ruling it out either.'

The idea is that these extraterrestrials charge themselves up in places with strong geomagnetic fields.

'Of course,' he added, 'extraterrestrial stands for anything that doesn't belong in the material world. Which gives us infinite possibilities. You see, the material world is a prison. We are trapped in a prison of perception.'

Perhaps that's why so many men in the village rarely sobered up.

Volleys of lightning fell near the closed mines too. Nedko the book lover had once been struck by a bolt of lightning near a mine while herding his single goat in the company of an old shepherd and his big flock. Nedko saw the lightning split a birch, then the electricity went through him and threw him to the ground. He didn't know if he was dead or alive until the old shepherd poked him with his crook.

In the neighbouring village lived Mr N.'s aunt, an old woman who read your fortune in a handful of beans the way African witch doctors read cowry shells. After first tossing the beans for me, she told me the following story. Her husband had worked in the nearby copper mine in the years of the five-year plan. Deep inside the hill, the miners had found tunnels and tools dating from the Thracians and the Romans, but had been instructed to destroy them. The tools turned to dust on contact with air. Before his death, the husband had a stroke and became demented. Night after night, he would climb out of the window and they would find him limping along the ghostly road in his nightclothes. Where are you going? his wife asked, and each time he said: To the mine. They're waiting for me. Soon after his death, she had a dream.

'We were in an ox-pulled cart, like the old times,' she said. 'We came to a river with an old name that doesn't exist any more. He couldn't cross the river with me because he was a spirit, so I went on alone. I turned and saw him, by the mine entrance. All around him were calves, pigs, lambs, like in the old days before they took our animals. He loved those animals.'

Writing about the psyche, Carl Jung said that 'when an inner situation is not made conscious, it appears outside as fate'. Perhaps the ball of fire was Strandja's way of manifesting collective fate.

Mr N.'s ninety-year-old father had lived in Strandja his whole life, though he and his nonagenarian friends liked to joke, 'There goes half my life!' One evening I sat with him under the hazelnut trees of his village square, where the gentry gathered for morning coffee and evening gossip (the women at one long table, the men at another), and he told me about a recurring dream. He wakes up and sees 'a girl' in the room – about your age, he said – though the house is locked. How did you get in? he asks her, but she shakes her head and disappears. Each time, she looks more familiar and he wakes up with a heavy heart, so heavy that he went to see his sister the bean reader. She tossed her beans and said: 'Why, you know her. There's nothing to fear.'

Forty years ago, he had a daughter who died in infancy. The day before her death, he saw a ball of fire hovering above the river. Hearing this, I felt uneasy. I wondered if he was being summoned to the Other-world and why he shared his intimate dream with me, a stranger, unless in me he saw his daughter's revenant.

Either way, the ball of fire was always seen by a river or a mine, and always in the evening or at night – in a liminal space, at a borderline.

On my last day, Blago's mother was hosing her garden, a few doors down in my street. Her husband had just died and she was in black. She straightened her back.

'We'll see it any day now,' she said.

'See what?'

'The ball of fire. I thought I saw it last night, but it wasn't it.'

Last night, I had lain in my bedroom with my bags packed, the dogs howling, the bodies of dead hornets on the floor, and I'd worried. These few weeks had been the longest time I'd spent in Bulgaria since leaving in 1992. I had worried that I was at heart a deracinated, drifting person, despite my delusion of being at home everywhere. That although I no longer belonged here, in the broken country of my youth, it was where I secretly belonged the most. That I fancied myself as an observer, but even after twenty years away, I was still a participant and always would be. That I had no distance from anything and cared too much about the doomed. That the Village in the Valley felt like paradise but might be purgatory. That I couldn't tell the difference. That I felt tainted, yet full of love for this plundered place.

And I had worried that so many of the young men of this village were dying. Every third house had lost a young man – to cancer, an accident, suicide. I wondered about that uranium mine, which others said hadn't existed, or else they'd said that the mathematician was confused, that it was only copper. I wondered about the sins of the fathers seeping like poison into the bloodstream of the sons.

Blago's mother shook her head. 'I've seen it before. They're keeping an eye on us. But the time hasn't come to communicate.'

Blago's mother was a sensible peasant woman with features death-less like the land. She wasn't what you'd call fanciful.

'But isn't that just lights reflected from the resorts?' I said.

'What resorts, dear?' she said. 'That over there is Turkey, empty villages.'

'A falling star?' I chanced. She shook her head.

'It ain't falling, it goes right over and hovers over the river. Thing is,' she said, and started filling a bowl for me with tomatoes, peppers, spring onions, 'I've seen them since I was a tot. Round this time of year.'

'That's too many tomatoes,' I said, stopping her, 'I'm leaving tomorrow.'

'Leaving? You only just arrived yesterday!' And she continued filling the bowl.

'What is it then, flying dragons?' I said, no longer joking.

'I'm a simple woman.' She came out of her garden and handed me the bowl. 'But there's something out there, I tell you. We're not alone.'

Back in my house that evening, I shared a last melancholy salad with the tortoise.

I called Marina in her border town to say goodbye. Her mother was expecting the ball of fire, she said matter-of-factly. Marina had no defined theory about the ball of fire. All she said was: 'Nothing exists in isolation. Everything is connected.'

'But is it physical?' I insisted. She laughed softly.

I said I was leaving Strandja the next day.

'Good,' she said after a pause. 'We are not saying goodbye.'

And she hung up. I knew I would miss her.

At around ten o'clock, my room was flooded with a pale light. I jumped out of bed and stepped out onto the balcony just in time to see it shoot off towards the river and Kreynero fountain. A turning ball of light. I glimpsed the tall, stooped shape of the retired basketball player in his garden, but it could have been a pear tree.

I waited some time, then I went back in and closed the curtains. I felt a bit drugged, as if a lot of time had passed and I couldn't account for it.

Did I really see that? Did Blago's mother? Did the basketball player? The forest walkers from Turkey, scratched by brambles, hungry, full of injury and loss, a long way from everywhere, with no way back, did they see it?

Here is what the old bean reader had said when she tossed the beans for me. Although I had posed my question mentally (Will I complete my border journey without anything bad happening?), she answered as if I had spoken it out loud: What you have begun you will complete, she said, tossing the beans in her desiccated hands, but you must heed the signs along the way. Never ever ignore the signs.

A good piece of life advice, if you can tell the real signs from the fake ones. Here, everything felt like a sign, and I had drunk thrice from the cold water fountain. Before dawn broke, I put my bags in the car, locked the house, put the key under the mat, drove across the empty square, past the closed Disco, and began the long, scary drive out of the misty valley. I locked the car doors and crept up the tight, winding road. It was like pulling myself out with a corkscrew. What looked like a giant hare ran across my path. In the spectral forest, an owl hooted a farewell.

I don't know what the ball of fire is, whether it's a visitation from another dimension, a projection of the collective unconscious, a glimpse of an Otherworld, a physical phenomenon of light. But I'm glad it's there. If it weren't for the ball of fire and the curative spring, people would go insane. The fact that the ball of fire doesn't really turn into your dragon–lover or visitor from outer space makes it better

– that way, metaphor keeps travelling. Over the muffled hills where no one sees the sudden torch beam, or hears you explain to the armed border patrol why you are here at this hour of the night.

PART TWO

THRACIAN CORRIDORS

All human populations are in some sense immigrants.

Neal Ascherson, *Black Sea*

thrace

Thrace today denotes a large geographical area on the map. But Thrace is also a dead civilisation, a contemporary of ancient Greece, Macedonia, and Persia. The Thracians, who never formed an empire, and whom we already met in Strandja, are perhaps the least known of the ancient peoples of Europe.

Ancient Thrace sprawled across what is today the territory of northeast Greece, including the islands of Samothraki and Thassos, as well as the European part of Turkey and all of Bulgaria; across the Danube, it covered Romania up to the Carpathian Mountains, and some of Serbia and the Republic of Macedonia. The Thracians left no written traces but a great deal of material ones. Their stone-hewn cult sites, painted tombs, and golden artefacts are second to none in the ancient world, but little is known of their lives. The Thracians weren't studied until the twentieth century, and now that they are (mostly in Bulgaria and Greece, and more recently in Turkey), new tombs and treasures are dug up by archaeologists every few years. The longest tomb corridor excavated so far is Mezek, in the Bulgarian border village of the same name. Found by villagers in the 1930s, already thoroughly plundered by treasure hunters after the Balkan Wars, and containing a life-size bronze boar among other things, it is said to be the tomb of a Thracian Odrysian king from around the fifth century BC. When you walk the thirty metres lined with giant stone slabs, your lonely steps echoing before and after you with a hollow sound, you feel the chill of twenty-five centuries in your bones. And you glance back to make sure the bored guide hasn't locked you in.

Herodotus, our main source on the Thracians, described them as the most numerous and powerful collection of tribes of his time. If only they could be politically united, he wrote, they would rule the world – but they just couldn't be bothered. If writing is one measure of civilisation, then the Thracians were literary barbarians, for they indulged in sensuous and mystical pleasures instead, song and craftship, revelries and solar–chthonic cults. Unlike the Macedonians, Persians, and practically everyone else, they had no great conquering ambitions. Perhaps they were just politically lazy, the first complete society of hedonists. They shocked their Greek neighbours by drinking undiluted wine, but they were also known for being formidable warriors and horse raisers and, because of their disunity and laissez-faire attitude, a source of mercenaries to others. The gladiator Spartacus, who led the biggest revolt against Rome, was a Thracian from a place near today's Bulgarian–Greek border. The peninsula was subsumed by Romans, Slavs, Vlachs, Greeks, Asiatic Bulgars, Tatars, and other ethnicities, so by the time the Seljuk Turks arrived in the late fourteenth century, Thracian blood must have been well mixed.

No nation-state has ever been named after Thrace (Macedonia is quite enough, thanks), but a geographic and cultural Thrace remains: bordered on three sides by the Aegean, Marmara and Black Seas, from north to south it is made up of southern Bulgaria, starting with the Balkan range (northern Thrace), then European Turkey (eastern Thrace), and north-eastern Greece (western Thrace).

★

Oddly, and perhaps symbolically, I couldn't find central Thrace on the map, but that's exactly where I was headed: to a fertile region of soft climate dissected by three national borders. During the Cold War, this is where the armies of Greece, Bulgaria, and Turkey were massed, because the low-lying hinterland provided an obvious military corridor for invasion. The Turks were nervous about the Soviets and the Greeks, the Greeks were nervous about the Soviets and the Turks, and the Bulgarians were nervous about everyone. A military buffer zone for half a century, this was the point where one ideology stopped and another began. Ideologies come and go, but one thing has stayed: several thousand years after the Thracians drank their undiluted wine, this is still a land of vines.

After the summer of Strandja, it was a late-flowering spring when I went to the twin border cities of central Thrace. The land was pale and exhausted with winter. Rivers thundered under, and sometimes over, bridges. Pink orchards blossomed, and rubbish lay strewn on the sides of the west–east motorway, as if every traveller had chucked out a plastic bottle in revenge for some old insult. Lorries with international plates and mysterious cargoes shook the road. Three alphabets, three currencies, three versions of history. I had never been here before, and I'd heard that since the relative softening of the border, the Thracian plain had become a hub of entrepreneurs and consumers, desperados and smugglers.

At the checkpoint between Europe and Asia, the fallen leviathan of a communist-era factory was twinned by a shiny giant mosque.

THE FRIEND WITH THE PIGEONS

I'd spent the last week in the leafy neighbourhood of a Bulgarian border town called Svilengrad, in a small hotel called Villa Columbina. There were three types of guest at Villa Columbina: Turks and Greeks of both sexes, visiting the town to feed their addictions; engineers prospecting in the gas-rich area; and rare tourists who came to see antiques like the Mezek tomb and medieval fortresses nearby.

The gamblers never visited historical sites, and the culture buffs had no taste for gambling. The only place where these two species met was in the garden at breakfast, where the air was thick with lilacs and cooing doves. Every morning from the garden, I watched the aerial promenade of a flock of pigeons. About a hundred of them flew over-head, clockwise, casting quick rustling shadows over the land where the Merlot grapes ripened. In reception was a glass cabinet that sold gold-plated Zippos and individually wrapped condoms. Everyone was welcome, no questions asked, and the tourist season was all year round, except August, when the Thracian plain became so sun-baked that those who could afford it went to cool down in one of the three available seas: the Aegean, Marmara, or Black Sea.

The owner of this establishment was a cheerful entrepreneur called Ventsi, and Ventsi had volunteered to be my driver across into Turkey. I pointed out that I had a car, but he insisted that I couldn't handle the 'oriental' streets of Edirne, and that he should place me in good hands there, just to be sure. True, a lone woman in a rented car was at best puzzling in these parts, and at worst suspicious (the typical drug mule caught at the checkpoint was a youngish woman from a Balkan nation, often in a rented car). Nervous about my first border-crossing, I left my car in the leafy street outside Villa Columbina and headed to Edirne in Ventsi's Land Rover.

There was another passenger in the car: Emel. A guest at Villa Columbina like me, Emel was returning to Edirne after visiting friends in Svilengrad. We had swapped greetings and biographies at breakfast in the garden. She was long-divorced and worked as a civil servant. Emel was large, beautiful, and immaculately appointed, like a wealthy estate. Her eyes shone, and her nails and lips too, as if she continuously snacked on life, and even her name meant Desire. When she walked into the courtyard of Villa Columbina for breakfast, she brought with her a sense of opulence – you just wanted to lie down and purr. When she laughed, her fleshy throat like a dove's, it was impossible not to laugh with her.

'Honey, you look young for your age,' she said to me one morning, 'But if you don't quit smoking, I give you two years before you suddenly start looking like a hag.'

I stubbed out the cigarette. She had never smoked or drunk alcohol, and had a complexion like a dewy meadow.

'It's interesting, isn't it, honey,' Emel said now, strapping on the seat belt in the back of the Land Rover, much to Ventsi's umbrage – what, she didn't trust his driving? 'I have a man in my life, but he doesn't need me any more.' She winked at me and relished Ventsi's startled look. Her man was her grown-up son. 'God, it's a man desert out there! Can you imagine what it's like being single in Turkey?'

'What is the difference between the Turkish man and the Greek man?' Ventsi joined in. We were leaving town now. 'The Greek marries his wife. The Turk marries his wife's family.'

Emel laughed with a fleshy throat and said:

'What is the difference between a Bulgarian man and his Greek and Turkish counterparts?'

There was a tense silence.

'The Greek and the Turk are romantic, at least in the beginning.'

Ventsi looked put out.

'That's because women measure things by money and call it romance,' he said. 'And the Bulgarian man is poor.'

Emel closed the conversation:

'Bring me a Scotsman, honey, if you find a suitable one,' she said. 'He can wear a skirt if he wants to, I don't mind.'

From Ventsi's dashboard mirror dangled a silver crucifix and a *nazar*, the Turkish blue 'evil eye'. Like Emel, Ventsi was on friendly terms with the checkpoint and the twin cities on either side.

They were twins because what you couldn't get in Edirne (alcohol, sex, casinos) you could get in Svilengrad, and vice versa (good shopping, infrastructure, family values). In Svilengrad, you could almost hear Edirne's chanting imams, and in Edirne, the beat of Svilengrad's nightclubs. Svilengrad meant Silk Town, though the silk industry died with the planned economy in 1990, to be replaced with an industry of pleasure. Now Greeks and Turks came over the border to Svilengrad to gamble all weekend, drink good cheap rakia, and get their bodies rubbed with essential oils.

In that city, Ventsi tried to do honest business.

'I hoped the restaurant would be a gourmet destination, but it's too fine for people's tastes. I'm putting in gambling machines. A man's got to survive.'

Ventsi was once fat and married, he said by way of an introduction when I first met him in his own bar. So fat that when he went shopping in Istanbul for a pair of Levis, he couldn't find a size large enough.

'I got so pissed off, I immediately went on a diet.'

He called it the separation diet, though I wasn't sure whether that was because of the division between proteins and carbs, or because he got divorced soon after. Now Ventsi ate tender lambs' tongues, salads drizzled with olive oil, and plates of black Turkish olives, no bread. This was why he went to Edirne: to buy wholesale supplies for his gourmet restaurant, because everything was cheaper across the border.

'Hm, the *border*,' he said and lit another Marlboro, silver chains singing from his wrists and neck, as his Land Rover sped along the short stretch of road to the border, past disused factories and still-wintering fields. 'It's time they abolished borders. They only make it harder for people to do the things they need to do.'

'It's true, honey,' Emel agreed from the back and waved the cigarette smoke away from her face with a plump hand. 'The only good thing about a border is that you can cross it.'

It was the first warm day of April, and Ventsi wore flip-flops. On his thin foot, not at all the foot of a once-fat man, I saw a tattoo of a bird in mid-flight, but tattoos and feet are personal things so I didn't ask.

To Emel's relief, Ventsi stubbed out his cigarette in the already full car ashtray because, within ten minutes of leaving Svilengrad, we had reached the checkpoint and a modicum of seriousness was required. Ventsi and Emel both chatted to the customs officials in their kiosks, who called them *arkadash*, Turkish for mate.

But I felt a pang of angst as I handed over my passport. I'd never crossed this border before. When I last lived in Bulgaria, this checkpoint was closed to all except the privileged and the doomed. The privileged were few and included the customs officials who were so corrupt that Svilengrad has been a wealthy town ever since. The doomed were more numerous. In particular, there had been three hundred thousand of them in 1989 who overnight became exiles in refugee camps on the outskirts of Turkish cities. They were the ethnic Turks of Bulgaria, the last victims of European communism, one of whom was Emel. In short, for half a century this was a checkpoint that you crossed in a state of fear and loathing. But those days were long gone, weren't they?

Then I saw them. A group of young men, skinny, bedraggled, with rucksacks on, blinking against the bitter April sun, already in handcuffs. They had just been flushed out of a lorry on the EU side.

The lorry driver was there too, throwing up his hands in despair at the cops. He was a heavy, tired man on the point of tears.

'What are they going to do with him?' I asked.

'Arrest him, what else?' Emel said.

'Nice sunglasses.' The Turkish customs officer handed my passport back.

'Thanks, arkadash,' Ventsi said, and bang, we were in Turkey.

'What do you notice about the non-European side of the border?' Ventsi asked.

A red flag with a crescent flapped above, and two massive buildings loomed: a mosque and a shopping mall. The road was bigger and better.

'Exactly,' Ventsi said. 'What kind of a border is this? Stopping the Turks from coming into Europe with their *merak* and money.'

'Merak is a Turkish word,' Emel said and smacked her lips. Merak: keenness, passion, interest. But Turks needed visas to visit EU countries, and visas were in short supply.

We drove towards Edirne, past the day-long queue of lorries with their sealed-up bulks. The bored drivers camped with little stoves on the side of the road and shuffled up and down, souls in transit between Baghdad and Hamburg, Istanbul and Calais. I'd passed their watering holes along the motorway, their lonely roadside eateries, the parking lots where they sleep, the shops that sell them yogurt and beer. Once they cross into Bulgaria, the thin prostitutes wait for them, swaying in the motorway haze like reeds.

'An arkadash of mine runs this roadside joint for lorry drivers.' Ventsi lit up again. 'The kind of place where women go only if they have something to sell. Says the drivers moan it's a dog's life but wouldn't give it up for the world.'

I wondered if I could've been a transcontinental lorry driver. Something about it appealed to me – the open road, to be precise. Ventsi scoffed and Emel laughed.

'There are two women in the industry, honey,' she said. 'A German and an Englishwoman. The Englishwoman lasted a year. And I don't blame her.'

'Welcome to Edirne, ladies!' Ventsi beamed as we approached the city.

Edirne: once the city of the Roman emperor Hadrian and later the second Ottoman capital, where the sultan adjourned to when Istanbul was gripped by plague, it was now the closest Turkish city to the border with the EU, Emel informed us with a local's pride.

Edirne was an impressive minaret-studded sprawl smack in the middle of the fat Thracian plain. Its modern name carried echoes of the first Thracian 'nation' – the Odrysi tribe, who built their capital Uskudama here. Modern Greeks still refer to it by its Byzantine name, Adrianople, as if time hadn't passed and the Ottomans hadn't arrived yet. But they had, and Edirne had marinated in centuries of oriental excess followed by centuries of decline. Coveted, assaulted, and inhabited by Thracians, Byzantines, Bulgars, Turks, Greeks, Armenians, and even Russians during two imperial Russian–Ottoman wars, today Odrys-Odrysia-Hadrianopolis-Adrianople-Odrin-Edirne was a city of mosques the size of stadiums, tulip gardens, public sculptures of figures that included anatomically explicit mermaids, a famed dish of fried liver called *ciger tava*, and a nominal alcohol ban.

The air was heavy with fumes and fragrant with lilacs.

'I told you you'd get lost in these streets,' Ventsi said as he sped through traffic cacophonous with hooting, Turkish style, and the closer we got to the point where he would drop us off, the more he threw at us small morsels from his restaurant and hotel, as if to make sure Emel would visit again and I'd go back to reclaim my car, and not be too seduced by Turkey's sticky almond sweets, syrupy coffee, and baskets of soft white bread that were put before you as soon as you sat down because the nearby fields were the granary of Thrace and there was no economic crisis here.

'There's this Greek guy from Kastanies,' Ventsi said. 'Used to come over in his car and sit in the corner. Widowed, lots of time on his hands. And a good Greek pension, though it's less good now. He'd have dinner and a few rakias, chat to people and drive back. Until the police took his licence away. Too many rakias.'

'So he stopped coming?' Emel said.

'Oh no, he still comes. In a taxi. A man has his habits.'

Kastanies was a sleepy Greek border town. From its outskirts you could see Edirne, spread out like a concubine in the haze. But the Greek man didn't like Turkey.

'There's this Turkish client who comes en route to a shooting park in the Rhodope ranges. Once I gave him a bottle of my home-made rakia, and on the way back from the shoot he brought me a boar. He didn't eat pork you see. Problem is, I don't like pork either.'

So what did you do?

'I thanked him and took the pig. A Turk has his pride.'

Edirne was central Thrace's third-biggest secret (in my own classification), after Strandja and the enigmatic tombs. How come it wasn't more famous, with its arched bridges touched by the swollen waters of the Maritsa River, which briefly became the Meriç before it headed south and became the Greek–Turkish border for 135 kilometres under the name of Evros, then joined the Aegean? The tourists who clogged Istanbul, the Greek islands, and the Bulgarian Black Sea resorts didn't stop here to see the Tower of Macedon from the time of Philip II, the arched medieval caravanserais, and the stadium on a river island where the world's oldest sport was still performed every summer. Oil wrestling: where men of all ages and sizes put on leather trousers and cover themselves in oil. How come it wasn't more famous?

'It *is* famous, to those who come for the Friday market.' Ventsi pulled over.

Today was Friday, and the people-darkened streets led to the market like arteries to a beating heart. Ventsi deposited me and Emel outside its maw-like entrance where 'Friday Market' was written in four languages: Turkish, Greek, Bulgarian, and English, one of which wasn't needed because all the shoppers were from the three countries of the border. Ventsi had errands to run, involving olives and toma- toes, he said – and I wondered if that was a euphemism, but Ventsi didn't do euphemisms. He was a straight-up optimist running an honest business in a country of poor people, he said.

'Instead of emigrating like normal folk. I must be crazy!'

The poor people were here in their thousands, in this kingdom of kilims and kitsch, or if they weren't poor, they weren't rich either, because here, for a few euros, you could buy baby clothes and snake oil, 'genuine' Levis and extra-large underwear, glittery make-up and patent-leather shoes. The sellers, in their movable Aladdin's cave of skins stripped from endangered African animals, yelled and cajoled you in every language, including Arabic and Russian.

I said goodbye to Emel, who was being picked up by a friend ('Remember to give me a call, honey,' she waved from her friend's car), and the crowd processed me. History dissolved and was replaced by voices. Visiting Greeks and Bulgarians, Bulgarian Turks who still spoke both languages after their 1989 exodus, milky-skinned Muslim women in baggy trousers from the Rhodope Mountains who spoke archaic Slav dialects, and beautiful fierce Gypsies who spoke everything. For these shoppers with the right passports, the border was something to do at the weekend, something to bring back. It was a magical line, a game for grown-up children. Now you're here. Now you've stepped across that line.

The border had reverted to its natural state of bargain and barter, curiosity and commerce, tricks and tariffs. Three cheers for the border!

'*Marka markaaa!* Genuine brands!' the seller of fake Levis called out, and the women of Thrace bought them in bulk. Everyone looked delighted. At a jewellery stall, I bought a ring with the head of Mustafa Kemal Atatürk on it for one euro, put it on, then took it off.

Against the rising tide of autocratic Islam, the face of Atatürk had become a banner of resistance. The man whose stony frown has dominated public spaces for a hundred years unchallenged, who homogenised the hell out of post-Ottoman Turkey, who approved when the fires of Greek Smyrna raged, the Armenians were slaughtered, and the Kurds were denied existence, this man was once again a symbol of something hard-won that could be lost: the secular Republic, the rights of women. I put the ring back on. It's a sad day when nationalism becomes the lesser evil.

Ventsi was waiting with a well-stocked Land Rover at the entrance to the market. He drove me to the luxury Hilly Hotel at the top of town where Emel had somehow arranged for me to stay for half price. The car park was full of buses with Istanbul number plates. A pro-Islamic AK (Justice and Development) Party demonstration was to take place the next day, and they had brought in covered women and sour-looking men from out of town because Edirne couldn't muster enough of those for the rally. These were the kind of folks who were organised by the ruling AK Party into furious protests against the anatomically explicit mermaid sculpture in Edirne, as well as an emblematic sculpture of a woman with open arms, claiming her posture was not representative of 'the traditional Turkish woman'. Presumably, *they* were: creatures in shapeless brown mantles; their faces looked as if they were continuously sucking on lemons.

'Just because Turkey's economy is doing well, doesn't mean its society is healthy,' Emel had said on the subject. Like the majority of those I met in European Turkey, she was a staunch supporter of the Cumhuriyet, the Kemalist Republican People's Party.

Back in the car park of the Hilly Hotel, I said goodbye to Ventsi.

'Call me when you're done and I'll come pick you up,' he said. I could smell the warm fragrant tomatoes in the back of the car. 'Meanwhile, it's Easter weekend in the Christian world. Gotta go and stock the restaurant for all the Turkish visitors.'

Then he produced something from under his seat and handed it to me with uncharacteristic shyness.

'You're a writer,' he said. 'You might understand.'

He got into the car heavily, and I saw for the first time that he had been a fat man. A fat man with skinny feet.

It was a large notebook with quartered pages, a remnant of his schooldays, which were my schooldays too, and it was filled with hundreds of handwritten poems in a still-childish hand. They were all dated 1988–9.

At nineteen, Ventsi had been enlisted in the border army. His brief was radio communication, which meant being locked up in a small room at the top of an observation tower for twelve hours by yourself, he told me later, where you had to be forever vigilant against the enemy.

'Once, the alarm was raised for a hedgehog in the middle of

the night. We had to go and liquidate it, in case it was a capitalist hedgehog. Once, this guy was brought to our barracks, in handcuffs. Fresh recruit. He'd gone crazy in the night and shot dead five of his arkadashes. He was like an animal. He wouldn't even look you in the eye, he just made these noises you make when you're beyond help.

'Once, I saw a man cut his son's throat. It was at the time of the name-changing campaign against the ethnic Turks. The boy wanted to take the new name and stay; dad wanted to keep their names and move to Turkey. We surrounded the house. We handcuffed him and handed him over. I'll never forget that boy lying with his throat cut in the vegetable garden.'

Ventsi went quiet. 'So you see, I had two options. Go nuts and start making noises like an animal, or start writing poetry.'

He wrote a poem every day, up in his tower. Then he tattooed his mates.

'I always liked drawing,' he said. 'There are now eighteen guys somewhere in the world with identical tattoos of birds on their feet. The last and best one I did on my own foot. Yep, I know it's crap, you can imagine the rest. I did it the night before I was due for leave. Twelve months shut up in that tower. I was so demented, I cut the tattoo with a rough needle that night. The foot swelled up and I limped home. My parents got a fright when they saw me, they thought I'd been wounded.'

In one of his poems, he *was* a bird, flying over the Furrow of Death. In another poem, he was the soldier who shot the bird.

Later, when I returned to Silk Town to collect my car and took a room in Villa Columbina again, I found myself waiting each morning for the rustle in the sky, and of course the pigeons were Ventsi's. They lived in the attic of his house. He told me what had happened on his way back from dropping me off in Edirne that afternoon. They had gutted his car and put it through the X-ray machine. They always did that on purpose when they saw the car was full. He had to take out every single box, and then put them all back in again.

'They know me by name! They know my restaurant!' He shook his head. 'By the time I got back, guess what'd happened to those tomatoes after a day in the heat?'

I guessed.

'Now here's the title of your book: What Have Borders Ever Done For Us, question mark.'

His pigeons all had names. But he kept talking about one particular dove.

'Columbina always came back,' he said. 'Once all my pigeons were stolen, but she came back. Another time, they were all strangled by a weasel, all except her. She was like a human, she loved me so much she flapped her wings when she saw me. I miss her.'

Columbina died thirty years ago: the week Ventsi became a soldier.

'Why don't we give you a couple of small ones in a cage, to take back to Scotland?' he said before I left.

I laughed but he could see I was tempted.

'You can release them and they'll fly back, no problem. They know the way home. No need for passports. Or you can keep them in Scotland, so you know that somewhere in Thrace you have an arkadash.'

A homing pigeon follows the main roads, he told me, instead of taking the shortest route as the crow flies, as we commonly think. Sometimes a pigeon even follows the roundabouts. A homing pigeon can fly thousand-mile-long stretches and reach ninety miles per hour, but even so, how could it make it from the Scottish Highlands across the North Sea, over millions of ghostly roads, to an attic in the Thracian plains?

On the other hand, perhaps the pigeons would adapt to the northerly climes, to the weasels and foxes, to the seagulls that blow in from the firth. Though they would never flap their wings when they saw me, and occasionally they would look at me with an oblique eye, and I would wonder.

memleket

Homeland. From the Turkish word *meme*, breast – a place that nurtures you. Naturally, a much-milked word in the mouths of politicians, which is why we must look to the poets.

Described as a utopian communist, Nâzim Hikmet is perhaps Turkey's best-known twentieth-century poet. He was much imprisoned and exiled during the Cold War, and even became an 'enemy of the state'. He died in exile in Moscow, some say of a broken heart. His last wish – to be buried in a village cemetery, any village cemetery, in Anatolia (though, like Kemal Atatürk, he was born on European soil, in Salonica) – wasn't carried out. He remains exiled in death as in life. Here is how he used *memleket*:

> *I love my homeland. I swung in its lofty trees;*
> *I lay in its prisons. Nothing relieves my depression*
> *like the songs and tobacco of my homeland.*

GIRL BETWEEN LANGUAGES

From the windy rooftop of the Hilly Hotel in Edirne, each day I watched the progress of a shepherd and his flock from one hill to another, across the road that ran from Istanbul to the checkpoints with Bulgaria and Greece. This is where I met a couple called Ayshe and Ahmed. They were friends of Ventsi's.

When they arrived on the hotel rooftop for our dinner date, a double hush fell over the empty restaurant. Actually it wasn't empty – there was me at one white-clothed table, and at another a retired, lost-looking Dutchman out of a Graham Greene novel, who seemed to drift towards the East, dressed in light linens.

They looked like a movie star and her bodyguard. Ayshe stood tall and distracted in her high heels and tailored trousers. Under a short fringe her green, wide-set eyes were made up but otherwise her face was naked with high cheekbones, the kind of face you want to gaze into, as if into a calm pool that would ease your pain. Ahmed was broad and heavy, with his feet planted on the ground, and a face that wasn't so much old as aged, though he wasn't yet forty: a face that had run out of youth. They sat down, lit up thin cigarettes, and ordered a bottle of Turkish raki, which is fragrant with aniseed and turns white when you trickle water into it.

'Bring us the best of what you have,' Ahmed said regally in Turkish to the waiters who hovered over us. To me he spoke a rusty domestic

Bulgarian, the language of his interrupted childhood in the tobacco-growing country west of Svilengrad.

He had picked tobacco from the age of five, with the rest of the family.

'You pick it before dawn, sometimes at night, 'cause the morning dew makes the leaves stick together. My fingers were always cut. Eight kids and one pair of shoes. You know the meaning of poverty?' He leaned across the table and I sat back, startled by his intensity, but Ayshe regarded him with friendly eyes.

Like Emel, Ayshe and Ahmed were Turks, but their homeland was Bulgaria. Their story is part of the bigger story of Bulgaria's Muslims, a tale of the countless ways in which nationalism doesn't work. It remains as little known as the story of Oriental tobacco.

By the 1960s, Bulgaria was the world's number one tobacco exporter. The aromatic indigenous sort was known as Oriental tobacco, and the traditional growers were Muslims, while the vine growers had been Christians. When the Bulgarian Turks were forced to leave the country in 1989, the tobacco industry that (along with fruit and vegetable growing) had been a driving economic force for over a century collapsed overnight. There was no one to collect the harvest.

'But I still miss it. Even if in Bulgaria they call me a Turk, and in Turkey they call me a Bulgarian. What am I, tell me!'

Ahmed banged the table and stared at me. Purring one moment, aggressive the next, one thing never left his baggy eyes – the melancholy, even when he told me how popular with women he was, which he did frequently, in front of his wife. The waiters brought a platter of seafood with dips and salads, a huge basket of bread. Ayshe and Ahmed drank steadily, as if anaesthetising themselves. While he spoke at length, using Turkish words where he couldn't remember the language of his childhood, she rummaged in her salad.

'That summer of 1989, the militia came and said, You have three days to leave. My dad kept saying, The money's gone, the house is gone,' Ahmed went on.

The money stayed in the State banks, and the house went for a song. Years later, Ahmed's family went back and bought their house again – at double the price. But it was worth it, Ahmed said, it's where our memories are. Everything is still there, somehow.

The older members of the family ended up returning to their Bulgarian villages; the strain of remaking themselves in a foreign country – Turkey – had been too great. This resulted in what was the norm across this border where so little was normal: fractured families.

'We loaded up the Lada and a lorry.'

Ahmed's large family joined the line of cars, trucks, pedestrians, and carts piled up with bundles and heading south. The carts were pulled by men, like the rickshaws in Calcutta, because the State didn't allow people to take their horses, cattle, or even pets – everything was confiscated. People wept over cows, dogs, cats, goats, and each other. Some shot their pets. Some shot themselves. All this only months before the Berlin Wall came down and the Cold War was suddenly over.

It is tempting to draw a parallel between the expulsion of the Bulgarian Turks and the hell that was about to be unleashed on Bosnia next door by Serb nationalists, because both crimes sought justification in an asinine anachronism, invoking the ghost of 'the Turkish yoke'. But there were fundamental differences. The Yugoslav war was driven by a reactivated Serbian and Croat nationalist virus that had lain dormant for decades just under the skin of the federation, and in essence was an act of extended territorial aggression, whereas Bulgaria's ethnic purge was the last cretinous crime of twilight totalitarianism.

'There was a neighbour in our town,' Ahmed said. 'He wasn't a

Turk, he wasn't subjected to any pressure, but he still hanged himself. Out of disgust at what was happening to his neighbours. That was us, we were the neighbours.'

What *was* happening?

Bulgaria has the largest population of native Muslims in the European Union. Not recent migrants like the Turks of Germany, but indigenous Turks who have lived there for generations, the human legacy of five ethnically mixed Ottoman centuries. Although many Turks had already left Bulgaria in various waves of voluntary or involuntary resettlement in the wake of the Ottomans' retreat from the Balkans, by the time the Iron Curtain was in place ethnic Turks still accounted for 8 per cent of the population. By the 1980s, because of the depressed Bulgarians' low birth rate and the slightly higher birth rate of ethnic Turks (who were less urbanised), the 8 per cent was more like 10. What if, in another twenty years, 'they' outnumbered 'us', the State argued?

A solution presented itself to the problem the Party politburo had fabricated: rename Turks, Christianise them, and ban mosques (although *all* religion was, strictly speaking, already banned). Assimilate 'them' before they assimilate 'us'. In any case, didn't they Islamise us once? In 1986, a name-changing campaign began, complete with top-notch propaganda. The language used by the State against its own people could have been lifted out of Orwell, had Orwell not been banned by the State, and anyway, party apparatchiks weren't great readers. For example, the process of forcibly changing Turkish and Arabic names to Slavic ones, the desecrating of Muslim graves, the beatings and rapes by organs of State Security, and even the changing of the names of the dead – this was all called the Revival Process. It was a cynical nod to the nineteenth-century movement for Bulgaria's liberation from the Ottomans. Now, it was time for the Bulgarian Turks to be revived into remembering their 'true' origins. Later, we will see how this experiment was performed on the Pomaks of the Rhodope. Unlike the Turks, the Pomaks had nowhere to go.

In truth, the Turks of Bulgaria only seemed to have somewhere to go. Turkey had enough problems as it was and couldn't really afford them, though it made a great show of giving the refugees Turkish passports. There is a photograph from that summer in which a great crowd of freshly arrived, exhausted men and women hold up their new Turkish passports to the camera, as they've been instructed to do, but on their faces can be seen the anger, the tears, the grief, the confusion. Their tragedy became a PR opportunity for one state against the other in the great scoring match of the Cold War in which everybody lost. But some lost more than others.

The hate campaign against the ethnic Turks was a bit like the Falklands War for the Argentine junta, pointless and poisonous, a way for a police state in decline to distract the populace from the real issues of the day: the failed economy, the empty shops, the habitual lack of human rights, the environmental problems, and the rising winds of change called Glasnost and Perestroika. A minority is always easy prey.

Overnight, Ahmed became Assen. Ayshe became Assia.

There was a resistance movement among the ethnic Turks which resulted in several acts of public terror that have gone down as 'the May events', though the real terrorist was never named. That was the State. A story I didn't tell earlier involves my older guard, the one who seeks atonement from Saint Marina. In 1989, it fell to his division to liquidate (his words) a father and his two sons, ethnic Turks who wanted to cross the border before it was officially opened by the State. They were said to have grenades strapped to their belts. The soldiers circled them in a clearing by the patrol booth where I met the older and the younger guards.

'I saw them for a second before we machine-gunned them,' the older guard had said. 'Three strapping men. And that made it much worse when we had to clean them up from the trees. Turned out they had no grenades. I kept thinking of the mother.'

I keep thinking of the mother too.

In a final brainwave, the State declared that the border with Turkey was open to those who didn't like the Revival Process and preferred to go on a Big Vacation. By then, the road to Turkey looked like the only option left to hundreds of thousands of confused people, even if it was a desolate one.

Ahmed was thirteen years old.

'That road was black with cars. And everyone was crying and smoking. Where are we going? To fuck's end, that's where. Go to Turkey, they said, you're Turks, but what *was* Turkey? Nobody knew.'

Because both city and country lived without freedom of movement or information, it was hard for us in Sofia to know what was happening in the countryside. I remember my mother crying in front of the TV when airbrushed footage of the Big Vacation was broadcast, because she saw the truth on the faces of the exiled, in their carts piled with mattresses and TVs. But some of my parents' friends didn't, and the living rooms of Sofia's intelligentsia became battlegrounds. Many bought the State propaganda wholesale, complete with a mega-film production called *Time of Violence* that was the must-see event of the season and that, bafflingly, remains Bulgaria's favourite film to this day, indicating a neurotic fixation on a doctored version of the distant past, the kind of fixation that drove murderous nationalists next door in Yugoslavia. If the film's title left anything to the imagination, the action finished it off. It was a fictionalised portrait of the Islamisation of the Rhodope region in the seventeenth century, complete with the country's finest actors, soulful music, and impalement scenes to haunt your lifelong nightmares. Its message was as simple as the production was sumptuous, and the message was: the good guys (Christian Bulgarians) were quietly heroic and their women were pure. The bad guys (the Turks) were sadists with shaven heads whose women signalled their moral turpitude by eating baklava. The main villain was a janissary, once taken from the same Christian village he was now converting by fire and sword. People gobbled it up with a masochistic relish, and collective self-pity lubricated the exodus of the ethnic Turks. Their carts were loaded not just with their possessions, but with the undigested weight of the nation's orientalist complex.

Ayshe and her sisters didn't speak Turkish. They only found out they were 'Turks' when the police knocked on their door – impossible not to think of yellow stars. The exodus of three hundred and forty thousand people with families, futures, and sometimes bodies broken by their own State was the largest movement of people in Europe since World War II. And it happened in peacetime.

Ayshe was eight when her family left. Her parents had worked in a cement factory in an industrial city, away from their home town, and the family lived in one of those free flats gifted by the State to workers whose lifespans were halved by heavy industries. Workers like Ayshe's father, who had sickened with cancer and died when the changing of the names began, at the age she was now. Her mother loaded up a cart with their possessions, packed up her three daughters, and joined the queue to the checkpoint. They didn't have a car. It took several days to reach the border.

Once in Turkey, some fared well immediately – they had relatives who hosted them while they found their feet, like Emel and her parents (even if they had to take Turkish-language classes). Emel's older brother stayed behind.

'He thought we were mad to up sticks and go to a foreign country,' Emel said. 'But now I'm glad I'm here and not there. Except for the man issue. Can you imagine being a single woman in Turkey?'

Others fared well eventually – they had the advantage of a solid socialist education and were highly employable, including the women, so one country's loss became another's gain. Then there were Ayshe and Ahmed.

The waiters padded between our table and the bar. The Dutchman looked desperate to join us. He was drinking a bottle of wine and sitting at an odd angle. We moved on to a platter of grilled meats. Ayshe was still picking at her salad – she didn't like parsley – and she laughed at my use of *maydanoz*, because it's one of those Turkish food words that have seeped into Balkan mouths permanently. The words for food can't be ethnically purged.

Then I got to ask my question: how did they meet?

They looked at each other and something passed between them that was almost too raw to witness.

'*Chaduri*,' Ayshe said. The tents.

'She called me bro,' Ahmed said. 'We were living in tents. You know the old bus station? One thousand five hundred families. Mud, rain, flooding, no sanitation, for two years. Then they built these prefabs for us. A present from the Turkish state. Because we were Turkish. Right?'

Ayshe's face had grown more distracted, and she was looking out to where the newest suburban sprawl filled the plains. Entire neighbourhoods of Edirne, Istanbul, and Kirklareli were populated by Bulgarian Turks who had crossed the border that summer and were well established by now, many of them in top professions. Just as many had gone back.

The shepherd was bringing his flock back across the road, onto the hillside and out of sight, with his three dogs beside him. One of them was missing a front leg but hopped along with such optimism that something about the scene squeezed my chest.

'Memleket,' Ayshe said suddenly. Homeland.

'That's the thing. I looked out for her,' Ahmed said and topped up everybody's glass with raki. 'We were in the same boat. But they were much worse off than us. No father. She called me bro.'

After a few months in the tents, Ayshe and her two sisters were taken away from their mother and placed in an orphanage. Their mother, a woman who looked like Nefertiti even in her sixties, when Ayshe showed me photographs on her mobile, lived on alone and worked as a hotel cleaner; in the evening, she went to Turkish classes. She could visit her daughters in the orphanage once a week. How had she survived those evenings in her leaking tent, on the sodden mattress, everything she loved ripped from her? The words of the younger border guard came back to me: 'One thing you learn in this job is that people survive things you can't imagine.'

'How come,' I asked Ayshe, 'you don't speak Bulgarian any more?' But I saw the answer. It was in her eyes. She understdood the question and looked at Ahmed.

'One day,' Ahmed said, 'it was early days in the tents, these cops came. One of them picked on Ayshe. He grabbed her like this, shook her, and said, What kind of a Turk are you if you don't speak Turkish?'

She never spoke a word of Bulgarian again. For a time, she fell between languages.

Ahmed and his family fared better in the first instance: at least they had spoken an archaic Ottoman form of Turkish. All they had to do was update it by a century.

'Actually,' Ayshe cleared her throat and Ahmed translated, 'the orphanage was okay. We had good food, a good education. There were kids from all over.'

What she didn't say was that unlike the other kids, she and her sisters were special orphans – orphans with a mother.

Ahmed visited his new friend at the weekends. 'I never forgot her,' he said. 'Also, her sister was very cute.' He winked at me. 'I was a real heart-throb, you know. All the girls wanted me.'

He grinned and the dark circles of his eyes deepened. It was as if his machismo narrative was a defence against hardship. Ayshe regarded him impassively. They married when she was twenty. Ahmed had already embarked on what would become his fate: working for rich men. Today he was a chauffeur to a wealthy entrepreneur.

Ayshe said nothing. I assumed she was a housewife.

'Memleket.' She smiled again and handed me the salad dressing made of olive oil, lemon, and pomegranate.

'That's the question, sister,' Ahmed said. 'When you have roots, the world's your oyster. But when you don't...'

He studied me with intensity.

'Where is your memleket, huh? What are you doing here?'

A year after Ahmed and Ayshe found themselves in Edirne, Turkey, our family found itself in Essex, England, where my father had taken an academic fellowship. Two years later, we emigrated to New Zealand. We didn't cross *this* border but some other invisible one over the Pacific, and we didn't live in tents but in a nice big house in Dunedin where my father taught at the university. We brought a container with us, which was supposed to contain our possessions, but for some reason the only sizeable item in it was a piano made in Czechoslovakia, a country that soon would cease to exist. Everything else stayed behind in the crumbling landscape of post-communist Bulgaria: furniture and friends, grandparents and seasons. The trees and birds in New Zealand were different, the stars were rearranged, the seasons were inverted, the vowels in Kiwi speech made words sound as if something was wrong ('fush and chups'), but what was it?, the beaches were devoid of lust or menace, and the water in the sink drained the other way. It was an upside-down world, but then it always is, for the immigrant.

Those first years are almost a blank in my memory. As if, on the way over the Pacific, I had fallen into an atmospheric pocket, and couldn't get out again. I had become stuck between continents and languages, adolescence and maturity, silenced yet full of things to say, to ask, to learn, yearning to be in Europe. It was always cold at the bottom of the South Island, and the people – descendants of Scottish, Irish, and English immigrants – were pale and puritanical. My fellow students at university were mostly interested in rugby and beer. Where were my people?

Meanwhile, the war in Yugoslavia raged on our TV screens, surreally distant yet familiar with its Balkan faces and passions. My mother watched the news and wept: *those* were our people. From time to time, not trusting the news, she dialled our family in Yugoslavia to find out if it had spread there too. In the 1940s, my Macedonian grandmother had left her ancient lake town of Ohrid to marry a man in Sofia, my grandfather. Shortly after she emigrated, the two countries fell into a Tito–Stalin dispute and the border was frozen; she couldn't see her family for eight years. In my childhood, though, we visited the family across the border in Tito's Yugoslavia, a land of plenty to us poor cousins, practically the West. They had everything there, and now they had war too. The war hadn't spread to Macedonia, our family was safe, but many others were dying barbaric, nearby deaths, and nothing would ever be the same. In the late 1990s, the first European war refugees since the 1940s began to wash up on antipodean shores: people who until yesterday were cosmopolitan Yugoslavs and were now souls drifting across the Pacific like us, their homes in ruins, their nationality non-existent, their ethnos and religion carved out against their own will, as Croat, Serb, or Bosnian; Catholic, Muslim, or Orthodox. From my faraway Pacific outpost, I wondered: was the world getting smaller, or was it being diminished?

We were lucky not to be running from the middle of a hot war, only from the end of a cold one, and not to be living in tents. But like

Ahmed and Ayshe, we had been spat out by the same loveless mother-land. Things improved when I moved up to the North Island and immersed myself in more diverse experiences and people, living inde-pendently and embarking on a writer's life, but my yearning for the old continent undermined whatever happiness I had. It would take me twelve years before I returned to live in Europe, aged thirty.

'See what I mean?' Ahmed stubbed his cigarette and leaned back, almost triumphant. 'You don't know what you are, sister. That's why you're here.'

'*Bademi*.' Ayshe smiled and pushed the dessert platter towards me. The plate was piled with the famed almond marzipan of Edirne, sure to give you diabetes if the baklava next to it hasn't already.

'I'll tell you a story,' Ahmed said. 'The kids were six months old. I had a lowly job, couldn't get a better one. I had five euros in my pocket. This guy I knew, he lived in Marseilles and said, Come over and I'll find you a job. So I spends my last money on a bus ticket to Paris. Not a word of French.'

The guy didn't answer his phone. Ahmed slept on a park bench.

'And I prays. Allah is great. But three nights later I'm still on that bench. So I went to the nearest kebab shop. *Salaam alekum*, I said. They were Arabs, not Turks, so they said *Alekum salaam*. Anyway, I work for them and sleep in the back of the shop. And the TGV ticket to Marseilles was one hundred euro. So I boarded and locked myself in the toilet. Three hours in the toilet, all the way to Marseilles. How many times did I say *engagé, engagé*? Sitting in that toilet and thinking to myself Where am I going? To fuck's end, that's where.'

Ahmed slept on benches again, but this time he didn't pray. He took himself to the nearest construction site run by Turks and offered himself. He ate for free in kebab shops and slept in a basement. In six months, he made fifteen thousand euros. When he finally came home, Ayshe opened the door and shut it in his face.

'She didn't recognise me,' Ahmed said in Bulgarian.

'I did,' Ayshe replied in Turkish. She just didn't want to let him in. He'd lost half of his body weight.

'Anyway, what's been has been,' Ahmed said and rose from the table unsteadily – the bottle was empty. That weekend, they were planning a trip to Svilengrad, to stay at Ventsi's hotel and spend the nights in the casinos.

I wondered how it felt to go across *that* border, back to Bulgaria.

'"Nothing relieves my depression,"' Ahmed recited, '"like the songs and tobacco of my homeland." I love going back.' He was drunk.

'Here, men stare at you like starved wolves,' Ayshe said. 'There, I feel free.'

With our translator gone to pay the bill, Ayshe and I clinked glasses in silence. There is a black-and-white photograph from 1989 that is engraved on my mind. I found it in a book by an Edirne photographer who made it his mission, that sweltering summer, to record the faces of the three hundred and forty thousand people who came across the checkpoint. In that photograph, a boy and a girl sit on a suitcase.

The girl has wide-set eyes and a short fringe. A doll with big 80s hair is propped next to her. She is about eight, the boy is older. In the background, piles of baggage. The kids are in a suspended world. The boy is looking at the ground, angry and ashamed. The girl, however, is looking straight at the camera. She wears a summer dress, and it is her expression I can't forget. It's the expression of a soul who knows something has been lost for ever but doesn't yet know what it is, who is between crying and being brave for the camera. In the next moment, she will comb the doll's hair, a gesture of normality restored.

When I passed the drunk Dutchman's table on the way back from the toilets, he leaned out from his chair at a dangerous angle and asked: 'Is your friend a star?'

I glanced at his restless freckled hands, and saw that he too was looking for something. Perhaps the story of all our lives is the story of what is lost and how we go about looking for it.

'She looks like a movie star,' he insisted.

'Yes,' I said. Ayshe sat smoking on her own, lost in a dream. 'She *is* a star.'

When Ahmed returned, tucking his wallet into his back pocket, I asked if Ayshe had a job.

After leaving the orphanage, Ayshe and her sisters studied. Her eldest sister was now a colonel in the armed forces. Her youngest sister ran an agency for orphans. Their Nefertiti-like mother was retired and often travelled to her home town across the border where she still had a sister, a house, a garden where in the summer of the exodus she had buried a few jars of plum jam and her best set of china – in the hope that someone might return, one day.

Over dinner, Ahmed had kept mentioning 'Ayshe's kids' and I thought he meant their own. But what he meant was the kids at the special school where she worked. She had never stopped working, not even when Ahmed was sleeping on French benches. Ayshe was a teacher of deaf children. In the holidays, she took them on bus trips around Turkey and across the border into Bulgaria, which involved heavy paperwork, but she didn't mind because the kids loved it.

While Ahmed explained this, Ayshe's face lit up and she said something in sign language, but neither Ahmed nor I understood it.

I saw her standing in that school bus, saying something to the kids that no one else understands, not even the driver, and the kids laughing. I saw her with her kindred spirits, in the homeland of silence, where no one can tell you what you are.

komshulak

Neighbourhood, neighbourliness, the spirit of being next door peace-
fully. From the Turkish word for neighbour, *komşu*.

TO SEE A DANCING PRIEST

It's not often you see a priest dance, and especially not an Eastern Orthodox one. They aren't known for their joyful abandon. It was past the polite evening hour, past the speeches, and Father Alexander was dancing to an Anatolian *kuchek*, with its rhythmic drums that produced vibrations in the lower chakras and made you want to dance on the spot. Which is what he did. He moved his hips with remarkable agility in a cloud of fig-scented eau de cologne, his arms in the air. The small white collar on his black shirt flashed like a smile.

His wife sat at one of the tables with other women, all in headscarves except her, and although her face was carved with the severity of a caryatid in a Thracian tomb, she sent him dazzling smiles across the hall.

They had brought me along to the wedding party of their Muslim neighbours' son, and like all public events this was an alcohol-free zone – except for the large glass of raki that had been brought for Father Alexander as a special treat by the groom's father, a shopkeeper in a dapper suit, with a matinee-idol face. I sat next to the ancient grandmother. She had a collapsed toothless face and hennaed hands that touched my face and my hair with a casual intimacy that took me aback, then she asked in a Macedonian dialect, '*Ubavo li si?*', 'Are you good?' Yes, I'm good, I'm fine, I said. She was the child of Macedonian exiles from a hundred years ago, as were the silent, wizened couple next to her, here with their towering son and his Russian wife. They had come all the way from the city of Lüleburgaz.'

The bride and groom, their fronts pasted with banknotes, were now dancing to a slow piece. They worked at the airport, had university degrees, and were marrying in their late twenties; the upward social movement of the family was in evidence. They were clearly the pride of their village relatives, the women with covered heads, the kids happy as the centre of attention, the men massed in dark-clothed groups at the entrance, where a bridesmaid welcomed the newcomers with chocolates on a tray and a spray bottle of eau de cologne for a touch of glamour (or perhaps hygiene). After the party, Father Alexander drove in a remarkably straight line all the way home, humming along to the folk beats on the radio.

Father Alexander and Maria Chakaruk lived in a town house with a rose garden and resident pigeons next to St George's Orthodox Church. This quiet neighbourhood of Edirne had been a Christian *mahala*, or district, in a city that once had Greeks, Bulgarians, Armenians, Jews, and Muslims. Maria was from Plovdiv across the border and Alexander was from here. He spoke an endearing old-fashioned Bulgarian, just as she spoke a careful Turkish. Their young son was bilingual and flitted between languages, social milieux and religions, as if this was still a pleasant cosmopolitan corner of the Balkans and not a recently demilitarised border zone.

'Thrace without borders. Just as it should be,' Father Alexander said when I first visited them at home, dropping in without notice. I hoped they didn't mind, I said.

'Mind?' Alexander said and bit into a cheese pastry. 'We *only* like guests who drop in without notice. Because we're *komshulak*. That's what we are.'

Maria served aromatic Turkish coffee, and the tiny cup looked minuscule in the hands of their other drop-in guest – a blue-eyed giant who sat there in his socks. Now he was a mechanic and a married man, but in the summer of 1989 he'd been a teenager in that long convoy of cars and lorries.

'You ask what we are here,' Father Alexander said suddenly. 'We are not Europe and we are not Asia. We are Thrace. Notice: those who live in the European part of Turkey don't tend to cross the Bosphorus. They like to stay on the Balkan peninsula, close to Europe. This is Thrace.'

And you? I asked.

'Don't ask me what I am!' Father Alexander cried theatrically. 'I'm a human being. Isn't that enough?'

The giant nodded over his tiny cup. In the rush of the exodus in 1989, he'd left behind his puppy, and when he'd gone back to visit ten years later, he found that the neighbours had adopted it. The dog ran after his car, so for the second time he drove away in tears, but he couldn't take the dog from the good neighbours. It was a question of komshulak. And it was for komshulak that he came to the church, the closest he could get to Bulgaria without crossing the border, though he was a Muslim.

'Komshulak is what keeps you sane,' Father Alexander said and dropped two lumps of sugar in his tea. 'That, and remembering what the good old Bible said. And the first shall be last, and the last shall be first.'

'It all comes out in the wash,' Maria translated.

I looked down at the immaculate tiles and realised I hadn't taken off my shoes. Everybody else was in socks or house slippers.

'Don't worry,' Maria said, 'we're religious but we're not heavy on rules.'

'That's right,' Alexander went on. 'In Thrace, we don't like rules.'

But he did like talking and being listened to, and he had such charisma that it didn't much matter what he said, it was enough to enjoy his mellifluous manner and bilingual baritone.

'To be told what to wear, what to think, who to vote for, and how to love? No. We are free and relaxed, and you can't take that away. This is Thrace.'

Maria passed around a basket of dyed eggs. It was Easter weekend and tonight was the midnight Easter service. Their house was fragrant with sweet bread and incense. Father Alexander's gold-embroidered ceremonial outfit was laid out in another room, so splendid and stiff, so unlike the relaxed priest on the couch, that I almost expected it to get up and walk into the church by itself.

The blue-eyed giant came to the midnight Easter service with his wife, dressed in jeans, also a Bulgarian Turk. And so did the neighbours with the now-wedded son. And so did Emel, with a rouged smile, chatting to friends and acquaintances and snacking on the sweet raisin-studded body–bread of the Christ.

In fact, half of the Easter service guests who stood and patiently listened to Alexander and Maria recite the arcane, sorrowful descants of Eastern Orthodoxy were Muslims.

The other half were a motley of Christians: a large group of visiting Greeks who periodically chanted, when conducted with dramatic flourish by Father Alexander. 'Christ is Risen!' he intoned in old Bulgarian. 'Indeed he is risen!' they piped back in Greek. But there were also Bulgarians, Romanians, Turkish students of Orthodox Christianity, and a Russian woman with a crucifix necklace. I recognised her from the wedding, and then I saw her towering husband next to her, along with his parents.

'Christ my Lord,' she sang along with the rest, 'set my heart on fire with love for You, that in its flame I may love You with all my heart, with all my mind, and with all my soul and with all my strength, and my neighbour as myself. Amen.'

The charismatic couple were both financial analysts.

'Actually, I studied to be a diplomat,' he said while we sipped red wine in the vestry afterwards, 'but I spoke my mind and fired myself from the service.'

'At least money takes no sides,' his Russian wife said.

'You see, you have two choices in life,' he said. 'Move on as if there is nothing behind you and repeat the past, or look back and try to learn something. People in Europe often ask me, where are you from?'

His parents stood by, silent, small, excluded from the English conversation. Next to their urbane son, they were people from another chapter of history. His mother squeezed my hand and, in a Macedonian dialect, I was asked again, 'Ubavo li si?', 'Are you good?' His parents' story was the reason why he couldn't be a diplomat, he said – because he knew the truth about nationalism, and truth is inconvenient to most governments.

'Amen,' the Russian said and the three of us drained our plastic cups full of the alcoholic blood of the Christ. His parents didn't drink.

A hundred years ago, his mother's parents had been kids in the Macedonian lake town of Kostur. They were indigenous Muslims known as Pomaks. The Balkan Wars redrew the borders and put an end to that kind of frivolity. Kostur had a Bulgarian-speaking majority – a mix of Muslims and Christians – but as large swathes of Macedonia became Greece, its indigenous people were purged and replaced with other purged people (Greeks from Turkey and Bulgaria). The financial analyst's family were forced to migrate to Turkey, though they spoke no Turkish. The same treatment was briskly applied by other newly independent Balkan nation-states, which is how many Muslims from Bulgaria, Macedonia, Bosnia-Herzegovina, Albania, and Serbia ended up in the Republic of Turkey. The Christians of Turkey ended up in Greece and Bulgaria. Their empty houses in the towns and villages of now-Turkish Thrace were occupied by the incoming Muslim refugees whose aged children and grandchildren kept squeezing my hand as soon as I sat down for tea in village squares, and saying with emotion, 'Ubavo li si?', 'Are you good?'

'I'm good, I'm fine,' I kept saying with a lump in my throat, and I squeezed back the mother's hand as if I had some good news from the ghostly land of her ancestral past. Kastoria is now on a triple border, where there was once none, mirrored by my grandmother's lake town of Ohrid on the other side. The husband, a quiet man exhausted by the long Easter service (and who wasn't?), was the child of Greek-speaking Muslims from Salonica who had ended up Turkish by the same accident.

'You know another irony?' the tall analyst said. 'They found an icon and a crucifix inside the dowry chest of my great-great-great-grandmother. They had once been Christians. Probably until that final wave of Islamisation in the seventeenth century, when Sultan Mehmet IV swept through the Balkans.'

'Do you think they were converted by force?'

'I don't know. But that's what decaying empires and failed governments do. They force people to do things and then call it by some stupid name like Revival or Taking the True Faith.'

I could see why he wasn't a diplomat.

'My parents never stopped talking about Salonica,' the father suddenly said.

'I have the opposite problem with Russia,' the Russian said. 'I wouldn't miss it if tomorrow they closed the border. In my eight years here, I've not once had bad food, bad language, or bad attitude. Turkey is the opposite of Russia.'

'So when people in Europe try to guess my nationality and ask,

What are you, Greek, Turkish, Bulgarian, Macedonian, or Albanian? I say, Yes, that's right,' her husband said in conclusion.

After midnight, Father Alexander and Maria circled the church three times anticlockwise with lit candles, and the rest of the Christians (plus me) followed, but not the Muslims. The trick was not to let your candle go out in the night breeze, and the matinee-idol-faced father of the groom stood at the entrance and handed out small plastic cups to protect the Christian flame. 'Ubavo li si?', 'Are you good?' he smiled, recognising me from the wedding.

It is small gestures like these that make human history – the history of komshulak – how it works, how it breaks down, how it is healed.

Although the red flags of crescented Turkishness were everywhere in Edirne, there were also road signs leading to this quiet street with St George's Church, and all the taxi drivers knew it. And just as the occupying Bulgarian army during the Balkan Wars was under orders not to touch the mosques, so this church, here since 1869, had been recently restored. Along with the other church and the synagogue.

The synagogue was built in 1906 by order of the city governor, to replace the Jewish temples that had burnt down a few years before. The first Jews in the area were exiles from the Spanish Inquisition who in the 1490s found refuge in the Edirne *vilayet* under Sultan Bayazid II's protection. As did many during the Holocaust. Today, the synagogue of Edirne had no community any more and its restoration in 2014 was purely symbolic.

Adrianople was besieged by Goths, Huns, Avars, Pechenegs, and Slavs; over fifteen epic battles echoed on the plains between Edirne and Svilengrad, between antiquity and the twentieth century. The most dramatic of all was perhaps the fourth-century battle of the Goths against the Romans, who had abused them for too long, with the surprising victory of the Goths, who remained in the Thracian plains for a hundred peaceful years. They even ended up adopting Christianity voluntarily.

Chroniclers describe how Adrianople fell to the Turks in 1363, nearly a century before Constantinople, and in a markedly less violent manner. The Evros River was high. In the night, the Greek commander of the fortress saw that all resistance was futile, got into a boat, and sailed to Enez on the Aegean coast. Though back then it was still Aenus, the Thracian city of Aeneus, son of Apollo and the nymph Stilbe. Meanwhile, at dawn, the gates of the fortified city of Adrianople were opened by the commandless Christian defenders, and an agreement was struck with the Turks. For centuries, Adrianople remained a wealthy, cosmopolitan hub of trade, agriculture, and arts, and the 'infidel' Christians lived undisturbed in twenty different neighbourhoods.

The fall of Constantinople was a blood-drenched affair, but even then, in 1453, Sultan Mehmet II had the wit to call an end to the rape and pillage of the city by his regular and irregular soldiers after one day, instead of the traditional three. He must have known that his tribe were here to stay and the sooner reconstruction began, the better. He touched his forehead to the floor of the plundered St Sophia Church and proclaimed that there was no God but God, and Mohammed was his Prophet. Agia Sophia became a mosque.

In portraits, Mehmet II appears with a cold-tipped nose, his face that of a man who has never been young or healthy. He must have had a difficult childhood as the only surviving son of Sultan Murad II and a Christian slave–concubine, reviled by the royal household, so it's no surprise he threw himself into scholarship. By the time he took the throne in Constantinople, still a teenager, the Conqueror was fluent in Turkish, Arabic, Greek, Latin, Persian, and Hebrew.

The Ottomans ran a vast empire with richly mixed results for six centuries (the 1300s to the 1900s). I'm not a historian and in my appraisal of it, the worst came last – with its devastating dissolution whose aftershocks are still felt a century later across the Balkans, the Middle East, and in Turkey itself. Popular appraisals of the virtues and vices of the Ottoman Empire vary dramatically, depending on the nationalist and cultural prejudice of those making the appraisal. So for the once-subjected peoples of the Balkans, the Ottoman Turks remain an arch-enemy and the explanation for their past, present, and possibly future woes. (It's either the Turks or the Gypsies.) In Bulgaria, the all-time favourite term is still 'the yoke' or 'the slavery', although the actual slaves in the Ottoman Empire didn't come from its European lands, and it was not a slave-based economy; it was based on taxes. In reality, it was the Gypsies of Romania who endured centuries of appalling slavery, and 'the Turks' had nothing to do with it.

Meanwhile, for some of the contemporary Turkish elite and ordinary folk the Ottomans were the pinnacle of glorious pan-Turkishness, woefully gone. When I spoke to a senior Turkish diplomat and asked him the question that everybody asks (Does Turkey belong in Europe?), he went from urbane charisma to red-faced apoplexy within minutes.

'Turkey is a great, *homogeneous* country that has belonged in Europe since we reached the gates of Vienna!' he shouted, spilling coffee in his saucer. 'Can you cite the date? See, your historical knowledge is zero. Or you wouldn't ask such stupid questions. And get this: Greeks and Bulgarians whine about their suffering, but nobody, nobody has suffered more than the Turks. We lost an empire!'

I could see why he wasn't a financial analyst: his logic was rotten. But he had an important point, and the point was this: in this first and last corner of Europe, emotion still ran high on the issue of the Ottoman Empire. You'd think nothing else had happened in the region since the Balkan Wars rearranged people's destinies and Mustafa Kemal Atatürk forced the Hat Law on Turkish men's heads.

Emotion aside, one of the most interesting policies of the Ottomans was the sowing and nurturing of human talent regardless of class or race. It served them well and gave their (Islamicised) subjects unlimited upward social mobility. The bridges of Edirne and many of its mosques are the work of the greatest Ottoman architect, Mimar Sinan. He was not an ethnic Turk, though you must whisper this in today's Turkey, split as it is between Atatürk's rusty nationalist 'homogeneity' dogma and the conservative Islamists' post-Ottoman tristesse. He was taken from his family in one of the *devshirme* raids, the regular blood-tax collections of young Christian males, which left peasant families bereft across the Balkans. Though some were glad to have their children join the imperial elite. Educated at the palace school in Istanbul, and later in the Janissary Corps, by the age of fifty he was the chief architect of the Guild of Palace Architects. Sinan's parents had been Orthodox Christians, either Greek or Armenian, or both; some even trace him to a stonemason father called Christos.

In the vestry, Father Alexander was sipping wine, surrounded by friends and neighbours. It was hard to imagine that before this church had opened again for service in the early years of our century, it had been left to the elements from the day the Christians departed. The only unofficial custodian had been a local Bulgarian man called Philip. For decades he cleaned the gutted building in his free time and literally propped up the crumbling walls. He died just in time to see his dream fulfilled: the church would be restored. Father Alexander was his son.

While delivering the tragic Easter service, Father Alexander stood with his back to the congregation, addressing the Holy Trinity. But I will always think of him dancing with his face turned towards the people, his white collar smiling. His face was no different from the many faces of Thrace I was to see, in villages and towns, faces with teeth yellow from tea and tobacco, faces that had one thing in common. They had all travelled a long way down the corridor of history and lost everything they had before they started here anew. And I don't mean here on this side of the border, but here to the point where they saw how the deeper story went: the first shall be last, and the last shall be first. Is faith or ethnos all that you are, any more than eye colour?

Then you may as well dance, dance with your arms in the air and let your lower chakras vibrate.

rosa damascena

Among the ten thousand species of rose, only one genus has the qualities to produce attar of roses, the oil used in perfumes and aromatherapy. For reasons too tied up with soil composition to be quickly grasped, only two regions of the world currently have the right conditions for the *Rosa damascena*: the plains of upper Thrace in Bulgaria, known as the Valley of Roses, and Isparta in Turkey.

In the nineteenth century and up until the Soviets nationalised the rose, the rose attar of Bulgaria had a monopoly on the world's perfume industry. But unlike the more robust tobacco industry, the rose didn't react well to communism and production went into relative decline. Today, the Valley of Roses near the main rose-producing town of Kazanlak (from the Turkish *kazan*, cauldron) still produces fifty per cent of the world's rose attar. To obtain one kilogram of rose oil, you need 4,000 kilos of flower heads.

The other fifty per cent is produced by Turkey. Like Oriental tobacco, the rose is a bitter love story between Bulgaria and Turkey. When Bulgaria broke away from the Ottomans in the 1870s, workers from the rose industry travelled south across the border with cuttings from the Valley of Roses and planted them in the soil of Anatolia. They must have really loved their roses.

★

But the central plains of Thrace are suited to less poetic crops like wheat, sunflower, and pumpkins, so the rose is confined to private gardens.

IF YOU ARE TRUE

'There's a rose garden on the outskirts of Edirne,' he said. 'You must see it, if you can find it. The guy is nuts about roses. Of course, if you knew the basic facts of rose history, which I can see you don't, you'll know that the *Rosa damascena* is called this because it was imported from Damascus in the sixteenth century, when Ottoman envoys brought it to the south-east Balkans. Some say the first rose garden belonged to a Turkish judge in Bulgaria, who was also nuts about roses. Damascene roses, you understand, not just any roses.'

I was sitting with the archaeologist in his old car with sagging seats, used Diet Coke cans, and ash everywhere. It was one of his rare days off and he had agreed to show me Edirne's sites. He coughed a pre-emphysema cough and continued.

'In that garden, the colour of the petals changes with the ambient temperature. Normal folk don't know about it, but botanists come from all over. Because it might be a new kind of rose altogether.'

I asked him where the garden was.

'That's why I said *if you can find it*,' he said. 'I found it. Once. But when I tried to take a lady friend there, guess what. Of course she didn't believe me about the garden, she thought I'd made it up. I stay away from women now. And rose gardens.'

He had the low, dense physique of a wrestler, like several short men packed into one, and a dark ruin of a face that didn't bode well.

But then you saw the wit in the saggy eyes, and the contagious enjoyment when he broke into laughter – briefly, as if laughing too much would give something away.

'Most people take one look at me and think, There goes a common thug,' he said. 'They're surprised when I start speaking languages.'

He knew Bulgarian, Turkish, English, and Russian, and, I suspected, a couple of other languages he didn't mention. The more he spoke about himself, the more remained unspoken, an inverse self-revelation.

He'd been coming to Turkey for twenty years. One day, he was between jobs and had just had a vivid near-death experience, he said and laughed, briefly.

'I thought, what do I really want to do from now on? The kids were grown up. I'd done my duty. Two marriages, two divorces, though to be fair the first divorce was more joyful than the second, but the second confirmed a long-held prejudice.'

What was the prejudice? I asked.

'That falling in love backfires sooner or later, but mostly sooner. So I thought, I want to learn about ancient civilisations now. And eat Turkish food. Every day, not just from time to time.'

Though he wasn't eating much. It was because of his illness, the one that gave him the near-death experience.

'The three classic illnesses of the service,' he said. 'Ulcer, diabetes, heart attack. You're sure to get one if you serve long enough, and if you live, you must find something else to do. Of course many don't. Live, that is.'

'Which service do you mean?' I asked, a bit alarmed.

We were driving across the humped stone bridge over the Maritsa–Meriç River, a stunning arched construction 263 metres long.

'Observe,' he said. 'This bridge looks old but it's only mid-nineteenth century. Sultan Abdülmecid built it, though there was a wooden one before that. This is Turkey. History begins and ends with the Ottomans. A bit like the Scots with the Battle of Culloden. Nations are like neurotics, they fixate on one thing.'

'Which service do you mean?' I said.

'There's only one service that's referred to as *the service*,' he grinned, relishing my surprise, and tossed his cigarette out of the window. The car bumped over the cobblestones of the road that led to Karaağach, on the other side of the river.

I don't know what a retired spy should look like, but he didn't look like one.

'The word is "operative",' he said.

I had met him through a friend in England, and all I knew about him was that he studied archaeology. After this I was hoping he might come on another day trip with me, to look at Thracian and Byzantine ruins about which I knew nothing. Yes, he said, it's hard for someone to know less than you do, and laughed at my expression, but not meanly.

'So I moved here, rented a bachelor flat in Karaağach, which incidentally means Black Wood and used to be a Greek and Jewish neighbourhood. By the way, it was a Greek who introduced the sunflower to Turkey, the biggest agriculture of Thrace to this day. His name was Papas. How do you know you're in Thrace?'

The tumulus-shaped hills with Thracian tombs inside them? I said, failing to impress him with my knowledge.

'No. When you start seeing people spitting sunflower skins. You know the old saying: The mountain gives birth to people, the plain gives birth to pumpkins?'

I didn't.

'That's Thrace for you. Pumpkin heads spitting out sunflower seeds. Anyway, I moved here and began a new life.'

We reached Karaağach. Silent 'g', he corrected me, Karaach. Can you feel the European vibe?

I could. The leafy streets were in a tidy grid, no 'oriental lanes', and the houses were huge, with balconies. He didn't invite me to his place though we passed it.

'This is Turkey,' he chuckled. 'Men don't fraternise with women. And I don't want complications with your Scotsman.'

The park on this side of the Meriç River was dotted with restaurants. Families would come on a summer's evening to picnic, and couples to snog.

'But not me,' he said, 'I come here alone to read.'

Today, though, the restaurants were flooded by a released dam upstream across the border, the houses in the field bore watermarks halfway up their walls, and the black wood was sodden like a mangrove.

'Rivers have always been borders between realms,' he said. 'Are you paying attention? I don't think you are. Because we're on the Greek border.'

I hadn't seen the barbed wire. It was behind a monumental concrete sculpture simply named *Lausanne*, after the treaty that ended the Greek–Turkish War (1919–22), and that meant so much to the countries with redrawn borders and so little to the Great Powers that redrew those borders on a map of the Balkans that some heads of state (Disraeli, in a previous treaty) couldn't even hold up the right way. Because the periphery can be sacrificed to the centre and, to the likes of Disraeli, the entire Balkan peninsula with all its nations was a periphery. Almost every city in Greece and Turkey has its unhappy monument called *Lausanne 1923*.

'The Turks love grandiose monuments,' he said, but he wasn't that interested. This history was too recent for him.

The Lausanne monument had three prongs: the highest column represented Asian Turkey, the shorter one European Turkey, and the small amputation nestled in the middle was the piece of land here, around Karaağach with a silent 'g'. This piece was what the Turks had wrenched from the Greeks. The Meriç–Evros River was the boundary between Turkey and Greece, and the small diversion of that boundary here was what these three sad phalluses celebrated.

Or it could be that after a time, all monuments look sad.

'Cheer up,' he said. 'Have your sugar levels dropped? Welcome to my nominal stomping ground.'

Next to the monument was Trakya University's Faculty of Fine Arts, restored from its late-nineteenth-century glory to Secession style by a famed Turkish architect and considered at the time 'the most beautiful railway station between Vienna and Istanbul'. Students milled around the lawn between *Lausanne* and the old railway, because this was the student district of the University of Thrace. The streets were glamorous with cafés and we took a seat at an outdoor eatery.

'These kids are thirty years younger than me,' he said, 'but I don't spend time here. I just try to make it to my lectures.'

He now had a job as mysterious as the service. His employer was an international company with an HQ in London; it had people like him all over the world, and he was responsible for Turkey. All of Turkey. His job: to supervise the handling and safekeeping of shipments in warehouses and depots around the country as they waited for further dispatch through the ports of Bursa and Izmir.

'What kinds of goods?' I asked.

'Anything you can imagine,' he said, 'or can't. Coal. Coal travels from Africa and Russia to Europe. But supervising a hundred tons of coal isn't a gripping tale.'

Actually, it is, I said.

'Don't ask,' he said. 'Some of the things in those depots aren't good news.'

I choked on my cheese toastie.

'Careful with that toastie, I don't want complications with your Scotsman,' he said.

Is it a good job? I asked.

'For me it's perfect. I'm an adrenaline junkie,' he said. 'I know I should be careful because of the old health, but it's a professional deformation. Whenever life calms down, I get twitchy.'

Sometimes he'd drive all night to make it back on time for a morning lecture. He'd just been to the Syrian border where the firm had a depot and where the Kurds were fighting 'Islamic State'. He had seen smoke.

'I like the Kurds,' he said. 'How can you not? They have to have enough guts for everybody, poor buggers. And they always get the rough end of the stick.'

He was not religious in any way, he said, but every time he drove across this country, he had a mystical experience. One time, he found heavenly olives – in a little house by the coastal road where they culti-vated them but didn't sell them.

'They wouldn't take any money although I wanted several kilos. This is Turkey. It moves you in unexpected ways.'

He munched his toastie and I munched mine.

'Now here's the strange part. It's true that it was night time, but I was sure I could locate that house again. It was just before the sea cliffs. Guess what. I've tried every single time I pass that spot. The olive grove is gone too. As if the whole thing has slipped into the sea. Come on, time to see Bayezid.'

We were off to see not the sultan, but the complex after his name, where one of the first medical schools of the Islamic world had thrived. There was a curious section for the treatment of mental illness. At a time when in Europe they were shackling the mentally ill to the floor, here they treated them with water, flowers, and music.

'Isn't that something? And then you hear Balkan people whine The Turks this, the Turks that. Let me tell you a true Balkan story.'

This happened in the late 1700s. His great-great-great – or whatever

– grandfather, he said, lived near Istanbul with his wife and daughter. He was a wealthy cattle herder with four thousand head of cattle. One summer while he was away grazing his herd on the Aegean plains, a band of rogues broke into his house and raped his wife and killed her, along with the young daughter. Someone got the news to him. He sold his cattle on the spot, gathered a band of trusty friends, and went on a mission of revenge. His band killed the guilty men, but then he couldn't stop – he took to brigandage with such gusto that they started robbing and murdering all and sundry. The Sultan finally put a price on his head and when the army went after him, the brigand disbanded his men and skipped north to the Balkan range where the authorities couldn't be bothered to look for him. He established himself in a place called Eagle's Nest and remarried.

'That's where I'm from. That's why I look like a thug. What is the lesson of the story?' he grinned. 'Exactly. There is no lesson. Now here's another one from the family archives.'

His great-great-grandmother-in-law would beat her stepson. The eldest stepson, a descendant of the brigand, beat her back so savagely one day that the family had to slaughter thirty sheep to cure her wounds. They wrapped her in the sheepskins full of herbs and ointments, a traditional healing method.

And? I said. That's an awful lot of sheep.

'She lived. And they ate mutton for ages. People sentimentalise their families the way they do their national history. The truth is a lot more unpleasant. But more interesting too. That's why I hang out with the ancients in my old age. I feel more at home with them.'

'In what sense?' I asked, though I could guess.

'As you'd know,' he said, 'if you had basic knowledge of magic, all ritual is an act of magic. There are two kinds of religious experience. Experiential, when you personally have an ecstatic or mystical experience. And canonical, when someone tells you what to think and believe, and you bleat in agreement, moving with a large herd. Ancient cultures were all about the former. And all the troubles of the world today come from the latter.'

I looked for the rose garden but nobody knew of it. And I never saw the archaeologist again, though I tried. After he'd cancelled a couple of appointments, or hadn't turned up at the agreed place, saying afterwards that the instructions weren't specific enough, he seemed to disappear altogether.

Then one day, sitting in a café by the Meriç Bridge, I thought I saw him on the stone hump, in his leather jacket, several short men packed into one, but something stopped me from getting up. The same day, I received a message from a faraway port city where he said he was supervising a depot, but really – I saw that now – the job was a cover. Just as his time in the service had been a cover.

The real life of men and women is the one you don't see.

He had sent just two lines, taken from the tomb of Yunus Emre, a Sufi mystic and poet from the thirteenth century:

> *If you are true, your words will be true.*
> *An untrue person cannot say true words.*

That was all. Under the various covers, he could pursue his true religion: the freedom to roam. To never be pinned down. The price he had paid was to write himself out of all official narratives – the family narrative, the national narrative, the cultural narrative, the career narrative – and to make his own small road stories. What about women spies? I'd asked him.

'Women make excellent spies. But they're no good as operatives, they become too involved. Though I can't talk. I've made so many mistakes.' He coughed and returned to his refrain, 'That's why I stay away from women now. And rose gardens.'

He laughed, briefly, but he needn't have worried about revealing too much. Even though in the space of a day he hadn't asked me a single question, I was certain he knew more about me than I knew about him.

'Still,' he said, '*you'd* make a decent operative. You operate solo and speak languages. But you rush too much, like all Westerners. You know the Turkish *yavash-yavash*? Like the Spanish *mañana*, but without the sense of urgency. Now, excuse me…'

He slipped his hand into the inner pocket of his leather jacket, and I thought he was going to get his mobile out and call someone in the services, but it was where he kept a small notebook in which he scribbled words and sketches from his nocturnal drives. I could see him quickly sketching something, but before I could ask to see it, he closed the notebook and returned it to his pocket, then suddenly excused himself from the table, the evening, and my life. His face had gone white. I watched him walk away to his car, a small plastic bag in his hand, with a syringe and a single shot of insulin.

His feet described small circular patterns as he walked, as if he was turning on himself, and in a flash, I saw him in some remote monastery of Anatolia, whirling in a white cape like an open tulip, his face turned up under the high arches with an expression of inscrutable bliss.

corridors

They don't change. Everything else changes, except the corridors.

Heroin travels from Asia to Europe. Cocaine travels from Latin America to Europe, Turkey, and the Arab states. Humans travel from Asia via the main sorting country (Turkey) into Europe. The corridors once used by the Palestinians and the Kurdish rebels are now used by refugees and all manner of fugitives. The corridors used in the Cold War remain the same. Only the direction of travel has changed.

EVERYBODY COMES TO ALI'S

In a Turkish café not far from the European border, the TV showed the world's longest belly-dancing show. A woman in gold gyrated on the screen, her greasy red lips fixed in a smile, with the sound off. But none of the men in the café paid attention. They had other things on their minds.

The café didn't look much from the outside. It was a featureless shop front without a name. But when you stepped inside, it was a pressure cooker. The atmosphere was so thick with suppressed emotion, with cigarette smoke and the tumble of rolled dice, and with that particular male burden of having to take action against the odds, that my first instinct was to flee. It was physically difficult to advance beyond the doorway.

I sat down and ordered tea, fielding heavy looks from the tables until they subsided. The waiter, a silent man of fifty with haunted eyes and the broken nose of a boxer, brought me a glass of tea with three lumps of sugar, and put it down with a flourish. A stained tea towel was draped over his arm, someone laughed and coughed in the corner, cards were slapped down, and for a moment this felt like a return – though I had no idea why. I had never been to a tea house like this before, where nothing was consumed other than tea and no woman set foot.

Though Ali's tea house was special. Everybody came to Ali's –

everybody who had nowhere else to go and everybody who was in need of passage across the border, which was the same thing. There were two categories of customer in Ali's Café. The first were from the neighbourhood. The second were those who came from troubled places, and you could tell who they were from the faraway look in their eyes.

All the tables were taken except the one where I sat, and the silent waiter never stopped circulating with a tray of tea glasses and sugar lumps. The table of locals played a game of something that looked like dominoes, but they played for money. Even though no cash changed hands at the table, you could tell what was going on from the fact that once the game was over, one guy bought a round of tea for everyone. That was the winner. At that point the players relaxed and laughed, chatted, lit another cigarette, went for a pee.

Those at the other tables didn't play. They huddled in groups but there was little conversation, they were too busy scrolling down their mobile devices. They scrolled, drank tea, occasionally looked up with empty eyes. And they waited.

'Kurds from Iraq.' Ali the owner pointed at one table discreetly.

I had plucked up the courage to go and meet Ali, out in the crepuscular back of the café where he perched behind an old-fashioned desk and scribbled something in a big logbook, like a tired teacher at the end of term.

Ali was tall and dapper, with a photogenic hawkish face and long greying hair, like an ageing rock star. He invited me to sit across the desk from him, like a student, gave me Turkish coffee as a special treat, and told me how much he liked to go to Bulgaria. There was another table, occupied by four skinny young men with hollow cheeks and once-smart jackets who looked like university drop-outs. One of them was texting furiously with his jaw clenched, eyes red from crying. When I had walked in and startled the rest of the clientele by being a woman, everybody had looked up, except this table. This table was sealed off from the rest by a heavy energy field. I felt it before I could articulate it: the loneliness of the leper, that's what they shared.

'Syrians,' Ali said. 'Life is crap for them.' The Turkish word was *pis*.

Ali was from Rize, the tea-growing town on the southern Black Sea coast not far from the border with Georgia, but he rarely went home. His mother sent him tea and home-made cakes.

Rize chai, he said and pointed at his glass with a dark twinkle in his eye, as if he wanted to say something else altogether, ask what I was doing here, why I was bothering him with my presence, as if he didn't have enough problems already. Every few minutes, someone would come up to his desk and pay for the tea. A young guy with his hair sprayed hard into an Elvis wave produced a thick wad of US dollars from his pocket to pay for a round, and Ali quickly found change in his drawer. All currencies were welcome here, no questions asked. Then Ali would make a little mark next to the name in his logbook.

I saw now that there was a whole other part of the café, beyond Ali's desk. Decorated with a single faded portrait of Kemal Atatürk, it was desolate, like the waiting room at a provincial railway station where the train has been cancelled. The tables in this section were reserved for a faster kind of transaction that didn't involve tea. But it involved money. Every now and again, skinny men with rucksacks would slip into the back and occupy this inner sanctum.

I did as Ali did and pretended this was normal. I pretended it was no big deal to see smugglers sealing deadly deals with the already-robbed of this world by robbing them further. The money came in bundles tied with elastic bands, in exchange for the promise of a lorry ride across the border. In many cases, people were dumped off before they even reached the border, and so they were back to square one, back in Turkey, back in Ali's Café, but this time without money. It was groundhog day, a Sisyphean sentence – to endlessly go up and down the airless corridor that never changed, though everything else changed. And never to arrive.

They said Turkey was the final destination for those who had no money to go further west.

I couldn't tell the smugglers from the clients – they all looked similar, unshaven, dingy. That's because it's not actually the smugglers you see there, I was told later. No trafficker worth his salt would turn up in person or give you his real name.

One of the younger Kurds at the Iraqi table had a different, softer look – he actually smiled at me in a carefree, relaxed way that didn't chime with the heavy vibes. He looked as if, in a different life, he could be happy. His name was Erdem, though I only found that out when I ran into him a few weeks later in Svilengrad.

He was here with his sister, staying in a cheap hostel, and waiting to get smuggled into Bulgaria in the back of a truck. He wore a smart cream jacket from another era, like some Great Gatsby who had gone down the wrong corridor of history.

'One more tea, Murat!' Ali ordered and the waiter brought me yet another glass of strong tea. Murat sneaked outside for a quick cigarette whenever he could, although everybody inside smoked constantly. I guessed he needed time out from the pressure cooker of human souls.

Ali was always here, from early morning to past midnight, he said. In any case, Ali said, and looked at me hard, if I told you some of the things that have gone on here, you would break out in a rash.

While Ali was putting a few marks next to a name, I heard piano chords on the radio somewhere in the back, or maybe it was somebody's mobile. It was an old melody, and after a few chords, I realised I had somehow been expecting to hear something along the lines of a kiss being just a kiss.

This was no place for romance, but it brought home to me why Ali's Café felt familiar in an atemporal way and why Ali cut a timeless black-and-white figure, though we were here now, in colour, in the middle of the 2010s, facing something resembling Europe, with the ransacked Middle East behind us.

Perhaps there is a Casablanca for every moment in time when war exiles people from themselves and catapults them to transit realms. A place with Rick's Bar, or Ali's Café, a safe house where the homeless of the day come in search of passage. Or just to sit and take comfort in something that never changes: 'One more tea, Murat!'

Once, Ali told me, a man with a rucksack came to the café, and when Murat went up to him and asked 'What would you like?', he broke down.

In Istanbul, he had paid eight thousand euros to a trafficker to get him across the border in a truck. But the truck dumped him and the others on some godforsaken Strandja hill, and when they ran up to a shepherd and asked him Bulgaria, Bulgaria?, he shook his head – Turkey, Turkey.

He walked back all the way to Ali's Café because he had no money left.

'And you know the worst part?' Ali said. 'He could have taken the bus from Istanbul to the border. It costs fifty euros.'

The man had lost his family in Syria.

'Every time I look at his corner, I see him,' Ali said. 'When I close up at night and everybody's gone, you won't believe me but that's when the café really fills up. With ghosts. Twenty years' worth of ghosts, coming and going.'

And then the next morning he would get up early to open the café, for business as usual.

via antica

It was a bridge from a dream – too perfect. I stood on one side of the river and counted. Eighteen stone arches hummed and harmonised. It was 300 metres long. It was spring, so the water was high and fast and dragged entire uprooted trees. I caught myself searching the murky water for something, for example the head of Orpheus. You just never know with mythical rivers, and they say that this is the one into which his head was thrown by the bacchanalians who tore him asunder.

It's about five hundred years old, so locals call it 'the old bridge'. But before there was a bridge, the Roman Via Diagonalis passed nearby. It was eight metres wide and connected Rome with Constantinople, which is why its other name was Via Militaris, and why all other roads sooner or later joined it. Via Egnatia, Via Pontica, Via Trajana – these roads are still around like ghosts. Sometimes they run parallel to the motorways but you can't see them. Sometimes you *can* see them, but they are so deep in the border hills that only treasure hunters and woodcutters tread them. Old people on each side of the border still point vaguely and say 'There goes the old road', and you have to figure it out.

Like all travellers to or from the East, I came to this crossing on the river. Until the Ottomans built the bridge, you had to paddle across or get ferried by boatmen. Springtime with its full waters was especially dangerous and you could easily drown. Or become stuck with your baggage, unable to go forward or back until the current pushed you downstream. The end of the journey is the Aegean, where, freed of your baggage, you would drift back to where you came from.

TALES FROM THE BRIDGE

Once upon a time, there was a Bosnian-born vizier called Damad Mustafa Pasha. He decided to build a bridge over the river for two reasons – to make the eastern leg of the journey between Vienna and Istanbul easier, and to immortalise himself, though he didn't yet know that he would die young. The bridge turned out to be so spectacular that when Suleiman the Magnificent and his army passed on their way to 'holy war' against Buda in the Austro-Hungarian lands, Suleiman was gripped with unholy envy.

Would the vizier allow the sultan to take credit for the bridge, in exchange for four hundred bags of gold coins, the cost of the construction? Mustafa Pasha asked for a night of reflection. Faced with an impossible choice – disown his life's work or disobey his master – during the night, he took poison. In the morning, the furious sultan cursed the bridge. Anyone who passed over it, he said, would lose the thing most precious to them. And his army paddled across the river, snubbing the bridge. It was a costly snub: the sultan's two precious pages drowned in the crossing.

For a while, no one dared use the bridge. Then, one day, Mustafa Pasha's old father was seen making his way over it. He had already lost the thing most precious to him. His symbolic act lifted the curse, and from that moment on, the bridge lent its back to tons of silk, wool, tobacco, rose oil, and everything else the empire ate and smoked, bought and sold between Budapest and Mosul. It served tradesmen, soldiers, wandering dervishes, envoys, pilgrims, bandits, travelling hippies, and lorry drivers.

The tale of the bridge, the vizier, and the curse is just that – a tale – but the fact is that, because of the bridge, the Roman road went out of use. Until the early 1900s, when it was renamed Svilengrad or Silk Town, Mustafa Pasha was the name of the bridge and the town, because the town *was* the bridge. First, of course, there sprang up a caravanserai inn by the bridge that slept and fed untold numbers of travellers and their camels and horses. You could cook on one of the three hundred fireplaces inside the courtyard, and tie your horse next to where you slept, with the saddle as your pillow and your money tied in a bundle underneath. And if you were gripped by a sudden urge to stay on and become a student of Islam, you could eat for free and even get a daily allowance.

Around the caravanserai grew a mosque, a hammam, a school, an orphanage, and a commercial district. For a long time, Mustafa Pasha was described in traveller chronicles as a chaotic market where everything was for sale. But especially some things: silk which rivalled the best in the empire; 'the best watermelons in the Levant', as a French aristocrat noted; 'frivolous women of the tribe of the wretched nation that in France they usually call "Égyptiens"', in the words of an Austrian traveller; and wine made from the small aromatic Muscat grapes.

Wine was the domain of the bibulous Christians – Greeks, Bulgarians, and Armenians – though Western travellers were divided on the pleasures of inebriation. The seventeenth-century English traveller John Burbery waxed lyrical about the wine, but with the advent of Victorian puritanism, disapproval crept in, and two rather dull British diplomats wrote in 1860 of the 'morally and physically degraded' Christian peasants of the area who 'idly lie dead drunk upon a dung-heap'! Austrian and French travellers described the customs of locals who carried out their rituals right beside the bridge. Local Muslims frequented a Sufi saint's tomb studded with deer horns, where 'lots of dervishes and holy men came', and they spent the night on sheepskins by the tomb. The local Bulgarians had a habit of slaughtering sacrificially anointed rams on stone slabs under certain trees in kurbans reminiscent of ancient sacrifices.

Although for centuries it fulfilled its colourful destiny as a crossroads, in the wake of the Balkan Wars, Svilengrad suffered the fate of borderlands – it was sacked and burnt, in this case by retreating Turks. Those who didn't die fled – both Muslims and Christians – but first they buried their treasures under their houses and inside garden wells. Some returned to find their houses gone, but at least the set of fine china was still inside the well. Others (the Muslims) never came back, and new refugees from Aegean Greece moved into their empty houses.

Silk Town drew me in the first place for two reasons: because of its silky name, and because it had been one of those unvisitable places in the barbed grip of the klyon when I was growing up.

The caravanserai was long gone, the mosque was a church, the hammam an art gallery, and the communist-era silk factories lay gutted. Instead of production, Silk Town had consumption. Instead of the centuries-long trade in watermelons, sesame-butter, cotton, tobacco, figs, and silk, now there were *services*. All kinds of services.

One road into town was lined with today's caravanserais – the hotel–casinos. Ali Baba, Pegasus, Monte Carlo, and Pasha all promised 'Shows, cash prizes and many more surprises!'

Another road was home to a refugee camp that promised nothing. These were once the buildings of the border army.

A third road led to a hill called Hissar, or Fortress, where treasure hunters from three countries buzzed with metal detectors over bumps that contained thousands of human years.

And just behind Silk Town are the low-lying karst hills of Sakar, a natural continuation of Strandja to the east: a realm just as riddled with antique tombs, subterranean passages, sanctuaries, and mystical theories of a Swiss-cheese nature.

A sanctuary recently excavated by archaeologists threw up artefacts dating back not three thousand years, as had been thought, but six. The local museum director confided that treasure hunters had come to her with mind-boggling finds, but the museum had no budget to buy them.

'This Turk came once,' she said. 'A treasure hunter. He had nothing to sell, but!'

But he had a tale to tell. There's a rock niche nearby, he told her, deeply hewn into the rock face. A treasure hunter in Athens had told him about it and they had travelled here together to look for it because it was said to contain a hoard of ancient gold-crafted jewels. They had found it. Steps cut in the rock led up to it and the Turk, picking up a bad vibe, had waited at the bottom while his Greek colleague had climbed up. The Greek didn't come out for ages, and when he finally emerged, something had happened to his skin. They ran. The visitor wouldn't say what his friend had seen inside, but he was keen to impress on the museum director that they should seal that place off because it was cursed.

When the museum director asked him to take her there, he said he was too scared.

'The thing is,' she said to me, 'we know all the rock sanctuaries in the region – some Byzantine, some Thracian – and the one he described is unheard of. We're still looking for it. But that's what you get with Strandja-Sakar. A mystery inside an enigma.'

Crossing the bridge, I found the original stone paving untouched. Cars and pedestrians mingled as they always had. I walked the 295 metres to the upmarket restaurant The Bridge, which offered fine Greek food upstairs and jackpot machines downstairs where the addicts sat hunched and hollow-eyed in the artificial light pressing buttons, and fat, eunuch-like male croupiers circulated with wads of cash.

Further along on that side of the bridge, where the old, poorer Christian neighbourhood of Gebran (Unbeliever) had been, the largest casinos in the Balkans were being built by international entrepreneurs of complex reputation. Clearly, demand was high. The Turkish state's clampdown on public pleasure was pushing people across the border. Past the mega-casino-in-progress was the end of town, and after that, the Polish-owned Katarzyna Estate, a huge stylish winery whose interior featured startling erotic murals of fantasy creatures engaged in Dionysian orgies. The winery's name seemed to be in memory of the absentee owner's daughter who had died young in a car accident. The vine plantations stretched over the hills like a mirage as far as the eye could see, and you wouldn't have guessed that just a generation ago, this had been a militarised border zone. The old border outpost had been converted to offices and painted an elegant pink. Cabernet, Merlot, and Malbec now ripened in the Furrow of Death.

Like Edirne, Silk Town was a town of three countries, and just before the Greek border checkpoint was the lorry drivers' joint owned by Ventsi's mate, where women don't go unless they have something to sell. Old 'Free Zone' signs from the 1990s and gutted border-post kiosks dotted the flat hinterland where not a soul could be seen for miles except a stray dog that I hoped wasn't too hungry. As I walked across the fields, my shiver of disquiet eventually grew into panic. I turned round and walked back to the outskirts of town fast, soon breaking into a run, and this time the dog felt obliged to run after me.

For half a century of Cold War, this fertile area of three countries was a buffer zone. Nothing grew, nobody visited, but the traffic kept passing over the hump of the stone bridge: lorries, Turkish *Gastarbeiters* on their way to and from West Germany, foreign tourists. The locals lived in a hothouse of twitching curtains and paternalistic privilege, since this was a town of bribe-rich customs officers. Europe's traffic passed by their doors, but in a Tantalus-like suspension, civilians were prohibited from talking to anyone with a foreign registration plate.

Once, a retired teacher told me, a Czech car stopped outside her house. It was the 1970s. The couple were thirsty and lost, on their way to Istanbul. She gave them water, cheese, and tomatoes. The Czechs were about to drive off when the militia arrived and a long interrogation began.

'So I never offered anything to passers-by again,' the retired teacher said.

She had been a propagandist at her school, and had solid faith in the regime, somewhat chipped now, and mixed with the sadness of loss because otherwise life was pretty safe and comfortable then, she said, not like now. The people themselves were extremely vigilant and there was no crime.

There was no crime.

Her job as propagandist consisted of this: taking her school kids to the local army barracks to see 'lessons in patriotism' – for example, how the dogs were trained to hunt *diversanti*, which means saboteurs and was the official term for people trying to cross the border. In an agitprop performance that she particularly enjoyed, she took a cooperative of female tobacco workers to the top of the hill, from where they could see the tobacco workers below, across the Turkish border.

'I called it "Two Worlds, Two Youths",' she said. 'And the idea was to show our workers the backward West.' She bent down to pull some weeds from her lush garden, because everything grew by itself here, even silk cocoons.

'Though tobacco picking is hard going however you look at it?' I suggested, as if tobacco was the point. No, the point was hope.

'It might sound strange to you now,' she straightened up and said with a stoical smile before she fetched a delicious lamb-and-yogurt casserole from the oven that we shared that evening under her silk trees, 'but I was proud of what we had achieved. The silk factories, the sesame oil, the watermelons, the star workers, the overproduction in our fertile region where everything grew. We were the vanguard of Socialism. And now? There's no cultivation, no care. We are the back door of Europe.'

It was here at the back door of Europe, and more specifically at a street café called Dream which sold cinnamon-dusted semolina pudding and Italian espresso, that I saw a familiar carefree expression and Great Gatsby jacket.

We exchanged greetings, and Erdem – who had just been released from the local refugee camp – introduced me to his father. They were scrolling down their phones.

His father's name was Soran and he spoke good English.

'Visiting Svilengrad?' Soran said, grinning sadly, and offered me a Bulgarian Parliament cigarette. 'Welcome.'

ghosts

The traveller Evliya Çelebi (born in 1611, died sometime in the 1680s) journeyed across the 'seven climes' of the Ottoman Empire like a medieval Herodotus. One of the most exuberant and eccentric travel writers of all times, he described himself as a 'world-traveller and boon-companion to mankind'. Here is a free translation of a *tarikh* (poem–memento about an event or a person) he wrote when passing through Silk Town:

> *There goes the ghost of Mustafa Pasha.*
> *He knows this world is nothing but a bridge.*
> *And so I utter this tarikh:*
> *There goes the ghost of Mustafa Pasha.*

In the second decade of the twenty-first century, Silk Town and its surroundings were full of ghosts, once again, but nobody was writing poems about them. They had travelled down the corridors that never change, and washed up here in Thrace, between three seas and, yes – 'two worlds, two youths'. The world of those with the right passports, and the world of those who came from places with ancient names: Babylonia, Mesopotamia, and Kurdistan.

*

These ghosts – men, women, children – walked along rural roads between the border towns of Europe, with plastic bags and eyes that locals didn't want to look into for fear of seeing all the world's trouble. And while they waited for their papers to be processed, their past lives lay behind them in ruins. But they couldn't afford to mourn because of a more pressing problem: their new lives couldn't begin.

A KURDISH LOVE STORY

Alal was a broad woman who moved like a royal frigate in her free-flowing dress and bare feet. She carried her uncovered head high, her gaze hard and unflinching, her skin a bit pale after the long Balkan winter of waiting and smoking, cooking and hoping. When she walked into the room, something else entered with her: a sense that everyone would be looked after and everything would come right, even if things were desperate, utterly desperate now.

They had just received the official letter they'd been waiting for, for eight months, the letter that they hoped would finally green-stamp the family with a Yes. Yes you are released from the waiting corridor, yes we acknowledge that you fled your home in Iraqi Kurdistan because it was nearly overrun by Islamic State and your lives were at risk, yes you are legally allowed to travel onwards to Western Europe, settle down, work, begin to live again.

But the answer was No.

'Sit,' she said in Kurdish and pointed at the bare kitchen table. While she made me a Nescafé and lit a cigarette, she leaned on the kitchen sink and gave me a good hard look to work out where I sat on the spectrum of well-meaning but ineffectual do-gooders. I put my notebook away.

They were renting this flat in Silk Town because the refugee camp for families had been noisy and depressing. They had seen a young

Syrian man die of grief for his wife who was stuck on the other side of the border, she said – it started as a migraine, but it was his heart that gave out in the end, and the doctor came too late. She sat beside him to the end, so he wouldn't be completely alone.

For the time being, they could afford the rent, though the money from the sale of the family house was running out, Soran said, and sat down next to me with his *n*th cigarette of the day. He was a short, stocky man with an easy laugh and eyes that had seen too much.

'I know I smoke too much,' he said. 'I can't sleep at night, believe me. Thinking all the time. What to do, what to do. In the morning, I am tired but there is no answer.'

Alal was fourteen years old when she married Soran. They had eight children, aged between four and twenty-seven – and the twenty-seven-year-old was Erdem.

'I'd like two more,' she said, 'but not now. Maybe when I'm happier.'

Soran had a second wife for a short time, because that's the custom, he said – but it wasn't working, he said. So I stopped after one child and divorced the other wife. Because Alal is perfect for me.

'Dead right I am,' she said and sat next to him at the kitchen table.

'Thirty years we've been married,' he said and put an arm around her. 'I'm a lucky man.'

'You can say that again,' she said with the same deadpan expression.

It was their game. In reality, this was the first time they had all lived together for more than a few weeks. Soran had been absent from the family most of their lives. On his mobile, he showed me photographs from the 1980s and 90s, the kinds of scenes I had only seen in magazine articles and films.

Soran and two friends with 80s hair, moustaches, and Kalashnikovs, high in the bleached dusty northern mountains of Iraq.

Peshmerga, he said. Kurdish guerrilla fighters. We were fighting Saddam.

Soran and a friend – my best friend, he said – in a cave, grilling something over a fire, grinning, tired. He was already a father of five by then, but rarely went down into the village because it was dangerous, he said.

'It was dangerous to be Kurdish, under Saddam,' Alal said.

Soran and one of his brothers at a low table, under a pomegranate tree.

'All dead,' he said matter-of-factly, and clocking my appalled look he smiled, as if I was the one needing comfort.

'Yes, my friend, that's what it was like. To be Peshmerga. Believe me, it was not a Hollywood movie. Many people died in the mountains and the birds ate them. My brother, my friends, killed by Saddam. I'm a lucky man.'

He got away with two bullets, one in his shin where a hole gaped the size of a plum, and another one in his stomach. I looked at Alal.

'Yes,' she said. 'Every day, I wondered: Am I a widow? In Kurdistan, you're never too young to be a widow.'

Alal means red rose in Kurdish. She said she never thought she would have to run without looking back. In her home village in the mountains, she had lived as if she would always have that life.

Don't we all.

Their three teenaged daughters came out of their room, in jeans and T-shirts, completely different from their parents – tall and skinny with youth and despondency, fragile transplants that had been ripped out of their soil but could find no nourishment here. They understood English but were too timid to engage with a stranger beyond polite greetings. The two youngest boys were four and seven, and as far as they were concerned, this was an adventure. Dressed in camouflage outfits with 'Peshmerga' badges on them, they played all day. Once in a while, as a special treat, Soran took the kids out for a lunch of fried calamari and chips at the Café Central, opposite the flashing promises of the Pasha Casino.

'If we'd stayed in Iraq, all my boys would have had to become Peshmerga too, like me when I was young,' said Soran. 'But now they'd be fighting Islamic State.'

'The girls too,' said Alal. 'I don't want that for them.'

When I asked the girls about their friends back home, the friends they'd last seen eight months ago, the eldest girl simply began to cry, though she made no sound. Her tears fell on the kitchen table. I touched her hand and I was suddenly seventeen again.

I was back in our Sofia apartment, in our family's deepest winter of the soul, the winter of waiting for emigration visas in 1991. Snow fell in the darkness outside. There was no fuel for cars, so people walked everywhere on the ice, and every night the power cut out. And because bad things always come in bunches, my mother had been hospitalised for an emergency operation for a tumour. Stunned with angst, the three of us sat in the dark apartment, waiting to find out what kind of tumour it was (benign), and to hear back from the British Home Office (the answer was No). My father, still working as a professor but with a salary made nonsensical by mega-inflation, sat in the cold kitchen filling in emigration papers. He hadn't shaved for days, and his hair had gone grey overnight. While things unravelled in slow motion, my younger sister kept a low profile and quietly did her homework in candlelight, while I simply stopped eating in protest.

I looked at the skinny girls next to me and felt everything with them: the humiliation, the injustice, the mindfuck of having to hate where you come from but having nothing new to love, your parents desperate to give you a better life, struggling against impossible odds. The sensation of being invisible, unwanted, speechless, a disembodied soul waiting in one of history's drafty corridors.

'The girls might never see their friends again,' Soran said.

Alal made no comment. She lit another cigarette and gazed out of the window from which you could see the many-arched bridge. It definitely looked cursed from here. What is a bridge for, if you still can't cross the river?

During a winter expedition through the Caucasus, so cold 'the sun rose in four places', the travel writer Evliya Çelebi's retinue came to a great river: 'But it was not frozen over. Nor were there any boats. We were overcome with a grieving sensation difficult to describe.' They could neither turn back nor go forward.

The girls had planned to go to university.

'I don't want my daughters to just get married, like us,' Soran said. 'But in Kurdistan, that's the culture. In Europe, maybe the girls have a chance.'

'This is not Europe,' Alal said with energy. 'We can't work, we can't move. This is a prison.'

But what is Europe?

'Europe is where you are not afraid. That's freedom. And that's home,' Alal said, with the fury of a brave heart who had been forced to live in fear for too long.

In the garden of their home, on the proceeds of whose sale they were now surviving, Alal grew roses. Theirs was the land of pomegranates and citrons, honey and musk. When Evliya Çelebi travelled to Kurdistan with the retinue of Melek Ahmed Pasha in 1655, even his high Ottoman standards of decadence were jolted by how the people of the Tigris delta lived in the summer, in their river gardens. They 'are the envy of the world for the delights they enjoy for seven or eight months of the year along the bank of the Tigris; thinking to snatch a bit of pleasure from this transitory world'. He marvelled at the giant basil that grew into a dense forest so that 'the brains of the men and women living there are perfumed night and day with the fragrance of basil and the other flowers in these gardens, such as roses, judas trees and hyacinth… Here on the bank of the Tigris there is a merry tumult day and night, with music and song, for a full seven months. Everyone parties in his hut with his lovers and friends.'

Soran had lived and worked in London for many years, sending money home. During those years, he had missed home so much that sometimes, in a bout of nostalgia, he'd jump on a plane at Heathrow and fly to Erbil.

'Just to smell the air and kiss my wife. Then I'd fly back on time for my next shift.'

'Iraq was okay for a few years,' Alal said. 'After the fall of Saddam.'

What the world doesn't realise, Soran went on, is that what threatens the Kurds also threatens Europe and America. But once again, like in the time of Saddam, the Kurds are alone. Fighting a global war on behalf of the world with home-made weapons. The girls get enlisted to be Peshmerga guerrillas too. Nobody is spared.

'Where is the justice in that, tell me, my friend,' he said.

'Kurdistan was doing well, for a while,' Alal said. 'The future looked hopeful.'

Then Islamic State began to make incursions into Iraqi Kurdistan. Soran and Alal made a decision to flee while they still could, and sold the house. Crossing into Turkey wasn't difficult, and once in Turkey, buying British passports for the whole family was a doddle, he said, if you had money.

But at the Bulgarian border they were detained. Only one of the nine British passports was genuine.

Why hadn't Soran got real British passports for his family earlier, while he still could?

'I applied, believe me. Many times. Many thousands of pounds. It was not possible.'

Our old friend the British Home Office required evidence of sufficient income to support the whole family in London, and Soran was
on a kitchen hand's wages.

'I had a car, a Lexus.'

When the Bulgarian border guards detained the family, they confiscated the car.

'It could be worse.' He grinned his painful grin. 'It was just a
car.'

Stressed people came and went from the apartment, scrolling down
phones, scrutinising documents, discussing the next step, or sinking
into anxious torpor and gazing into space. One of the visitors was
their lawyer, a young local woman with dark circles under her eyes,
who held a cigarette for an hour without lighting it. She was appealing
the government's decision.

'Actually, it's a matter between three countries,' she said. 'Bulgaria,
Britain, and Iraq. It's complicated but at least they have a chance.
Many don't.'

Her own great-grandparents were Aegean refugees from the Balkan
Wars. They had arrived robbed of their possessions by road brigands,
and moved with nothing into one of the big houses of this neighbourhood. The big houses vacated by Muslims fleeing to Turkey.

'As the descendant of refugees, it's my duty to help these people.
Otherwise the story will never change. You know the legal definition
of a refugee?'

A refugee is a person persecuted by their own government or
living under a government unable to protect its own citizens, she said.
If Soran and Alal don't fit that, then nobody does and governments
should go hang.

But no legal paper records the emotional definition of a refugee:
someone with 'a grieving sensation difficult to describe'.

Alal lit a portable gas wok on the floor of the kitchen and began cooking. When she and the girls had prepared a huge pile of spicy fried chicken, rice with raisins and nuts, and pickles, a roster of feeding began. There was a pecking order. First, it was Alal and Soran with the guest (me). Then Erdam came with a friend, an effete type with pomade in his hair and a midnight-blue velvet jacket who had the air of habitual privilege. He was angry, angry and aware that he had one last thing to hold on to: his style.

'Oh I see,' he said tartly when we were introduced. 'Soran has got himself a second wife.'

Everybody laughed, even the girl who had been in tears just before.

'You're writing a book?' the velvet jacket said. 'That's very nice for you, but not for me. I need a visa.'

'Be quiet,' Alal said, 'or you'll eat somewhere else.'

'I'm so sorry,' I said, 'that I can't help you.'

'It's okay, I can't even help myself,' he said with a flourish, and everybody laughed.

He had left Iraq four years ago, with a friend. At the Turkish–Bulgarian border, Bulgarian guards beat them up, took their mobile phones and their money, and sent them back into Turkey. From there, they crossed into Greece.

'I like Greece, but in Greece there's only beach. No money, no work. Four years I didn't see Mama and Papa. I talk to them every day. They cry.'

I asked him if he spoke Greek.

'I speak six languages. English, Kurdish, Arabic, Greek, Persian, and Italian. I want to go to Roma,' he said. His flamboyance contrasted with the family's down-to-earth style.

'Six languages my foot,' Soran said. 'He says he speaks English, and you see how good his English is. Can you imagine his Greek?'

Another round of laughter. I asked what his job had been in Athens.

'Job: gay,' Soran answered for him and the room went down in giggles.

'That's not a job,' I said.

'It is for him,' Soran said, to another attack of mirth.

Velvet jacket didn't seem to mind, he liked being the centre of attention. Out of everyone gathered here, his situation was the most favourable – he was multilingual if not fluent, his parents sent him money, and he already had the precious 'green card' which was actually blue and which was not far from the refugee status that would allow him to travel to his precious Roma.

A week later when I walked past Café Dream I saw Soran, his seated figure packed with stress, an empty espresso cup before him. He was scrolling down his phone.

Erdam was gone. He couldn't take it any more, Soran said, and made a deal with a smuggler. Again. He boarded a truck in the night and made it across the Serbian border.

'Fifteen hundred euros,' Soran said.

Then from Serbia into Hungary.

'One thousand euros,' Soran said.

And from Hungary into Austria.

'Eight hundred euros. And yesterday he called me from a train in Austria or Germany. The signal was bad. I think he's been arrested. The phone cut off. I couldn't sleep last night.'

There was a chance he'd be sent back to Svilengrad.

'Believe me, my friend,' he said, 'four thousand euros is a lot of money for me. But I pay it because Erdam has a future. And a wife. In Germany, he can work.'

Erdam was a car mechanic and had worked for a Mercedes garage in Erbil. Three months on from this conversation, he was working in Germany.

Soran's eyes had filled up, but even so, he grinned because he had just opened the little luck scroll that came with the espresso. I opened mine too.

Mine said 'Travel'. His said 'You must break that wall with your head.'

'It's true my friend,' he shrugged. 'It's true.'

Back in their flat that day, when the afternoon of taking turns to eat was turning into evening and it was time for me to go, Alal had spoken to me.

Soran translated, but somehow I already understood what she said.

The only things we had in common that could be put into words were that we shared a century and a generation, yet I could sit with Alal and Soran and drink endless glasses of tea, with or without sugar. Alal and Soran were like human radiators. You could sit beside them and warm yourself. I was sad to be with them, but even sadder to leave.

'Why don't you just move in with us?'

That's what Alal said when I was about to leave. Her three daughters hovered behind her, smiling with red eyes.

'We have room and we have food. Don't pay for a hotel. Come and stay as long as you like,' she said.

'Yes, you are welcome.' Soran grinned sadly. 'You are welcome indefinitely.'

the spring of the white-legged maiden

Between Silk Town and another Bulgarian town called Harmanli, which means threshing place, there is a spring whose stone fountain bears an Arabic inscription: 'There is life because there is water. 1585.'

This cheshma entered the public imagination through a popular nineteenth-century poem called 'The Spring of the White-Legged Maiden', but the poem's author, Slaveykov, first heard the legend about it from locals, who had passed it on for generations.

There was once a fair maiden called Gergana. In the village she had a sweetheart, and one night in the village square, he asked for her corsage. She said I'm yours, but let's meet at dawn, out by the spring. The day is wiser than the night. At dawn, she turned up at the spring, but instead of the sweetheart, a vizier had set up camp with his retinue en route to Istanbul. Gergana washed her legs in the spring and the vizier was seized with lust.

Come with me, fair Gergana, he said, you'll be my favourite concubine. You will want for nothing in the harem – gold, silk, perfumes, gardens, birds of paradise, a thousand latticed windows, slaves. You can even bring your parents!

★

Thanks, she said, but I prefer it here. From my window I can see my garden with all my flowers in it, and I also have a sweetheart.

Oh, wretched girl, the vizier exclaimed, you know nothing of the world's ways! Don't you recognise the chance of a lifetime?

Take me if you want, she said, but you'd take my lifeless body, not my soul.

This went on for a while, possibly days. In the end, the vizier was so moved that he left her alone and continued on his way. To mark the encounter, he commissioned a fountain with twelve stone basins on the site of the spring. So Gergana could wash her legs amid opulence and remember him.

But while the fountain was being built and Gergana wedded her sweetheart, something strange happened: she began to waste away, as if an evil spell had been cast. By the time the fountain was completed, she was dead.

It was well known to the master masons of the time that when the spirit of a human being was built into a public work, it endured for ever. And the fountain has endured almost for ever. True, only three of the stone basins remain and the area around it is broken and full of rubbish, but the spouts continue to chatter, four hundred years on.

After Gergana's death, her sweetheart went into the hills and was never seen again. Sometimes you hear his flute, and on those nights, a white figure comes to the spring to wash her legs.

THE CHICKEN SHACK

The Chicken Shack was in a run-down square in Harmanli. It served falafel, spit-roast chickens that squirted delicious juices, and finely chopped salads. Half the clientele were locals, the other half refugees. The Chicken Shack was a fast-food joint, meeting place, employer, and therapy room. Those who came to the Chicken Shack had had different lives and dreams a few years ago. Now they were united through a single act: crossing the border and ending up in the Chicken Shack.

You were greeted discreetly by Bassil, who had a goatee and eyes that instantly got your measure. He spoke Bulgarian, Arabic, French, and English, and came from one of Syria's elite families. He was thirty-five and he said to me calmly – with the calm of one who has made the only peace available to him – that Syria would not become inhabitable in his lifetime.

'It is not a place for the living any more,' he said. 'It's hard to explain to people who only know peacetime what it's like when bombs fall on everything you've known your whole life. And everything is down on the ground.'

Bassil was the son of a broadcaster from Damascus whose first wife had been Bulgarian. Bassil was from the second marriage. That's how he and his siblings were able to settle here and begin to live again. Although his wife and young kids were in Sofia, Bassil had opened up here because of the large population of Middle Easterners near the border.

'Welcome to the Chicken Shack,' he said to everyone who walked through the door, then he left them alone.

Harmanli was once known for its sweet melons and aromatic tobacco, and for 'the finest travellers' inn not only between Vienna and Istanbul but in all of Europe', according to one captain's travel diary in 1740. And according to a local twentieth-century writer, Harmanli was always the kind of town that does not need to travel because the world goes through it.

In the mid-2010s, Harmanli resembled the set of a post-apocalyptic film. To reach the Chicken Shack, you passed derelict factories like mutants along the dusty road that followed the Maritsa River in the plain hazy with early-summer heat, and crumbling apartment buildings where the factory workers no longer lived. But Harmanli still had a green and homely heart, and a beautiful Ottoman bridge.

There were two types of pedestrians on Harmanli's streets – those who walked to get somewhere, and those who walked the way you do when you have nowhere to go, slowly, with a plastic bag. The refugee population of Harmanli was several thousand strong, and had created an alternative black-market economy, culture, and cuisine. The Chicken Shack had competition now, as other joints were opening up.

Can the shabby periphery be a cosmopolis? If so, it was a strange cosmopolis of people who had embarked on a forced adventure, and their roads had converged here, at the point between opportunity and catastrophe.

'Harmanli. Reminds me of Syria,' said Nizar, my travel companion for the day when I drove into town. He said it with a forgiving smile. 'Everything is down on the ground. But it's peace.'

Nizar was a cook from Damascus. He had worked in city restaurants for twenty years, and at weekends he went home to his wife in the countryside. Their house was bombed but they survived. His wife now lived in a safe house with relatives and their five-year-old twins, though he didn't know if she was alive from one day to the next, and every time he called, he didn't know who would pick up. When their village went 'down on the ground', Nizar and his brothers made a decision. They would first run to Turkey, then try for a safe passage to Europe and for asylum papers, and eventually get their families out of Syria legally. And in the meantime, they would pray. God is great.

Nizar had made it all the way to the Serbian–Bulgarian border, and that's where he was caught. He was a man of forty with dark, peaceable eyes and a mellow disposition. His destiny had been domestic comfort, fatherhood, and good food.

After months in a detention centre, he was back here, at the familiar border.

In the refugee camp outside Silk Town where the border army had lived for fifty years, there was no library, no sports centre, nothing but burnt yellow grass. People could leave the fenced compound for the day, go for a coffee, and come back. That morning I had passed the camp, and just before I joined the empty new motorway from Svilengrad to Harmanli shaken only by international lorries, I saw a man in a worn leather jacket walking towards the red roofs of the next village, and offered him a lift, because the only pedestrians on these rural roads came from the refugee camps. That was Nizar. I looked at his face and trusted him. I invited him to come to the Chicken Shack with me. It was something for him to do. But to leave the perimeter of the camp, Nizar had to take along his ID, a piece of paper that had his name, photograph, and civic status which said: 'Status pending'.

He had no friends in his sudden new life.

'Actually, I have one friend,' he said. They'd known each other back in Damascus through the restaurant trade, but had been distant. Here, they'd run into each other, and now, he smiled forgivingly, now they were best friends.

His nine brothers were scattered across Turkey and Europe. He only knew where any of them were when they called. I'm in London, I'm in Frankfurt, I'm still in Istanbul, I'm in the refugee camp in Edirne. Istanbul was the great sieve – in the daily shake-up, some would go through, others would stay.

'Welcome to the Chicken Shack,' Bassil said.

Nizar greeted Bassil like an old friend, although they were total strangers, and he ordered a whole chicken, although he didn't eat. He sat scrolling his iPhone, looking at the latest distressing news from Syria.

'Welcome to the Chicken Shack,' Bassil said.

A young woman in jeans had come through the door and was ordering a takeaway. She was heavily pregnant. She didn't sit down to wait, and kept checking her mobile and biting her lip. She was a Kurd from Iraq and her name was Ariya. She left without speaking to anyone, but I heard her story from a social worker called Nadia.

Nadia sometimes came into the café, not to eat but because she was part of the scene. She was large and cheerful, with a tired complexion, and when I visited her in the dilapidated communist-era offices of the Social Services, I saw that her work was her life. The light in her office was always on, and there she sat behind her old-fashioned desk, knocked back sugary coffees, and made phone calls to charities, sponsors, and inert government officials, and all the world's trouble poured in and out of her door.

'Words fail me,' she said, but they didn't, she talked at length. The first time the Syrians had arrived, the old army barracks were converted into camps overnight.

'Kids with diabetes. Babies without nappies. Men with shrapnel wounds.'

No help came from the State for months. Nadia and her colleagues at Social Services unplugged the fridges from their kitchens, took the sheets from their own beds, and brought them to the refugee camp. The only food and supplies came from civilians who arrived from nearby towns in cars and trucks loaded with provisions. Border guards came too, to help families they had seen at the checkpoint and whose plight they had been shaken by. A local pharmacist donated drugs and medical assistance. A local barber, Nadia's brother-in-law, offered shaves and haircuts. The owner of a local tennis court gave away sandwiches in his café. It's no big deal, he shrugged. A few years before, the river had flooded his courts and café. When that kind of thing happens, he said, you get a taste of what it's like to lose everything overnight.

'That was just the beginning,' Nadia said. 'Now it's off the scale. But how can you witness this at your doorstep and do nothing? No. I refuse to do nothing!'

Nadia had first seen Ariya in the street in Harmanli a couple of months before. She was running barefoot, bloodied and pregnant. When the police arrived, her story came out. She had paid two traffickers to take her across the Turkish border and then to Sofia, from where she would fly to Germany and join her boyfriend. They put her in the back of a truck, but instead of taking her to Sofia, they brought her here, to an apartment where they locked her in and – Nadia wasn't sure – either attempted to rape her or did. She had escaped through a window.

'That story has a happy ending,' Nadia smiled. 'Because the cops finally got hold of the traffickers, and because Ariya's papers just came through. She's flying to Germany as soon as the baby is born.'

Nadia herself had been widowed young, in her thirties, and I wondered if there might be some happy ending or other for her too, one day.

Yizie was still waiting for her happy ending. She was the always-busy cook at the Chicken Shack. A vivid woman of forty, she wiped her hands on her apron and showed me photographs of the sculptural cakes she had made in her previous life. She'd been a patissier in a cake shop in Damascus, and she'd been married to an army general. The army that was dropping bombs on people, Yizie said.

'I put the kids in the back of the car one night. And drove into Turkey.'

She spent a couple of years working in Istanbul, where she found a new boyfriend, and her teenage daughter married a Turk. But in Turkey, you run the risk of being repatriated. So, eventually, Yizie took her young son and drove to the border, and said to the Bulgarian guards: You can't make us go back. She and the boy were living in a small rented place in town. And though she was smiling bravely, not wanting to be an object of pity, Yizie didn't know when she would next see her daughter or her boyfriend. She showed me his photograph – a younger man, a Syrian from another province. He was a mechanic and he was trying to save money for a passage from Istanbul, she said. Because single men like him were turned away at the border, his chances were slim. Her red nails were chipped from the kitchen work. Bassil sat next to us and listened, unshockable, sympathetic.

'Welcome,' he said. The new arrival was delicately featured, like an Egyptian prince, with small round glasses and a shirt printed with tiny flowers. He ordered and sat down. He stood out by not smoking.

Kemal was the refugee of a love affair gone wrong. He had been working in an office in Casablanca when he'd fallen in love with a Frenchwoman. They made plans to marry, but she was older than him, which was perhaps why the Moroccan government didn't give them permission. Apparently, the government of Morocco had to approve all marriages, and in particular the King must give his blessing. It was impossible for Kemal and Julie, so after Julie had gone back to Paris and they endured a year of Skype, Kemal decided to follow her. But he couldn't get a visa. So he travelled to Turkey, then got smuggled into Bulgaria, and that's where he was arrested. After a few months in the same detention centre where Nizar had been, he took stock of his situation: Julie's failure to make an appearance or even reply to his phone calls was telling him something.

'She only *said* she loved me.' Kemal bit into a falafel. 'But she didn't.'

No, Nizar, Bassil, Yizie, and I shook our heads.

'It's time to go back to Casablanca,' Kemal said.

Yes, we nodded.

'But – problem,' he said.

Self-deportation was even harder than illegal emigration. Morocco and Algeria didn't want their errant citizens back. Algeria only accepted repatriates twice a year, and to fly back to Morocco legally Kemal had to board a plane that didn't fly over EU territory. But it wasn't easy to fly from Bulgaria to Morocco while avoiding both European and Middle Eastern airspace.

'Eat, my friend.' Bassil stubbed out his cigarette.

'At least you know what you're going back to,' Yizie said and got up. 'And you know what?' she added. 'Maybe Julie did love you. But she saw it was impossible and cut her losses.'

Nizar, who had listened to Kemal's outburst in Arabic with a forgiving smile, suddenly said:

'It's a nice story. You are having an adventure by choice.'

Nizar proffered his iPhone to show us the latest from his province. A church and a town on fire, fifteen people dead.

'What has happened to our country?' He looked up at Bassil.

Here were the two ends of the social spectrum – Bassil was the urban multilingual elite, Nizar was the rural working class who could only communicate with non-Arabic-speakers like me through Google Translate, resulting in some very strange sentences.

Bassil said nothing. He just offered Nizar another Coke. He had made his own peace, but Nizar was still in a state of daily shock that his country really was on its knees, more so every day, until there was nothing to recognise it by. And even if, God willing, he could get his family out of there, he would always have to live with the memory of his country before it was razed, with its bazaars and temples, its gardens and its dead children. God is great but that is not enough.

He conveyed all this to me in a mess of Google Translate.

When a Syrian couple with two young kids sat at the table next to us, I saw him look at the munching kids who were the same age as his twins. He saw me looking.

'Children,' he smiled, too private to show the depths of his distress.

Two months later, he posted on Facebook a photograph of himself in Frankfurt – in a white shirt, with slicked-back hair, in the picture-perfect centre of the Gothic-spired city. He looked like the loneliest man in the world.

After the Chicken Shack, we drove back along the empty motorway with the wide river on one side and absolutely nothing on the other, back to the refugee camp on the outskirts of Silk Town, because Nizar had to check in again.

'You didn't eat that chicken,' I said.

He smiled. At the Chicken Shack, he had quietly gone and paid for lunch behind my back. I had protested furiously until Bassil stepped in and said to me: Just say Thank you or he will lose face. He's Kurdish, he'd never let you pay.

Blinded by good intentions, I had made Nizar spend money he didn't have on a stranger he didn't need in his life.

We had reached the gates of the camp and the guards stood chatting, bored.

'Don't worry, they feed us well in the camp,' Nizar said, sensing my agitation. 'And it was my pleasure. Thank you,' he took my hand, 'for a wonderful afternoon. God willing you'll be safe on your journey.'

He waved goodbye from the prison-like gates, and the crumpled guards took his dog-eared piece of paper and filed it away in a box with three hundred others. I drove, swallowing tears, all the way to Villa Columbina, where the pigeons circled above in the lilac dusk, clockwise, casting quick rustling shadows.

It was my last night in the plains of Thrace and I went to say my goodbyes, though I didn't feel like talking to anyone any more.

Down in the restaurant, I found Ventsi, along with Ayshe and Ahmed, who were here for the weekend, and a square-headed man whose body was too small for his head.

'You look like you need a drink,' Ventsi said and plonked a glass before me.

The square-head was the only son of old Turkish money, and spent his time in the casinos and clubs of Bulgaria and Cyprus. He didn't speak, he sang instead. He sat at the table, with the rest of us talking, and in between large glasses of rakia, cloudy when mixed with water, he crooned bilingual pop ballads in a voice so honeyed, it was hard to believe it came from him.

Every day I pray to God! To fall in love. To have a woman by my side.

Then he tapped his head and said, 'Nobody there.'

He was still recovering, Ventsi told me, from a trans-border love affair. He'd fallen for a Bulgarian woman a few years ago. She had a jet-setting job that took her around Europe, but gave it up to be with him in Turkey. They first met in this restaurant, after hooking up on a dating website that specialised in trans-border matches. An extravagant wedding was set up on both sides of the border. It was going to cost fifty thousand euros, Ahmed added – he liked to name the price of things. Then she dropped the bombshell: she had a child. Actually, it was two children.

The thing is, Ventsi said, he didn't mind about the kids, it's just that she had lied to him for two years. The wedding was off, the relationship was off, but three years after that debacle, they still called every day. She called him and he screamed at her, then he called her and she screamed at him. Then they wept.

Every day I pray to God! Square-head crooned, then stopped. He wanted to show us something on his mobile.

'Last year,' he said 'I won fifty thousand euros in a night.'

The exact cost of the cancelled wedding. But he didn't need the money. What to do with it? In the photograph, he lies naked on a single bed, except you can only see his face; his body is covered in banknotes. A fifty-thousand-euro blanket. The room is filled with crates. He'd tried to drink himself to death, but failed.

'Nobody there,' he tapped his square head.

Then, leaving Ventsi to his restaurant, the Turkish company departed to gamble the weekend away in Ali Baba Casino that promised 'Shows, cash prizes, and many more surprises!'

True to style, Ayshe hadn't said a word. We just kissed hello and goodbye.

I had started to tell them about the Chicken Shack, but on their faces I saw why they didn't want to know. Ahmed and Ayshe because they had been those refugees. Square-head because he was wrapped up in his world of operatic excess. Ventsi because he disliked the way Arab men treated women, otherwise why would they leave their families behind? No, he didn't trust Arabs for a moment.

On my room's balcony I breathed in the smell of lilac and thought of the souls in the camps with their lives in a plastic bag, the punters in the casinos haloed by the glow of jackpot machines, and the rest who travelled up and down this ghostly corridor for reasons of our own, up and down, like the vizier of the legend, and less grandly, like me. How did we all end up like this?

Visiting Algiers during its bloody independence war against France and itself, Ryszard Kapuściński reflected on 'the two great conflicts of the contemporary world'. The first, between Christianity and Islam. The second, between two strands of Islam: the 'open, dialectical, "Mediterranean"' one, and the 'inward-looking one, born of a sense of uncertainty and confusion vis-à-vis the contemporary world, guided by fundamentalists who take advantage of modern technology and organizational principles yet at the same time deem the defence of faith and custom against modernity as the condition of their own existence, their sole identity'.

It was the 1950s. Perhaps our species is doomed to repeat its unlearnt lessons with each cycle of history, as families do down the generations. I kept thinking of Gergana the white-legged maiden, whose tale was not about religion or romantic love. Gergana was a sage in a maiden's disguise: she already had everything she wanted, and didn't want to travel up and down. Most of us live longer than Gergana but fare worse in life, not because of the two great conflicts of the contemporary world but because of somebody's greed and delusion, often our own, but just as often the greed and delusion of powers greater than us. That's what undoes lives in perpetuity, and that's why there were so many sleepless souls in Silk Town that has no silk. Only the odd humble Gergana can show a wiser way by saying Thanks, but no.

After midnight, the trans-border lovers on each side of my room made their beds bang discreetly against my walls, though not at the same time. If nothing else, they possessed a commodity that was in short supply on warm lilac-blue nights like this one, when so much was down on the ground and the Merlot grapes were ripening in the plains of Thrace. Even if it only sounded like love.

PART THREE

RHODOPE PASSES

… Versatile
and full of tricks, a thief,
a cattle-rustler, a bringer of dreams,
a spy by night, a watcher at the gate,
one who was destined to bring wonderful things
to light among the immortal gods.

from 'Hymn to Hermes', *The Homeric Hymns*

rhodopaea, rhodopaeum, rhodopensis

Queen Rhodope and King Haemus of Thrace were prone to hubris and liked to refer to themselves as Hera and Zeus. In punishment, the real Hera and Zeus turned the couple into mountain ranges far from each other. Not even their river-son Hebros could breach the distance between them. And so, in time, Hemus (from Haemus) became the Balkan range, also known as Stara Planina or the Old Mountain. It runs from eastern Serbia to the Black Sea, and gave the entire peninsula its name thanks to a lasting confusion, finally formalised by a German geographer in 1808. The confusion was that the Balkan range ran all the way from the Black Sea to the Adriatic coast. The River Evros (from Hebros) is the longest in the Balkan peninsula, and there's no confusion there: it springs from the highest range in the Balkans, the Rila Mountains, runs south for 480 kilometres, and ends in the Aegean. And the Rhodope is the oldest land formation on the peninsula, 18,000 square kilometres of limestone gorges and caves, ancient coniferous forests, Roman roads once trodden by crusaders and caravans, and Orphean melodies not quite of this world. Because the Rhodopes are not quite *this* world.

It must be because the Rhodope ranges straddle a biogeographical line between Mediterranean and continental spheres that crossing them feels like travelling across all of Europe, from Scots pine to silver birch, from pre-Alpine meadows to black granite peaks that spell the end of something, possibly reason. This is wolf and bear country, and there are so many endemic animal and plant species that they have suffixes like *rhodopaea*, *rhodopaeum*, *rhodopensis*. In various parts of the Rhodope, you can see vultures glide over vertiginous niches carved in the cliffs by the Thracians and whose purpose is unknown, the thundering water cave where Orpheus might have descended into Hades, and a megalithic rock sanctuary that (maybe) hosted the Oracle of Dionysus.

The Rhodope Mountains were heavily Islamised, resulting in a religiously mixed population that somehow survived the periodic purges of the twentieth-century nation-state. This is how the Rhodopes are still the heartland of the Pomaks, indigenous Balkan Muslims. Mosques of all sizes and shapes punctuate the furry hills, and the Orthodox churches are painted with rare frescos – here I saw a dog-headed Christopher, patron saint of travellers. Every type of traveller has passed through the Rhodope over the last few thousand years, but this is above all the realm of those who have the mountain in their blood. You see it in their eyes and in their tall stone houses like fortresses. They aren't going anywhere.

Travelling west from the warm plains of Thrace was like going back into winter. There had been a late heavy snowfall a couple of weeks before and the mountain passes had been closed. At first the flat open road into the eastern Rhodope was lined with white and pink blossoming trees that trembled in the breeze, and I drove through an intoxicating hour of confetti-like blossoms, like a guest at a bridal procession without people. But when the road began to climb above deep gorges, like a ribbon unfurling, the blossoms disappeared. Black fir trees hung over the road, barely attached to cliffs so high their tops couldn't be seen. Top-heavy lorries caterpillared ahead, with a sheer drop to one side. The tarmac was eroded by fresh snow melts and piled with forest debris, but accidents were surprisingly rare. Drivers knew that no one would come looking for you if you came off the road. You would biodegrade at the bottom of the gorge and vultures would pick your bones clean, so you clung to the tarmac for dear life.

Shadows fell, as if giant birds or clouds were passing overhead, but the sky was blue, paradise blue.

THE VILLAGE WHERE
YOU LIVED FOR EVER

The village was at the end of a mountain road so long that it surely
had to end with each next village huddled in the secretive hills, but
didn't. Big woolly sheepdogs called *Karakachan*, after the nomadic
Greek shepherds who bred them, ran alongside the car like shag-
pile carpets on long legs. Labyrinthine passages carved out cathedrals
and entire cities inside the cliffs, but the caving season hadn't started
yet. At dusk, a roadside inn sold me a jar of sheep's yogurt, fatty like
double cream, and while I ate spoonfuls of it, a bear crossed my path.
A small bear, maybe a lost cub. It didn't even look at the car before it
tumbled into the shrubs.

The forest of the looming hills was still twiggy-brown, with
pockets of snow. The days blazed with the sun of high altitude, but
in the morning, when I stood on my balcony wrapped in a goat-hair
rug, the hills were steamy with frost. The only warmth was the wood-
scented smoke of chimneys and the breath of barking dogs.

Then the faint call to prayer from the hilltop neighbourhoods
joined in with the dogs until their barking fell in sync with the imam's
voice, or the church bells if it was Sunday, and the sound rose over the
fortress-like houses and strangely human hills in a way that made me
feel I'd been here before.

But I hadn't. As a child, I had gone on summer holidays to the
Rhodope with my grandparents, picking wild berries and climbing

resin-sticky fir trees, but not here. This village had been doubly on the fringe, because of the wild terrain and because of the Iron Curtain. The village was officially known for two things: the spring in the hills where a major river began, and the long lifespan of its people. Every summer a Japanese team came to copy their methods of yogurt-making and animal slaughter, to the quiet bemusement of the locals.

But from the late 1960s onwards, the Communist State had made the most of the isolation of the village, and used it for the manufacturing of parts for armed vehicles. Those were then exported to friendly countries like Iraq and Algeria, and used in the USSR's war in Afghanistan. This top-secret factory operated under the auspices of an agricultural cooperative. It later became a sewing factory, but when that was privatised, the owner paid his seamstresses so little for the goose-stuffed jackets sold to Italian brands, that my hostess quit her job in anger, and went into business herself.

Now she and her teacher husband were running the four-storeyed family home as a guesthouse and shop. They were a peaceable, well-educated couple in their fifties, and looking at their faces, you'd never have guessed what they'd been through. Like most in these parts, they were Pomaks: descendants of long-ago converts to Islam. Their names had been changed three times in their lives.

As the human symbol of the Ottoman past, the Pomaks absorbed the collective angst about residual orientalism as if they personally stood in the way of Europe. Despite representing less than 2 per cent of the country's population, throughout the twentieth century they were perceived as a fifth column and endured all manner of indignities. In Bulgaria, even more than the ethnic Turks, the Pomaks were seen as having a double identity – they were Slavs or ethnic Bulgars anyway, but also of Islam. The more self-pitying students of history insist that the word Pomak comes from the old Slavic word *pomachen*, tortured (by the Ottomans). Another deconstruction of the word fancies that it comes from *pomagach*, or helper (to the Ottomans).

Whatever the truth, the bigger picture was this: large swathes of Ottoman Europe took Islam by choice, and the reasons covered anything from paying less tax to escaping persecution by the Orthodox Church if you were unlucky enough to be a heretical sect, like the Bogomils. Starting in Bulgaria and spreading west to Bosnia, France, and Italy, where the movement morphed into the Cathar Church, the Gnostic, dualistic Bogomils were anti-institutional. They suggested that the body of the Church was bloated, and that to be spiritual you didn't need the trappings of a corrupt, hierarchical institution. Although, like the Paulicians, the Bogomils were truly the tortured ones, they were influential for several centuries, until Islam subsumed them. It must have been a relief to get the Church off their backs. Some trace Bogomilism to a Manichaean teaching rooted in Persian Zoroastrianism, which further blurs the boundary between East and West.

Another group of early converts to Islam were Balkan landowning nobility, who quickly saw that the only certain upward social path under the new order passed through Islam. This included estate-owning Bulgars, Serbs, Byzantine Greeks, and Venetians.

And another thing: the imposition of Christianity in the Bulgarian kingdom in the ninth century had been astonishingly bloody even by the standards of the day. In order to quash widespread resistance from his powerful pagan boyars, still loyal to their shamanic roots (because the nomadic Bulgars had arrived from the Asian steppes), Tsar Boris I simply had them massacred. Along with their families. That was fifty-two families, and presumably he was pleased, but he also destroyed the entire aristocracy of the kingdom, a symbolic act of national suicide that some commentators see as only the first in the nation's history. Five centuries later, the Ottoman Turks rocked up and stayed, in their turn, for five centuries. There is a certain symmetry to that.

In the early twentieth century, the descendants of all indigenous Muslims were Christianised at gunpoint by the independent Bulgarian state, with the official aim of giving them back their Christian roots. A strange concept: to give back somebody's roots by force. This is when many fled to Turkey. Others took Christianity as a token gesture, but later reconverted to Islam. One Muslim village here that was forcibly Christianised a hundred years ago remains Christian to this day. I guess they just couldn't be bothered any more, they'd run out of energy.

A friend introduced me to a retired miner called Hairi who lived in another Pomak village near the local mining town. Hairi, or Good in Arabic, became the less Arabic Hari in the 1970s. And in the 1980s, he became the fully Slavicised Zakhari.

'At least you could choose the name by which your identity was destroyed,' Hairi smiled over his small moustache. He was not bitter despite supping on the bitterness of history for generations.

We were having coffee in the mining town of Rudozem, overlooked by blue mountain peaks and by the red brick of a 1950s ore-processing plant which, miraculously, and despite its broken windows, still operated. Across the top of the building ran an indelible slogan in white paint: 'This factory is the offspring of Bulgarian–Soviet friendship.'

In the last name-changing campaign, Hairi said, the local functionary was so embarrassed to be doing this to her own community *again*, she couldn't make eye contact as the queue of people signed the register with their new names. Don't worry, Hairi-Hari-Zakhari comforted her, I'm used to it.

'Of course I never used the other names. I was always Hairi to those who knew me, even if my passport said otherwise.'

One night in 1949, when Hairi's mother was a child, her family were rounded up in an army truck. Abandoning animals, harvest, fields, they were deported north to a village in the Balkan range.

When they arrived, their enforced new hosts were crying with fear, but Hairi's grandmother was crying with shock. Why are *you* crying? she asked the hosts, you're at home! Because they told us you come from the border and only criminals live by the border, said the hosts. They ended up laughing about it, and the two families got on fine under the same roof for a few years – they had no choice – until Hairi's family were allowed to return to their village, sow anew, buy new animals, pretend nothing had happened. Because no one was about to apologise, let alone compensate them.

'It's not about that,' Hairi said. 'We're not special, this happened to many other border families. It's about simple acknowledgement that this happened.'

Why had it happened? Because in the early years of Soviet terror, thousands ran across the border while they still could. Some Pomak communities mounted an organised armed resistance against the regime, much like the Goryani. The people of the border were deported for fear that they would help such 'bandits'. That they were a fifth column. Still, the Pomaks always bounced back. Those who worked abroad sent money home and eventually returned – to the fortress-like houses, to the villages where you lived for ever.

Unless you died a violent death.

'There was a German guy, in 1982,' my host recalled.

I was back in my guesthouse, eating a dinner of small meatballs in tomato sauce, with crunchy home-made pickles, while my hosts hovered good-naturedly, asking if I wanted more bread, wine, or heat from the booming log-stove.

'Actually, there were lots of Germans, back in the day. But I can't forget that one. He had made it across the wire without setting it off. They were looking for him. He climbed above the village, to a sunny meadow, and thinking he was in Greece, he sat down to eat some apples. He had a hunting knife and was cutting the apples when a shepherd saw him. That's how it went. Most were caught by shepherds and old women.'

My host shook his head.

'When the army came to get the German-language teacher from school, we knew it was endgame for some poor bugger. We were so brainwashed, it was unthinkable to see a stranger and not raise the alarm.'

Guilty until proven innocent, Pomaks were under double pressure to prove their loyalty to the regime.

The German with the apples was taken into the barracks.

'They didn't kill him immediately,' my host said. 'He died later in hospital. The barracks' commander took his knife as a trophy and showed it off round the village.'

School kids from border villages used to be taken in brigades up to the Furrow of Death. Their task was to smooth out the soil along the wire with rakes, so that not even a hedgehog could cross it without leaving a trace.

I guess it had to be the children. That way, by the time they weren't children any more, they were fully under the shadow of the wire. That way, handing a runaway to the soldiers felt more like housekeeping than murder.

Later, I was told by others that the barrack commander had a son. When he was in his twenties, the son was killed in an accident that may have been an act of revenge for his father's crimes.

My hosts were pragmatists who made their own world from what was at hand – their two family houses, their milk- and cheese-producing cows, sheep, and goats, the youthful in-laws next door who breathed down their necks every minute. It was this domestic economy of dependence from house to house that kept the village going.

'We have this mare,' my hostess said with an ironic smile. 'If you ride her, you become pregnant. Apparently.'

'I think you need more than a mare,' my host quipped. 'Still, we've had several guests with infertility. Until they rode the mare.'

'We had a specialist,' my hostess said. 'She said it was something to do with the lower chakras. The mare unblocks them.'

'Want to have a go?' the mother-in-law piped up. She was a small, brazen woman with pitch-black hair. My inexplicable childless state sent ripples of anxiety through the family.

'You know what they say,' her husband said and winked at me because behind the façade of dignified patriarch, he was still a flirt, 'if you don't have a house or a descendant by the age of forty, you're a write-off.'

'Better go hang myself now,' I said but nobody laughed. Perhaps they agreed.

'We had a guest once,' my host said. 'A young woman like you, charming. She said she'd come to get away from it all, get to know the area.'

It had been the 1990s, when the border was still 'hard' because Greece was in the EU and Bulgaria wasn't.

'She rode the mare all the way to the spring,' my hostess said.

'But she didn't get pregnant,' the mother-in-law said.

'The cops turned up and arrested her instead,' my host said. 'Such a charming woman!'

The charming woman had been a people trafficker on a reconnaissance trip.

'Which reminds me,' my host said, and I thought he was joking at first. 'I haven't seen your ID.'

I passed on the mare but went to visit a couple up the hill to get a peek into the world of longevity. They were ninety but you'd never have called them old. Uncle Radoy and Auntie Zlata lived up a steep cobbled lane in the Christian neighbourhood.

Uncle Radoy was pruning trees when I arrived, and she was planting tomatoes. We sat in their little garden with a plate of golden raisins.

'What can I say,' he shrugged, then smoothed his hair and prepared for a long spiel.

'It's not what it used to be. In the 1970s, there were dozens of centenarians. Now my sisters are dying in their nineties!'

'The men are potent until they fall off their perch,' Zlata said approvingly. Her eyes were clear blue like mountain lakes.

'These days, however, it's not so much about the sex,' Radoy said. 'It's more about the companionship.'

I stared at his smooth, cunning face where I couldn't find a single wrinkle. Not one.

In a Bulgarian mountain village, our 'boon-companion' the travel writer Evliya saw a crone turn herself and seven kids into chickens by rubbing her vagina with ash from the fire. He wrote: 'It really unnerved me.'

Likewise, these young ninety-year-olds really unnerved *me*.

'The garden keeps us on our feet,' Zlata said.

They had been together for over sixty years. They'd met in 1953, at a party in the army barracks where, thirty years later, the German guy with the apples hadn't been killed immediately. It was love at first sight.

'These city folk,' Radoy said, 'they come in their cars and try to drive up the lane to our house because they can't walk! We've come to the end of the world, they say. But they haven't.'

'The end of the world is not a place,' Zlata said.

'One day, before they strung up the wire, I walked over to Greece,' Radoy said. 'When the end of the world doesn't come to you, you must go to it.'

'They came here looking for food, poor souls,' Zlata said. 'We had food at least.'

Radoy changed the subject. 'Let me tell you how the Christian and Muslim neighbourhoods came about.'

There were three brothers. One took Islam, another didn't. When the third one came back from grazing his sheep, he found a new neighbourhood had sprung up, and one of his brothers was wearing a turban. Bro, he said, what happened? Run, bro, the turbaned one said. Or they'll convert you too.

'No no,' Zlata said, 'that's not how the story goes.'

There were two friends, a Muslim and a Christian. They were in love with Fatme. For reasons of faith, Fatme couldn't marry the one she preferred, so she went for the other. The two friends fell out. When Fatme was dead, they ended up living in the same neighbourhood, over there. It's completely empty now. One night, the Muslim friend got sick, or maybe the Christian. Anyway, it was winter. His friend set out across the blizzard to look for a doctor. It nearly killed him, but he made it and his friend was saved. They finally broke their silence and got drunk together, had a cry, remembered Fatme and the old days when the village was full of life. Then they went back to their silence and took it to the grave. They're buried next to each other. But the two neighbourhoods still bear their names.

'That's why we live in peace here. Muslim and Christian,' Zlata concluded.

'Women. They always go for the romantic story.' Radoy turned to me as if I wasn't one. 'Eat your Turkish raisins. They're good for the skin.'

When we walked to the top of their street where the incline was almost vertical, I struggled to keep up with them. Uncle Radoy wore brand-new trousers and matching waistcoat made from *shayak*, top-quality wool beaten at the river mills, the kind that stopped being made fifty years ago. The village spread out over several kilometres, a long walk to visit the neighbours. At the top, we took in the panorama of white peaks and awakening meadows. There was a small chapel at our feet.

'There's an agiasma inside it. You must wash there,' Radoy confided. 'It cures eye and skin disorders, stomach ailments and impotence.'

Maybe he did think I was a man?

'See that peak?' Zlata pointed at what was known as Kom Peak. It was 1,600 metres high and it was where the sun first rose in the morning. The Roman road to Xanthi passed along its ridge, the one where the knights of the Fourth Crusade had passed on their way to sack Constantinople. Everyone had their version of what Kom Peak contained.

'There's an old chapel with locked gates inside the hill, full of gold and silver dishes,' Zlata said. 'Pilgrims from the whole of the Rhodope came to pray there back in the day.'

'Wait wait,' Radoy said. 'Remember old Assan?'

When he was young, old Assan had served as adjutant to a colonel in the port city of Kavala. It was World War I. The Bulgarians wanted to retake Macedonia from the Greeks, and Kavala was a strategic point because from there, ships carried the 'aromatic gold' grown in Macedonia: tobacco. So they got talking and the colonel said to Assan: 'Since you're from that village, you must know something, in case I die. Kom Peak contains untold treasures. I've seen the key with my own eyes. They say if you find the key, you must go up there and wait till sunrise, when a hamlet appears in the mist. But only for a moment. That hamlet is called Tekir and people from another time live there. Only when you see Tekir can you unlock the iron doors to the underground chapel.'

The colonel died in the Great War, the wretched border remained the same, and Assan lived to tell the story. But did he find the key?

Zlata shrugged. 'They say there's a loom made of pure gold in there,' she said.

'All you're going to see at sunrise is treasure hunters. Digging till kingdom come,' Radoy said.

'Besides, who needs a golden loom?' Zlata said.

And we headed back down the lane, because they had tomatoes to plant.

I heard more about Kom Peak two days later. But first, on the following day my hosts held a baby shower for their granddaughter, and hundreds of guests poured through the house from neighbouring towns: stone-faced older women in flower-printed headscarves whose eyes scanned me to ascertain just what kind of wanton creature I was, their heavy men huddled silently next to them with awkward hands and archaic Balkan expressions of granite-like endurance. Together, they had survived the ritual name-changing campaigns, being written out of official national history, and the truth of life on the periphery – for example, ten days without electricity during the last snowfall when no authority came to help and the men had pulled their villages out of the snow by removing fallen trees from electricity cables with their bare hands. The younger generation were urbane, confident, and snappily dressed in jeans and tailored dresses, not a headscarf in sight. Sixteen kilos of the famous buttery local *smilyan* beans had been cooked in a cauldron, a calf had been slaughtered, and dozens of trays of filled pastry circulated, because it was a matter of pride for my hosts to show abundance. No alcohol was served, only herbal cordial, until the late evening, when a few of the men got sloshed and reminisced, and nobody drank more than the raven-haired mother-in-law. But the baby shower went on all day, and at one point I went to hang out at the only place in the village that wasn't a family house.

The boutique hotel sat idyllically beside a chatty weir. Its owner was a tall, effusive Greek called Kostas whose wavy mane was in a perpetual state of movement. Every time I sat in the restaurant, he would put a plate of roast lamb before me, 'on the house'. Oddly, he seemed to do that with everyone.

'It's only a bit of lamb. It won't make me poorer or you richer.'

Kostas was from Xanthi, a white city that appeared suddenly in the Aegean plains just as the dark Rhodope ranges ended. If you followed the Roman road over Kom Peak, you'd go south through the Xanthi pass, the way transhumant shepherds had done for centuries, dividing their time between the warm Aegean plains in winter and the cool Rhodope in summer.

Kostas was an exile of a special kind. In the late 1980s, when he was due for compulsory military service, he deserted.

'I went to Sweden. But the people were like the weather. I missed the Balkans.'

So he settled in Bulgaria. It was close to Greece and here you could smoke to your heart's content. Except Kostas wasn't a smoker. No, he said, but I like it when people smoke. Shirking military service meant that for twenty years he was only able to go home during a general amnesty, and that only happened during elections.

'Fortunately,' he said, 'Greece is quite unstable, so I went home regularly.'

Kostas laughed and his hair moved. The waiter brought another plate of lamb.

On the wall was a nationalistic map of 'Greater Bulgaria', the way it had been at its height as a rival to Byzantium, touching three seas – the Black, the Aegean, and the Adriatic. He had put it there ostensibly to please his customers, but on this border, the map looked like what it was: a sad joke thrown back at nationalism.

'You know the secret of longevity?' a voice suddenly said.

I hadn't seen him until now. He had materialised like a djinn at the table, and was already having a shot of rakia, on the house. He was a whippet of a man with a hatchet face and straw hair. His eyes were so pale, they looked bleached by too much time in the high-altitude sun.

'The secret is to have three hearts. One for loving people. Another for loving yourself. And the third one, to love the mountains. Kostas has three hearts,' said the straw-hair.

He reminded me of the scarecrow from *The Wizard of Oz*. His speech was fast and garbled, not helped by his mixing of Bulgarian and Greek words.

'That's the secret. Not yogurt, that's bollocks. Hi, I'm Ziko. Ziko's the name.'

He got up and bowed unsteadily.

'If they ever open up the old road between Greece and Bulgaria, so we can feel normal again,' Kostas said, 'as they've been promising for years, useless states the both of them, then I'll sponsor a statue, right by the border pyramid.'

The statue would be of Ziko, he said. Life-sized.

'Wow,' Ziko said, chuffed. 'Really?'

Like most in the village, Ziko looked ageless, but he had history. In his late twenties, he'd been stopped by a police patrol car on a deserted road above the village and beaten to a pulp. The beating had changed him for ever – the flesh fell away from him, his speech went funny. After a spell in hospital there was a spell in jail, because Ziko had been a notorious people smuggler.

'Drinks on the house today,' Kostas rose from the table, preceded by his hair, 'because I can see this is the beginning of a beautiful friendship.'

the judgement

The name of a cliff over a border gorge. The gorge is so deep, you can't see the bottom, only mist. The cliff is visited for only one purpose. From here, inconvenient people have been pushed into the mist since the beginning of people. Given the Thracians' fondness for sacrifice and their supposedly upbeat relationship with death, this was a good place for 'the chosen' to begin their journey to the Mother Goddess, with a message from the living.

That's speculation, but the following true story was told to me by a local as we stood by border pyramid number 47. This happened in 1981. The young couple had been perhaps Czechs. Nobody said any more and we were too scared to ask, he said. They had been moving in the direction of the Judgement. It was late summer, harvest time, and they had managed to cross the klyon without setting it off and entered an allotment in no-man's-land. Except there *was* a man, and they could see him working with his back to them. And they could see the basket with his lunch. Now let us imagine multiple takes of this story.

In the first take, the Czech couple took the lunch. When the man turned and saw his lunch was missing, he guessed what had happened, but had the choice of keeping it to himself because there were no witnesses.

★

In the second take, the Czech couple took the lunch and left some German marks. When the man turned, he guessed what had happened. But now he had a dilemma. Extra-zealous cadres were deployed in border areas to test the locals' loyalty through various ruses. Things could go wrong very quickly if you failed the test. If the missing lunch and the marks were a test and he said nothing, he'd be deported with his family or sent to a labour camp. His life would be destroyed within hours. If the missing lunch was genuine and he reported the fugitives, he'd be highly commended but he'd live with it for the rest of his days.

In the third take, the couple didn't take the lunch and arrived in Greece ravenous.

That man working in the fields was our neighbour, the local said. Of course, he was highly commended. But he stopped going to his allotment, and his own judgement ate him up like a cancer.

ON THE ROAD TO FREEDOM

'E-e-exactly,' Ziko said. When he got excited or very drunk, he stuttered. 'It's because of mind-fucks like that I started getting people across. It was my duty. To carve out a road for people.'

Ziko grew up in the highest neighbourhood of the village, behind the locked gates of the klyon, behind the barracks. His childhood perspective was the wire on one side, and Greece on the other. His playground was no-man's-forest. As a boy, he did errands for the army, for the locals, and for the Greeks.

Once, he was cutting wood when two Greek men came up to him and gave him a pistol and a photograph. They'd crossed the border illegally. Boy, they said, if you do this, we'll give you and your family a nice house in our village. Ziko's mission was to shoot a corporal at the local border barracks. During the Bulgarian occupation of northern Greece in the 1940s, he had murdered the men of a family and moved into their house. The men with the pistol were the surviving relatives.

Ziko was ten. He knew the corporal.

'But I left that pistol well alone. I'm not cut out for that kind of thing. And anyway, revenge is bollocks, man,' he said. 'Other times,' Ziko said, 'Greeks came to me in the forest to ask after relatives and friends. How's so and so?'

Because the klyon had cleaved people down the middle, like an axe.

Ziko knew every glade and ancient road, every deer track and carved initial.

'It's my fate, man,' he said. 'It's like I had no choice. First my grandfather. He was a tradesman. Between here, Xanthi, and Kavala.'

What did he trade in?

'Are you kidding? Everything you can put on a mule's back. From berries to guns.'

From the late 1800s until the start of the Cold War, the Rhodope ranges were a lively smuggling gateway between the independent kingdoms of Bulgaria and Greece. Arms smuggling was the most lucrative trade, and tobacco was the most lucrative crop. As a kid, Ziko and his friends had gone into the forest caves to look for old stashed weapons that they could sell on. His father had run both the local shop and the local choir which toured the country singing those otherworldly Rhodope songs.

'He loved three things in life,' Ziko said. 'And one of them killed him. Music, women, and booze.'

His father's shop in the upper village was still open, but it was a shadow of its former black-market glory. Because in those days, in this shop at the end of the world, Ziko said, you could find the world. Anything that could be bought, sold, exchanged, smuggled, and speculated on – his dad had it. From single malts to car parts. It was a booming free-market local economy within the planned economy of empty shops.

'And how many times did he see people making a run for it?' Ziko said. 'How many times did he just point the way to the lost? Because he took orders from no one. He wanted people to be free. Then it was my turn. God knows what my kids will do!'

Ziko was, by his own admission, a womaniser, drinker, and – yes – one-time smuggler. Now that this was a soft border between two EU member states and his people-smuggling days were over, he was

on the lookout for whatever else was going. This and that. Mostly
hunting dogs. A good hunting dog born and bred here used to go
for good money in Greece, but now the Greeks had no money for
dogs.

'God has always looked after me,' Ziko sighed, 'but lately, he's
been forgetful.'

When I asked him about the people he'd taken across the border,
he said that the only way I'd understand was if he took me along what
he called the Road to Freedom.

'Otherwise it's all words,' he said. 'Until you tread those paths,
you'll never get it. I'll bring two mates so you don't freak out,' he
grinned. 'You pay me if you have money, you don't if you don't.'

It was a deal. I trusted Ziko; I sensed goodness in his heart.

In the morning, when I stood on my balcony wrapped in a goat-
hair blanket, the hills were invisible with mist and the air was so
heavy with imminent precipitation, you could drink it. A snowstorm
brewed over Kom Peak.

Ziko's old BMW screeched to a halt outside the house. Ziko
emerged, beaming.

'Ziko,' I said, 'what's up with the weather?'

'Nothing's up, Kapi,' he said. 'It's weather like any other.'

Weather like this was ideal for a smuggler.

I was paying Ziko a daily fee. Within minutes, he spent half the fee
in my hosts' shop on provisions, including a two-litre bottle of rakia
(50 per cent alcohol) and a stack of smoked pork ribs.

'Ziko,' I said, 'I thought you were a Muslim.'

He shrugged.

'You know how many times I've been to a mosque? Once, when
my father died. All those Kurban Bayram parties with lemonade, and
I'm supposed to enjoy myself? Bollocks.'

My wholesome hosts, who liked their lemonade parties, looked on him and on our outing with dismay. Ziko was a legend but also a reprobate.

We took off with a screech, and in the car I put on the kit he'd brought for me – old boots and a man's waterproof camouflage outfit, several sizes too big, but it did the job.

'Now you look like one of us,' he grinned with approval.

Just before the cemetery, where you turned up the steep road to the top of the village, we passed a flock of sheep and goats. I glimpsed a shepherd in the mist. He was very young, wore a tatty tweed jacket, and seemed to be scribbling something in a notebook, like some poet of the elements. But when I looked again, the mist had swallowed him and his flock.

'Who was that?' I asked Ziko.

'Oh that's just the Predator,' he said.

'Why Predator?'

'Once, a long time ago, he found a wolf eating one of his sheep. He wasn't armed so he sneaked up from behind and strangled the wolf with his bare hands. Personally, Kapi, I'd have left that wolf well alone,' he concluded.

Never mind the wolf, I was taken aback by the words 'a long time ago'.

'But he's so young!' I said.

Ziko glanced at me strangely.

His friends were waiting for us at the top, where the last houses perched. Ziko abandoned the car. From here, it was on foot to Greece.

The younger friend was known as Indiana Jones, 'Jones for short,' he said and blushed, and the older one was 'Galen: the number one stag of the village', as Ziko introduced him. Galen smiled with his huge face and bent down to kiss my hand.

'Once,' he said demurely, 'a long time ago.'

Galen was eighty, but looked like a giant oak full of sap. Galen meant Beloved. His hands were like spades, I imagined them digging a tunnel all the way to the Aegean. He had a leonine head of hair and eyes squeezed in perpetual pleasure.

Jones by contrast was a small freckly man with sad grey eyes and a hunting rifle, who hid behind an easy chuckle. He scraped a living from woodcutting on both sides of the border, walking everywhere because he had no car. I said hello to his mother, a tiny woman bent over her garden. His father had been a shepherd.

'It's just the two of us now.' She wiped her face. 'We can get by on what I plant.'

'He's looking to get married, hehe,' Ziko said and Jones blushed again.

What kind of a wife was he looking for?

'Someone who's more or less a woman,' Jones said in earnest. 'Not too young, not too old.'

'Is it the hunting season yet?' I asked, looking at his rifle.

'It's always more or less the hunting season here,' Jones said. 'But not if it's a pregnant animal. We do it by the book.'

'Hehe,' Ziko said.

I really hoped I wouldn't have to gut a wild pig with them.

The mist began to disperse and we set off for Greece: me in the oversized camouflage outfit, Jones the woodcutter, Ziko the straw-hair, Galen the lion-head, and an excited dog called Mara.

The tracks in the forest were well trodden, but they were too many. Even without the mist, I could get lost within minutes.

'It's not that you could, you *will*,' Ziko said.

Ziko darted ahead of us and vanished, then he popped up right behind me, magically, saying, 'Look at this.'

And he showed me a fresh wolf print in the muddy track.

'Aha! Are you glad we took the rifle?'

You bet I was. The paw was quite large.

Ziko had a relationship not just with the land, but with the air. He could make himself appear and disappear.

'When I walk this road, all the faces come back to me,' he said, walking nervily ahead, then behind, his body so skinny he was almost two-dimensional. 'It's like they're still here. All the souls I took across. In snow blizzards, in rain and sunshine. At night. Some cried. Some collapsed. I've carried children on my back. Some came with bags. Some with nothing. Loads of Gypsies with just the shirt on their backs. There was no work in the country. And the smell of fear comes back to me. Fear has a smell, Kapi.'

Ziko only took money if people had it.

'When people cross a border, they don't run from good, Kapi. They run from bad. Sometimes very bad.'

Ziko admitted he'd made good money until the fateful beating and the prison sentence, which was supposed to be longer. That's where all his money went – into lawyer fees. They took the last shirt from his wardrobe, he said.

'My last Armani shirt. Can you imagine? I love my shirts. I'm a stylish kind of guy. Sporty yet stylish.'

Although he lost every penny, he was glad to be out of jail after a year. And anyway, the Armani shirts were all Turkish-made fakes.

'I managed to keep my arse. You're laughing, but it's not funny when you're behind bars in the company of giants who want to bugger you. Yessir, my head went funny but I kept my arse. You can't have everything.'

After we climbed through a dark glade where it seemed to be perpetual night-time, wading through knee-deep snow, Galen stopped by two initialled trees:

H
S

The year was distorted by the expanded bark.

'One night in 1963,' Galen said, 'we were sitting in the pub, me and my friend Hamid. I was talking about some motorbike part I needed. Hamid said, Bro, I can give you that part. Fuck it, you can have the whole bike, I won't be needing it.'

Galen knew then that his friend was going to do a runner that night. Locals like Hamid made the bulk of successful border escapes.

Galen never said a word to anyone and kept his friend's bike.

'Now Hamid is the richest Bulgarian in America,' Jones said wistfully.

'No, that's Shevket,' Galen said.

The families of Shevket Chapadjiev and Hamid Rusev had suffered the same fate as Hairi's family: they were deported to other parts of the country, in sealed cattle wagons with just the clothes on their backs, for the double crime of being Pomaks and being of the border.

Hamid's mother was forced to live in a stable with her four kids; her husband had been jailed. Eight years later, when the family were allowed to return to the Village Where You Lived For Ever, they found their house plundered by the army. Even the doors were missing. They had to begin again from scratch. No compensation ever came, quite the opposite: as a promising young Pomak, Hamid was enlisted as an agitator in the new name-changing campaign against... the Pomaks. He even considered it, because he didn't lack ambition, but quickly saw through its true intent, and from that point on, there was no future for him here.

Hamid and his friend Shevket escaped together, sailing from Athens to New York on a ship called the *Olympia*. Hamid Rusev ended up working for the International Monetary Fund, and Shevket Chapadjiev started by buying two printing presses which grew into a printing empire. Today the two men are philanthropists and pater familiases of the large Bulgarian community in Chicago. Their American dream had come true, at the price of exile. Galen stroked his friend's tree and smiled approvingly.

'It's not about the money,' Ziko said, 'it's about opportunity. How many times did I almost stay in Greece? But something pulled me back to this bollocks country.'

An hour later, we stood by the small concrete border pyramid. This was where the Furrow of Death had once been tended by the local children. The forest was bleak with a winter that wouldn't go away. Silence lived here, and not a single bird.

Jones paused by the pyramid to tell me about something called the Devil's Hole which is cursed for all time. But Ziko was nervous.

'Get a move on,' Ziko whispered loudly from the top of a hillock where he stood camouflaged among trees. How on earth did he get there in just a few seconds?

There were still border police posted in the forest and we were in effect crossing illegally. None of us had papers and we could be arrested. Jones had dismantled his rifle and put it in his rucksack, but as soon as we crossed into Greece, he assembled it again.

'The Roman road,' Ziko said behind me, and when I looked down, I saw that we were walking along a sloping Roman road in excellent shape. The white stones had not been dislodged by twenty centuries of use. This was where they met with their Greek mates every season for their deer- and treasure-hunting parties. There was a sharp bend in the road and this is where they had the first and last shot of rakia or ouzo.

Jones liked telling stories. Once he had a job across the border, logging, when logging was still good business in Greece. He'd walk four hours in the morning darkness, down this road, then four hours at night, back to his mother.

'Just as well I enjoy walking,' he chuckled sadly. 'And in the end, the bastard didn't pay me a single penny.'

Then for two summers he worked for a Greek friend who had a hotel on the Aegean coast. And in the end, he didn't pay him either. It was the economic crisis. And Jones was hurt as well as broke, but still he felt sorry for his friend, you know, a crisis is a crisis, though sometimes he felt like going there just to punch him.

Another time, Jones saw a Gypsy guy in Greece selling a set of earrings.

'Pure crafted gold. Old. I could tell he'd dug them up somewhere and wanted rid of them, and I bought them off him. One hundred euro.'

'How old, Ottoman?' I asked.

'No no, old I tell you,' Jones said. 'Antiques.'

'So you gave them to the national museum?' I said without hope.

He gave them to a 'lady friend' he was hoping to marry, but she skipped off to Germany. Somewhere in Germany there was a woman wearing Thracian or Roman gold. And Jones was still broke and wifeless.

The Roman road led to the Roman bridge. A fully preserved, high-arched Roman bridge that passed over the river, rushing with snowmelt.

'It *was* fully preserved, until last week,' Galen said and looked at Jones, who helped me across gallantly, because in the middle of the bridge, a single stone was missing and through the gap you could see the raging water below.

'Don't look at me, it wasn't me!' Jones said. 'Must have been the Greeks.'

'I don't know who it was, but I bet the Romans built it so that whoever tries to mess it up will have the bridge fall on him and kill him,' Galen said.

This had been an active thoroughfare until the Cold War. Many of the refugees from the Balkan Wars and the subsequent three wars (World Wars I and II and the Greek Civil War) had buried possessions and money along the way. Marauding bands of all stripes – Greeks, Turks, Bulgarians, a United Nations of roadside thuggery – robbed refugees, tradesmen, partisans, and each other. In this forest, if you were committed enough, you could find anything from Thracian, Roman, Byzantine, and Ottoman coins to British and German weapons. Bodies too.

'One day when I was a young lad,' Galen said, 'I came here for a spot of hunting. Time of the Greek Civil War. The *andarte* partisans came onto our side to hide and get food. I found this dead andarte, about my age. Pity about the lad, but he'd never be alive again and his boots were my size. I wore them for twenty years and thought of him.'

Galen's mother took food to the andartes. She couldn't bear it that they were starved, he said, people just like us, and not least because some of our army were shits who requisitioned their supplies during the occupation, Galen said.

'One such shit from our village raped a mother and daughter. His house back here was all decked out in looted goodies from across the way. When the war was over, one day we found him before the bridge. Castrated and nailed to a tree. The Greeks had come for him. And he deserved every bit of it,' Galen concluded evenly.

Jones's face had relaxed into its natural sadness. Ziko had gone on ahead to check out something called Bears' Cave in the karst cliff face above us. He was there in no time and called us to follow. It looked impossible to reach, but there was a steep path through the brambles and we took it.

The cave had a wide entrance and went inside the hill. Ziko emerged from the darkness, sniffing.

'What is it, Ziko?'

'I smell bear,' he said.

I laughed then I stopped. The reason why this was called Bears'
Cave was because bears spent the winter here.

'We're okay now, it's warm,' Galen said. 'They'll be higher up.'

But it wasn't *that* warm and inside the cave were the bones of some
large animal. 'A deer,' Jones said and prodded it with his rifle.

'Shall we go now?' I said.

The entrance was lush with geranium bushes that filled the air with
the new aromatic season.

'Speaking of bears,' Jones began, again choosing an awkward spot
for his narrative.

He'd been on a summer job in Greece, herding cows. Two
hundred head. One morning, he came out of his hut in flip-flops, and
what did he see? – a brown bear tearing into one of the cows. The
bear saw him and stood on his back legs, full height. A mature male.
Jones went back into the hut, latched the door closed, and loaded
his gun. But he was too scared to come out again and the hut had no
windows. He sat listening to the bear all day. By the evening, the bear
had dragged the cow away to a safe place.

'The Greeks ban the shooting of bears,' Jones said, 'so when he
came again the following week and tucked into another cow, I had to
move the herd.'

'So,' I asked, 'is it true what those tourist boards instruct you,
that when you see a bear you lie on the ground and pretend to be
dead?'

They burst out laughing.

'And when the bear starts pawing you and you suddenly spring to
life, then what?' Jones said.

'The instructions are: wear a nappy and run for your life,' Ziko
said. 'Works for me every time.'

When we descended to a point of safety again, Jones and Ziko went off after a roe deer, the dog barking with mad excitement. Galen made a seat in the ruins of what had been a dairy station.

In its days of abundance and free trade, the Rhodope had been dotted with dairies called *mandras*. Travellers stopped to fill up with cheese, yogurt, and *katuk*, the first fatty cream of the milk. At the turn of the twentieth century, after observing peasants in Rhodopean villages where you lived for ever, the pioneering Russian micro-biologist Ilya Mechnikov singled out the mandra, with its leather saddlebags that allowed milk to be transported over the mountains on muleback, as the key to the remarkable longevity of the locals. Mechnikov identified one product as the agent that made gut floras healthy and prolonged lives: yogurt. *Lactobacillus bulgaricus*, named after the Geneva-based Bulgarian student of medicine Grigorov who isolated the good bacterium that ferments milk into yogurt, is alive and well in our yogurt pots. But the only thing that survives from the mandras that gave rise to yogurt is these ruins. And dairy-derived expressions. For example, 'a woman like a mandra', an old-fashioned compliment. In the ruins of the mandra, Galen told me a story, his gentle voice punctuated by distant gunshots and barks.

There was a woman like a mandra who had a lover in the upper village. But she was married to a rich man. His sister was a busybody and found out. It's okay, the husband said, I forgive her, but the sister wouldn't leave it alone – people talk, she said – until one day, the husband had had enough. When the woman like a mandra hadn't heard from her lover for a while, she knew something was up and went to a seer. The seer looked into her coffee cup and said, 'Go to the Bears' Cave.' So she walked here. They found her lying next to her lover's decomposing body.

'And?' I asked anxiously.

Galen smiled peaceably.

'There is no *and*. You look disappointed but sometimes it's like that. You come to the end of the road and it's over.'

He then produced a geranium root and gave it to me. It was from the entrance of the Bears' Cave.

'To plant in Scotland and remind you of here,' he said.

We went quiet. Galen had been miner, logger, dairy farmer, labourer, hunter, poacher, nominal Christian among nominal Muslims, free man among the barbed wire. Somehow, he had preserved himself. His wife was a smiley, fine-boned woman who had thoughtfully packed his rucksack for the day with snacks for everyone.

'And the good news is,' Galen concluded, 'that the odd new mandra is popping up again.'

'Boo!'

I jumped up. The hunters were back. The deer had escaped, thank God!

In the late afternoon, when the smoked pork ribs had been barbecued on an open fire and the bottle of rakia was almost empty ('I n-n-never get drunk on the job,' Ziko said), we sat down to rest in the last meadow before the descent into the village. Even Mara the dog looked exhausted.

To the south, the edge of the meadow was still lined with concrete anti-tank barricades from the 1940s. Horses grazed below and a rainbow bridged the distant snowy peaks to the north, where the ski resorts had just closed.

'Is there any work in Scotland?' Jones asked and chuckled sadly. 'Nah. Can't leave my mum.'

'It's a shame we have to go abroad for work,' Ziko said.

Jones hadn't been to a big city for thirty years.

'What for? Everything I love is here. Except work.'

Kom Peak rose across the valley.

'Kom Peak is special,' Jones said.

'Kom Peak is where you start seeing things if you're not careful,'
Ziko said.

'There was a German guy in 1990, came and camped on Kom
Peak for two months. Digging. Went off his head and had to be hospitalised,' Jones said.

Germans didn't fare well here.

'They say all you see on Kom Peak is phantoms,' Jones said.

Reclining on the new grass, Galen sunned his face with his eyes
closed.

'What kind of phantoms?' I said.

'There's only one kind of phantom,' Ziko said. 'The one in your
head.'

I suddenly realised that this was the exact meadow where the
German with the hunting knife had eaten his last apples before the
shepherd saw him.

'I guess all the fugitive stories are forgotten now,' I said, prodding.

'No,' Galen opened his eyes. 'Everything is remembered. Everything.'

At these words, for some reason of his own, Jones leaned over, his
eyes brimming with alcohol and tears.

'Are you sure you don't want to marry me? I might find a pot of
gold, more or less. One of these days.'

Ziko pushed his friend out of the way, a conscientious look on his
face.

'Drink up, Kapi,' he said. I was drinking water from a bottle.
'Drink up 'cause the Road to Freedom is long and hard and we ain't
done yet.'

Ziko had offered to be my guide across the border into Greece.
We would take our own cars and drive in convoy through the labyrinthine mountain passes. He would take me to a ruined monastery on
the other side, where a monk lived who was over a hundred years old.

Once, Ziko went to visit him in the middle of summer and it snowed, but only around the monastery. You'll never find him on your own, he said, and I believed him. So it was a deal.

When we said goodbye, Galen produced a small bottle of home-brewed raspberry wine from his rucksack and handed it to me.

'Next time, come and stay with us. We have a big empty house.'

Despite his inebriation, Ziko drove the steep single-lane road to the lower village in a straight line. We passed the Predator in his tweed jacket, the flock's bells chiming in the dusk. They were returning to the village. I turned to look at him.

He was an old man. A huge old man with white hair, like Moses.

Ziko laughed like a hyena, but said nothing.

That night I sat on my balcony and drank Galen's aromatic raspberry wine. Despite the cold fog I needed no blankets, and despite my exhaustion I couldn't rest. It was the new sensation under my skin: there are beautiful places on earth where nobody is spared.

The shepherd unfortunate enough to see the German guy with the apples had been Jones's father. And the father's choice – if it had been a choice at all – was stamped onto the son's face. I mourned the German guy with the apples, his unlived life, his lonely death. Who was he? Who else mourned him? He was remembered by everyone in the Village Where You Lived For Ever, but nobody knew his name.

The night swallowed the village, window by window, until it was gone, and if it wasn't for the smell of woodsmoke, you could believe that no houses had ever been here. Only cold stars and distant barking dogs.

tale of two kingdoms

Once upon a time, there was a kingdom of the South and a kingdom of the North. What these kingdoms shared also divided them: a stretch of delicious land, some navigable waters, and an inflated ego. In short, the border.

The South was gloriously Mediterranean and its city-states invented European scripture, thought, philosophy, and religion at a time when Europa was still a girl abducted by Zeus under a bull's guise. Later, Europe was ascribed a physical location in the writings of Strabo: it began at the Hemus mountain. And Hemus was the North. The kingdom of the North wasn't actually a kingdom to start with. It remained for a while pagan, divided, and wild, ruled by khans and shamans who had arrived on horseback across the steppes. In order to be on a par with the great powers, the North took the religion of the South and therefore of Europe. Although it retained the harshness and wildness of the mountains, once consolidated by religion the North rose to be a vivid civilisation with its own scripture, art, and culture. And therein lay the border trouble.

At regular intervals, the two kingdoms slaughtered each other's people and declared definitive victory. An emperor of the North called Krum had a cup made from the skull of his rival Nicephorus, and drank from it for the rest of his short life. Despite that cup, he was the only ruler of the North ever to order the uprooting of vines (there is no information on whether the edict was carried out). An emperor of the South called Basil was so obsessed with the North that in one victorious battle he had fifteen thousand soldiers of the North blinded and led back to their emperor Samuil by a handful of one-eyed men. Samuil died of shock, and the emperor of the South died lonely and unloved even by his own subjects. He was the only ruler of the South ever to forgo intimate relationships. And so it went, with brief periods of horrible sanity during which both glimpsed the pleasures of peace and neighbourliness and the waste of the wars that went before. Until the next war. It's as if neither could rest until it devoured the other, and since the South was bigger and richer, that's what it did, for a time. But only for a time.

The East put an end to this by colonising both kingdoms, and the delicious land and navigable waters had to be shared under the new overlords. In the empire of the East, the Northerners were typically cattle herders and craftsmen, the Southerners were typically merchants, and somehow they got along and even mingled, though not their Churches: the Church of the South was always trying to devour the weaker Church of the North, the Church being the main organ of power in the East-subjugated kingdoms. When eventually the decaying empire of the East was pushed back with help from the West and the rising empire of the North-East, the ghost of the border reawakened, and South and North were at each other's throats again.

When you look back, it seems like a see-saw effect: when the North was up, the South was down, and vice versa. While in the later twentieth century the North was frozen in the long icy winter brought by the conflict between the West and the North-East, the South had enjoyed a season in the sun, propped up by the West. But the fact remained that they were always joined by the border, and would forever bear the brunt in the see-saw game of greater interests. Herodotus, a man of the South but also a man of the known world, wrote: 'Human happiness never remains long in the same place.' By extension, the same must go for unhappiness, and we must find hope in this. And now?

Now I was crawling down a serpentine road from north to south, behind Ziko's old BMW with its screechy brakes, hoping that neither of us would have to scrape the other off the bottom of the hill.

DRAMA

Although you could draw a straight line from Drama to Ziko's village across the border as the crow flies, the disconnected old road meant that the nearest checkpoint took hours of circuitous driving. Next to the abandoned military post on the Bulgarian side, an old board for hanging jackets was still nailed to a birch tree.

Spring had arrived in this part of the Rhodope. Deer jumped out of the dense canopy and woodcocks brushed the heads of the bored border police who stood basking in the spring sun. This was a small, recently opened checkpoint, little used because the roads were not for the faint-hearted. The border police waved us through – eventually.

'How come they searched my car but not yours?' I asked Ziko. He laughed.

'Because they've already seized everything I've got. If there's anything interesting, it'll be in your car.'

After the checkpoint, the road spilled down the mountain slopes at such a gradient that it was a wonder of gravitation to remain attached to the surface. We drove through secretive Greek Pomak villages that Ziko described as 'a wasteland of lemonade'. Women and girls wore headscarves, alcohol was not sold within many miles, and a spirit of puritanism hung over the scrubbed streets. Ziko felt no affinity with the Greek Pomaks, they were too pious for him, and we drove through villages without stopping. When we finally stopped to get some water, the locals in the street looked at our cars with cautious curiosity.

'Ziko,' I said, 'what do you make of the modern Greek theory that the Pomaks are originally Thracians, from the ancient Greek *pomax*, meaning drinker, meaning Thracian?'

Ziko looked at me in dismay. 'What do I make of it? Bollock soup. Come on, there's nothing here for us.'

Huge houses and mosques clung to the hillsides. Although people still spoke a Bulgarian or Macedonian dialect, they did so only in private, because anything that had a non-Greek whiff was suppressed by the nervous state.

Nervousness is the true reason why the long-awaited road between Pomak villages across the border has not been opened twenty years since it was first discussed. The road that would be overseen by the Judgement cliff. The road that would reconnect Pomaks across more than half a century of border blues.

Just as the communist Bulgarian state had been paranoid that the Pomaks were the fifth column of Turkey and Orientalism, the Greek state had been paranoid that the Pomaks were the fifth column of Bulgaria and communism. To reflect the paranoia of each state, in the second half of the twentieth century the names of Bulgarian Pomaks had been Slavicised (that is, de-Islamicised), while the names of Greek Pomaks had been Turkicised (that is, de-Slavicised). Do you follow?

Exactly. Hellenised and Slavicised, exoticised and demonised, homogenised and revised by South and North, fed up with promises about roads that never materialised, the Pomaks here had turned to the East. True, the East was now telling them that they were Turks, and possibly the oldest Turks on earth, the very vanguard of Turkishness. True, this seems like a throwback to the old blurring of ethnos and religion which has given so much grief to so many until so recently, but then nationalism is like that – it won't just let people be.

The original Slavic–Bulgar dialect of the Pomaks was called by the Greeks 'Pomak language', a fabrication as linguistically void as it was politically transparent. At least the East had something to offer the Pomaks: the certainty of Islam. There were three hundred mosques in tiny Greek Thrace. At the Xanthi–Drama fork in the road, the mosques stopped and churches began to appear.

Two huge factories welcomed the visitor to Drama, but I couldn't tell whether they were still in use. At the other end of the city was the old railway station of Drama, standing unloved like all terminuses of history. Hefty tobacco fortunes had been loaded up here for the ports of Thessaloniki and Kavala, from where ships sailed on to Germany, Britain, America, and Egypt.

By the end of the nineteenth century, the hills of Macedonia were producing huge quantities of tobacco. International hunger for the mild, aromatic 'Oriental tobacco' that grew here dislodged the taste for American-grown Virginia. As with the *Rosa damascena*, the unique properties of the crop were to do with soil and climate, a cross of soft Aegean and cool Balkan. The tobacco trade had become so mega-lucrative that in 1884 a British vice-consulate was set up in Drama. Some of the richest merchants of the Ottoman Empire had lived in the old town, in beautiful painted mansions by the river, next to the tobacco warehouses and the bubbling springs of the city's patron saint Varvara that were used in Byzantine times for cotton-dyeing and spinning mills. It was said that Saint Varvara was so outraged by the (successful) attempt to convert her church into a mosque that she flooded the whole neighbourhood with the thundering waters of her springs.

'This place is called, in the tongue of the infidel Christians, Dirama,' our 'boon-companion to mankind' Evliya wrote in 1667. 'The canvas of Dirama is famous, and is made from a choice variety of cotton grown on the plain. In a word, this city prospers. May God protect it!'

In his day, the city had twelve mosques and seven *mescit*s, mosques without minarets, many of which were of course converted Byzantine churches. With the Ottomans gone, the minarets were lopped off. Today, the Saint Varvara Church is inlaid with a commemorative stone dated 1912, when the city officially became Christian again. But this hopeful stone marked the beginning of a turbulent twentieth century for Drama.

One of the darkest chapters came when the tobacco warehouses of Macedonia and Thrace were used to herd the Jewish population of the region on their way north to Treblinka. The 11,343 Jews of Drama, Kavala, Xanthi, Serres, and the rest of Macedonia never returned, and British diplomatic attempts to rescue 4,500 Jewish children from this region failed, thanks to a combination of callousness and spineless-ness in the Bulgarian monarchy. The sealed-up trains of horror that started here passed through Bulgaria, where outraged ordinary people at railway stations tried to intervene. The deportations were energet-ically executed by the occupying Bulgarians, who allied themselves to the Axis powers for two reasons – a revanchist bid on the rest of Macedonia and Thrace, and total economic dependency on Germany. The two were connected through tobacco – the number one regional export product. Some of the major tobacco merchants were Jewish, and one of the most prominent, the Sofia-based Asseoff, escaped to the USA with his family and part of his fortune on a tobacco ship, in the nick of time.

In Bulgaria, thanks to public opposition and the courageous acts of church metropolitans and MPs (some of them communists), the Nazi-allied Bulgarian monarchy halted the deportation of its own Jews, though it didn't lift a finger to help the Jews of Bulgarian-occupied Macedonia and northern Greece. Much has been made of the physical salvation of the 48,000 Bulgarian Jews, but the anti-Semitic laws that were imposed disenfranchised them permanently, from the key tobacco merchants like Asseoff to the workers in the tobacco fields and warehouses. The result?

'World War II furthered... the unravelling of the complex ethnic tapestry of the eastern Balkans by pulling out the Jewish thread,' wrote Mary Neuburger in *Balkan Smoke*. And just as the Nazi-allied Bulgarian state of the 1940s pulled out the Jewish thread from tobacco and society, the Soviet-allied Bulgarian state of the 1980s pulled out the Turkish thread. It's a melancholy miracle that both North and South still have the odd ragged bits of this once-rich human tapestry. And that the odd Oriental leaf still grows.

Drama was in the blossom of spring and in the depths of economic collapse. The snowy peaks of the western Rhodope rose behind it with a majesty made poignant by bankruptcy. The old town was flooded (again) by the angry springs of Saint Varvara, and the merchant mansions stood crumbling next to the rotting tobacco warehouses. In the old lanes, still redolent of Oriental commerce, every second shop was boarded up. The oldest mosque gaped roof-less and full of weeds. A century of rain hadn't managed to fully wash off the painted murals, naive fourteenth-century scenes of fusion cities – Drama, Constantinople, and some other place that only existed in the mind of the artist. In the central square, a red sign saying SYRIZA had been spray-painted, then crossed out. The red KKE banners of the Greek Communist Party headquarters watched over café patrons as they perfected the art of making a single coffee last all afternoon.

Nikos lived with his parents in a house at the end of St Constantine Street. Nikos was Ziko's friend. They'd known each other for twenty years.

'He's like my father,' Ziko said. 'He knew me when I still didn't speak Greek.'

Nikos was not expecting us and didn't know what to make of me.

'I like to surprise him,' Ziko winked, 'just like he turns up on my doorstep out of the blue, hehe.'

I wasn't even sure why we'd come to Drama, since the ruined monastery Ziko had promised to show me was back the way we'd just come.

Nikos was everything Ziko wasn't. A man of sixty with a heavy machismo, he must have been a looker before booze and lack of exercise had got to him. For twenty years, Nikos and his brother Alexandros had run a notorious bar in town – only single malts and vodka, no ouzo or cheap stuff, Ziko said.

I peered through the smoke. I was now supposed to spend the night here and a simple truth suddenly caught up with me: I was in the company of small-time dealers. We were sitting in Nikos's seedy lounge, a mix of bachelor den and domestic kitsch: leather bar stools, gilded mirrors, and in one corner, an icon of Saint Nicholas on a doily. Alexandros was here too, flipping his worry beads, while the Greek parliament shouted on the TV screen. Alexandros had a gold tooth and a charming, ambiguous smile. His basic English made me feel safer. He must be okay if he speaks English, surely!

Ziko's Greek was as fast and garbled as his Bulgarian, I could see it from the bemused faces of his Greek friends. By his own admission, 'My Greek is a bit patchy, but if I speak fast I figure they won't notice.'

'Those were the good times,' Nikos grinned darkly. 'Who would have thought Greece would come to this?'

'I'd sit there all night,' Alexandros reminisced, 'playing with my worry beads, with a bottle of Scotch. And the money would roll in.'

'At the end of the night, they'd take out the cash in a wheelbarrow,' Ziko said. Now Alexandros ran a small pasta restaurant, and Nikos didn't do anything.

Their parents lived upstairs. The father planted tomatoes while I sat in a garden chair in the quiet of the neighbourhood. At first he thought I was Ziko's girlfriend, then he thought I was some kind of general 'girl for the weekend', Ziko breezily explained later, then the father gave up guessing and I changed the subject: what about him?

He had been an andarte during the war and had regularly crossed into Bulgarian territory, but I couldn't work out which kind of andarte he meant: red (socialist–communist) or white (pro-government, royalist). There was a big difference; the two factions murdered each other and were at the root of the Greek Civil War. He knows loads of stories, Ziko promised, but the old man was in a grumpy mood.

'The people in the Bulgarian villages were good,' he said, 'but your occupying army were worse than the Turks.'

When a Greek says that something is 'worse than the Turks', you know it's bad.

And he turned back to his tomatoes with a wounded expression. Later, he told Ziko that I looked 'like a pure Christian'. It's a compliment, Ziko clarified, seeing my alarmed face.

By now, I was quite keen to find a hotel, but Nikos protested with such a sincerely hurt look that I stayed and slept in the guest room. It was adjacent to the lounge, where the drinking continued until midnight. The smoke seeped through the walls. I lay on one of the single beds in what had been the kids' room in some happier time, watched the smoke curl above my bed in the darkness, and worried. The phrase 'girl for the weekend' kept returning to me and this whole trip was starting to seem like a bad idea.

The next day, there was a change of plan. It was Nikos's birthday and we couldn't leave town after all.

Okay, I said, annoyed that I'd have to spend another day and evening with these two, I'll go and see the town then.

'You think I'd let you get lost?' Ziko said. 'No, I'm a responsible kind of guy.'

So they tagged along like invalid bodyguards: square-shaped Nikos and spindly Ziko, propping up each other's hangovers.

The crowd was circulating in the sun. Sellers out-shouted each other at the stalls which, unlike the boarded-up shops, were doing brisk business because nothing here cost more than a few euros. Ziko bought himself a fake red Costa tracksuit.

'Sporty yet elegant, that's me,' he said.

You're ready to go running, I said.

'Running? You think I'm mad?'

They could barely walk. On our way round the park, Nikos pointed to the flooded springs of St Varvara where they met the pink remains of the Byzantine cotton mills:

'There were swans here, but the Gypsies ate them. It's the crisis. Soon we'll be eating swans too.'

'Don't worry, bro,' Ziko said, 'we'll come up with a plan.'

Poor man's graffiti decorated the beautiful public sculptures. One said: 'I'm thinking of getting drunk, so when I'm drunk, I won't be thinking.'

Which is exactly what those two proceeded to do in the afternoon. Nikos sat receiving birthday guests in his lounge, thickset men of all ages in dark clothes, their faces overgrown with worries. Not a woman in sight. They drank, chain-smoked, coughed precancerously, ate pickled salads, flicked their worry-bead strings, and talked money and no money, schemes and cuts. The scene was oddly timeless, the men had thick Levantine features, and the absence of women gave the gathering an oriental feel. In fact, I was told by an elderly man in a mixture of Turkish, Greek, and Russian (he was an old communist who had fought in the Greek Civil War), many here were children and grandchildren of Asia Minor refugees, including him. After the death of his parents, he had gone to visit their birth-place, Smyrna, since they never stopped talking about it. And? I asked.

'And nothing,' he said and his eyes suddenly filled up. 'It's now called Izmir.'

The rest of the time, I was glad to be ignored in the corner. Have you locked your car? someone would turn to me occasionally and ask, you can't trust the Albanians round here! The Albanians were the least of my worries.

The booze was provided by Nikos, and I bought the food, expecting to learn something special, eventually, about life near the border.

Ziko put out a reassuring but blurry hand:

'Don't worry Kapi, as long as you're with me, you're safe.'

I suppose I *was* learning something special. Nikos and Ziko had been in woodcutting together, but that had dried up. They had dealt in hunting dogs. Ziko would bring them from his village to Nikos, who would then sell them here or in Turkey. But that too had slowed down. Now they thought about setting up a winery, but you needed capital for a start-up. What about those wheelbarrows of cash, I said, was any of that still around? Nikos and Ziko laughed.

I escaped the smoke den to check out two hotels in town. But they were closed, and on the way back to Nikos's house, I got lost in the leafy streets near the old railway. This trip was acquiring a dark hue. It all felt so different from the day out with the hunting party on the other side, and I didn't know anybody else on this side of the border.

Back in the house, Ziko and Nikos were in the late stages of lachrymose male bonding. They had been exchanging gifts. Ziko had given Nikos his prized hunting knife, and Nikos had given Ziko an outrageous striped velvet Italian suit, fit for a gigolo. They were both delighted and so drunk that they couldn't move from the couch.

Nikos's face was so red it looked boiled. Ziko was like stuffed straw inside his red tracksuit. He spoke very carefully:

'Now, Kapi, listen. There's a plan. Tomorrow…'

I slept badly in the smoke-infused guest room, while a bare-breasted woman stared at me from a poster on the back of the door.

In the morning, I gave Ziko *my* plan in a firm voice, while among the debris of the night, Nikos gallantly made me a mug of Greek coffee. Ziko didn't drink coffee. In his jail days he was the chief coffee maker because he alone could get coffee beans smuggled in, and now couldn't stand the taste of it.

And I could barely stand the way Ziko vanished and reappeared in unexpected places, babbling in his garbled languages, the hours and days like shifting sand beneath my feet, making me doubt everything now. He in turn complained that translating all my questions made him lose weight, while Nikos looked sick and tired of both of us. There was one place I wanted to see, though, and Nikos and Ziko grudgingly declared that they were coming along, as if they were doing me a favour. It was in this spirit that the three of us took our first and last drive together, in Ziko's BMW: west across the mountains to a hillside labyrinth on the border.

There was no traffic along the winding roads of Granite Valley, past sleepy villages called Stone and Granite, except for trucks loaded with giant cubes of marble headed for the port of Kavala. Drama lay in the shadow of a marble mountain. Ancient ore mines were still inside the hills, along with the new quarries that nibbled the many faces of the Rhodope like leprosy. Quarrying was the only thriving industry around here, and private fortunes were made from it, as they once had been with tobacco. Some hills were so badly hacked they were not long for this world.

We drove past abandoned military posts and shafts with buried dynamite that had been planted on the sides of the road in preparation for World War II, but that had also been handy during the Cold War. In the event of enemy invasion from the north, the road would be blown up, blocking the only access to the Greek interior on this side of the mountains. The dynamite was still there, Nikos said, and inside the hills were hundreds of fortified complexes. Some of them went on for miles inside the hills, and one of them was now open to visitors for the first time since World War II. This was where we were going. But it was only when we arrived at the foot of the fortified hill that Nikos said:

'In the 80s, I worked here.'

metaxas line

A military defence line 155 kilometres long that ran from the
Macedonian plains at the western end of the Greek–Bulgarian border,
along the Rhodope range, and down to the Aegean coast. The line
passed to the north of Drama and consisted of twenty-one military
fortifications. It was created as a defence against likely territorial
aggression from Bulgaria, sore from the earlier losses of Macedonia
and Thrace.

The fortifications were built with the help of English engineers
under the regime of General Ioannis Metaxas, who was no friend
of liberals, books, or minorities, but then it was the 1930s. In order
to 'hellenise' Macedonia, he had the Bulgarian and Macedonian
population of northern Greece deported to islands and labour camps;
others emigrated to the New World. The centrepiece of his corporate
paternalistic fascism was the grand, or *megali*, idea of manufacturing
a homogenised Greece with himself as father of the nation, in the
style of Atatürk. Metaxas went down in history for his famous '*Ohi!*'
or 'No!' to Nazi overtures. While Greek forces, including thousands
of Bulgarians and Macedonians from Greece, fought the Italians on
the Albanian front in March 1941, the Germans mounted an invasion
of Greece from the north. Had the British not been massed against
a plotted German landing on the shores of their own country, they

might have saved Greece. But British forces fled to Crete when the mainland fell – the first of two times in that decade that Britain let the Greeks down. The second was a few years later, during the Greek Civil War.

In April 1941, after apparent dithering, Bulgaria's Tsar Boris III decided that he would rather get into bed with the Germans than be ground down by their tanks. The tobacco-driven Bulgarian economy had been in the hands of German tobacco cartels for years, ever since Boris's father, the greedy and deluded Ferdinand, had dragged his country into war with its neighbours. The Bulgarian Saxe-Coburgs were dynastically linked to Germany, but that was the least of their shortcomings. Two years later, Boris would die suddenly after a meeting with Hitler, a clean death through which he escaped post-war judgement for his cabinet's war crimes abroad.

The German road to Greece was now open. The Nazis had promised Tsar Boris III the ultimate carrot: the rest of Macedonia and Thrace. On the same day, one million German soldiers crossed from Axis-power Romania into Bulgaria, and two days later they were here, at the start of the Metaxas Line. Against the massed German forces, a few thousand Greek soldiers held out inside the fort hills along the Metaxas Line for three days. Several of the forts refused to surrender even when the central Greek command surrendered in Athens. The high command shouted down the phone to embattled officers inside the bunkers who wouldn't come out. One particular gun post along the line was manned by a sergeant who single-handedly gunned down 232 German soldiers. When he ran out of ammunition, the German commander came to shake his hand. Then shot him.

*

There is a series of poignant photographs showing the surrender of Fort Lisse. As the Greek commander and his officers emerged from the anthill, the German field marshal congratulated the Greeks and ordered his soldiers to salute them. This field marshal later became known for savage reprisals and by all accounts was a maniac. But that April day in 1941, the surviving Greeks were let go under their own flag.

MOUNTAIN OF MADNESS, II

'Yeah, I worked here for a couple of years,' Nikos said evasively. 'Haven't been back since.'

Fort Lisse was a giant honeycomb. The tunnels went on for miles and it would take a full day to walk them all. Only a fraction of the bunker was accessible to visitors and I went in without Ziko, who said he wasn't a mole, and without Nikos, who didn't say why.

The tunnels were whitewashed. The commander and his adjutant's room, the dorms, the battle-viewing room, the communications room were here, fitted with original phone sets, maps, blankets, and uniforms – though the labels stitched on them said, oddly, '1989'.

It had been the job of soldiers and labourers like Nikos to dig out the debris left after the German attack and the Bulgarian dynamiting of surface structures along the Metaxas Line. The Bulgarians, ignominiously helping themselves to everything on the heels of the Germans, had wanted to reuse the steel from the concrete reinforcements, until they realised that the dynamite was costlier than the steel. The Germans were more methodical: they studied the forts in detail.

The reconstruction had begun in the 1970s, during Greece's junta known as the Regime of the Colonels, which persecuted those socialists and communists who hadn't died or fled in the Greek Civil War.

NATO funded and supported the project (as it supported the junta), and the idea was to refit the bunkers with modern weapons and living quarters for civilians, in the event of chemical or nuclear war. The threat from the north was still there, this time not with a swastika but with a hammer and sickle.

Now the plan was that the visitable part of the fort would be set up as an interactive games labyrinth for re-enacting the war through computer games in the bunkers. It would be called 'Follow the Fox' because Lisse was a derivative of the Slavic word for fox – like many place-names here, an echo of its ghostly Bulgarian past.

Bunkers, no matter how large, are not happy places. Within minutes, I was sweating in the heat of the artificial lights. You could almost hear the phone ringing with a voice from Athens shouting, 'Order to surrender!' You could almost smell the Oriental leaf that had kept them going. You could almost imagine that it was still happening, inside this time hole.

When I emerged from the hill, panting and faint in the dazzle of daylight, I found Ziko and Nikos photographing each other in front of a tank.

'There's a whole hospital in there,' Nikos said suddenly. 'I know because we built it. It's an underground city, but they'll never open it all up because they don't want you to know what's there.'

Why not? He shrugged and looked away.

From where we stood at the gates of the subterranean city, the plains opened up ahead like an avenue, and you could see how easy it had been for the German tanks to roll this way – as easy as it would have been for the Soviet tanks. And how desperately heroic the Greek defence had been.

What defeated Fort Lisse in the end was an aeroplane attack from the rear, on the side we couldn't see.

Ziko blinked in the sun, moved.

'War is total bollocks, man,' he concluded.

'One day,' Nikos said suddenly, 'I was clearing a tunnel at the far end. It was lunchtime and the others had popped up for a bite. That's when I saw something.'

What thing? I said.

'Something that looked like a person,' Nikos said heavily, 'but wasn't.'

Ziko looked completely sober.

'That's why I'm not going down there again,' Nikos said. 'There's madness in there. Madness gets trapped.'

'Let's hit the road.' Ziko started rushing. 'This place gives me the shits.'

After saying goodbye to Nikos in Drama, his relief as great as mine, our two-car convoy hit the road again, this time north-east, to what Ziko said was the last village before the border. It was just opposite his village on the other side, like a mirror image, only derelict. The monastery was nearby, he said.

'It really is the back of beyond. Go missing there and you'll never be found.'

For some reason, I didn't like the sound of that.

Ziko's mood changed on leaving Nikos. He looked shiftier than ever. Along the road, I noticed several brand-new BMWs with tinted windows and Greek registration plates. They travelled in a sinister convoy. At one point, they stopped in a lay-by, and as I passed them, I saw the drivers wave to Ziko, who drove ahead of me. They were men in dark shades. Why were they waving? Just a clubby BMW wave, I tried to tell myself.

By the time I'd parked my car outside a quiet marble hotel where I planned to stay at the top of a little village and took a seat in Ziko's BMW for our ride to the monastery, I felt things were slipping. No, things *had* slipped. But I'd be damned if I wouldn't see the monastery with that monk!

And now we were heading up the twenty kilometres of dead-end. Before us went two other BMWs.

'Where are they going?'

'Visiting someone,' Ziko shrugged, but there was no one to visit up that road.

Everything about him and Nikos was dodgy, I saw that now. They were desperate for cash, they were men of transactions, and I was out of my depth. As he strained his engine up the hill, I tried to make light conversation, but my stomach was in a knot.

'Ziko,' I said brightly, 'after this, it's bye-bye, 'cause we're finished here.'

He glanced at me darkly. He seemed like a different person from the sunny Ziko who'd shown me the Road to Freedom. Maybe it was just a hangover.

'Bollocks,' he said. 'The party's just beginning.'

I could get out now. We were only halfway. We passed an abandoned logging station, then we passed nothing. Absolutely nothing.

A huge canyon opened over the river, which was so far below I couldn't see it. Metamorphic peaks all the way ahead, a hell of granite disguised as a valley. The road was a slim ribbon clinging to the side of the mountain. I felt sick in several different ways. It wasn't Ziko himself I feared, it was his judgement of where to draw the line with other more malevolent forces.

A sign said: 'Warning: Dangerous Turns Ahead!'

I said: 'Ziko, I don't want to go to that village any more.'

'What?' he said. 'We're almost there. Nikos has a house up here, he asked me to have a look at it for him.'

The house had been mentioned before but only sounded like bad news now. Nobody knew I was here except Ziko and Nikos. I checked my mobile phone – no signal of course. The signal stopped once you passed the last building, the marble hotel where I had left my car and my sanity, or what remained of it.

We drove the rest of the way in silence. Starved-looking cows nearly crashed into the car. I had never felt so certain of imminent doom.

'We're here,' Ziko said, and pulled over with a screech.

We had reached the village at the top where the road ended. I got out. There was a water fountain that didn't work, an overgrown church, and houses with empty windows. It was a phantom village, and below it, the blue abyss of the canyon.

There is no silence like the silence of abandoned human dwellings.

'Don't drink from the fountain,' Ziko said flatly. 'Water's full of uranium.'

Maybe that's what killed off all the residents, I thought in a distant way.

'That's Nikos's house.' He took out a bunch of keys and unlocked a rusty gate. While he did this, I checked the ignition, but he'd taken the key with him.

The house was some distance from the gate and it looked derelict like the rest. The garden was full of wild flowers, knee-high. Red-tracksuited Ziko waded into the flowers and before my staring eyes, somewhere between the gate and the house, he vanished. He just wasn't there any more.

'Ziko?' I croaked, but not with any hope. 'Ziko?'

A curse fell over the scene. Time stopped, my heart stopped. Then I woke up and broke into a run, down the steep road. I'd never run like this in my life: like an animal, with astonishing speed and just one part of my brain working, the part called 'flight'.

The road snaked at angles that made it visible from higher up; this was not a road to hide on, and soon they would come down looking for me, whoever they were. The phantoms of the uranium village, the BMW drivers who had waved. I climbed the steep forested hill above the road, praying for mobile reception. When I gave up on that, I continued scrambling through the forest parallel to the road.

Various scenarios about what Ziko was up to crossed my mind, all of them crazy and all of them possible. The old bean reader's words suddenly came to me: 'What you have started you will complete, but never ever ignore the signs.' I'd been lured into a scheme and failed to judge the signs until now, because this was not my world. This was not anybody's world. It was not a place to come to. The land itself hummed with malignant intent. Everything was set up to trap you. Were I to spend the night here, which looked inevitable if I didn't want to be spotted on the road, there was the issue of the wolves, the boar. Was it high enough for bears? The clothes stuck to my body with sweat.

The futility of my flight suddenly struck me. The long road I had travelled was revealed as what it was: a dead-end. But more than that, life itself was a dead-end, and the border had delivered this simple truth to me, bodily.

It had happened to others before, why not me? The border was an equaliser. No one was too exceptional to die a stupid death. I was running to safety, but somehow getting closer to the German guy with the apples. Because he would have walked this exact road, his hunting knife folded in his pack, had he not stopped to eat those apples in the meadow, had the shepherd made a different choice, had the world been a better place. Galen's words rang in my head like a prophecy: 'Sometimes you just come to the end of the road and it's over.'

Still no cars. The scratchy forest emanated heat like radiation. No birds, no movement, no water except at the bottom of that ravine on the other side of the road. I could hear it now, which meant I was making a real descent. Crazy hope surged in me. Could I cover twenty kilometres by running?

The thought of Ziko never left me. In the event that my paranoia had fabricated this, he'd be panicking. But then he wasn't coming down in the car. No, he was up there getting beaten by the thugs in the BMWs for letting me slip away. It was his destiny to deal, smuggle, sell, and to get beaten by thugs larger than him. Surely if he really wanted to find me, he'd guess I'd headed down towards the hotel.

Oh, the world of hotels, a cold Coke, and the company of those who were not phantoms or dealers. All that seemed on the other side of something impassable. If I survive this, I must leave the border area immediately, go home to Scotland, lie down in a dark room, and give up. I passed the sign that said 'Warning: Dangerous Turns Ahead'. The blisters on my feet were popping like bubble wrap. Then I came to a point in the road where the river looked reachable. I crossed it and there, tucked under the road, was a beaten-up Land Rover. A dog barked. At the river, a woman and two men were loading up a small boat. I stopped and stared, not trusting my vision.

They were loading it with loaves of bread. Dozens and dozens of loaves of bread. I had stumbled into a biblical tableau. Were there fish too? Would they walk on water?

One of the men actually had a fallen Jesus look about him. Both men were long-haired and wore old faded clothes, like hippies. The woman saw me first and came over to me. She had a warm face and long dark tresses. Never was a face such brilliant news. I realised I hadn't spoken to a woman for days. The Jack Russell puppy at her feet sniffed my boots and looked up quizzically.

'What's happened to you?' the woman said in Greek then in English. I opened my mouth to explain, and long barking sobs came out, not human.

The woman gave me a bottle of water and invited me to their house on the other side of the river. They were setting up for summer, she said, and gave me a hug.

'It's okay,' she said. 'Everything will be okay.'

In the boat there were four of us plus the puppy, the bread, and some geese in a cage. The boat was the only way to their one-room summer hut camouflaged by forest. From the road, you'd never guess there was a house.

In the forest behind was an immense waterfall and a swimming hole. Chickens pecked at seeds. A paradise of lemon balm and fig trees.

The woman's name was Marta. The two men were, rather improbably, Orfeus and Achilles, and they were makers of things, including this house. Orfeus was in his forties but had a drastically aged face and blue eyes of such unnerving kindness that it was a test to look into them. His eyes seemed to say, 'Hey, don't cry over this little bit of life. Don't you know that all of life is tears?'

Marta made herbal tea with honey, and Orfeus gave me a roll-up and smiled with stained teeth – at me, at everything, because you had to. I finally regained my speech. They told me that a man from Drama did have a house at the top, and came to hunt with male parties, but their worlds never intersected. They couldn't understand how I'd ended up with these people.

But they weren't bad people. Were they?

This episode has a happy end and a sad end. The sad end came when I found Ziko waiting outside the hotel, his BMW parked next to my car. He looked like death. Death in a red tracksuit.

'K-K-Kapi,' he said, and his chin shook.

Marta had driven me from the hut to the hotel. She exchanged a few curt words with Ziko and left. Later that week, when I saw the three by the waterfall again, Marta said: That guy's Greek was incomprehensible, are you sure he speaks it?

I wasn't sure of anything.

Ziko had searched for me for hours, thinking I'd gone into one of the empty houses, or run the other way, up towards the border forest where we'd walked with Jones and Galen. He thought I'd fallen into the ravine. He thought I'd gone to report him to the border police. His voice was hoarse from shouting. He'd seen himself in jail, this time a life sentence. He had felt as desolate as me.

I was racked with guilt and confusion.

He said he could understand that I'd freaked out.

'It's the m-m-mountain,' he said, 'it drives you nuts. Unless you have three hearts.'

'I don't have three hearts,' I said. I barely had one.

And because there was nothing left to say, I paid him the agreed fee before he set off for the long drive back to the Village Where You Lived For Ever.

'You wanted to see the Road to Freedom,' he said, before he slipped into his car.

'I've seen it now,' I said.

'E-e-exactly,' he said, and I thought I could see tears rolling down his face.

'Will you forgive me?' I asked, suddenly appalled by his face; he seemed to have lost half his body weight in a few hours. And I was appalled with myself: that my good intentions had backfired, that I had made a mess of things, that it wasn't just Ziko who was full of shadows, I was too, and my shadows were even more treacherous than his because they were undeclared. He owned up to everything he did in life, but I had projected my own darkness onto him, asked him to carry the weight, and now wanted him to absolve me of it all, so I could be light and clean again. Though I only figured this out later.

He waved magnanimously from the car seat.

'I've forgiven worse. But what really hurts is that in the end, I wanted you to feel safe with me, but you just couldn't trust me, could you?'

In this mountain, I couldn't even trust myself.

agonia

It isn't just Greece, the whole world is in *agonia*, Orfeus said.

Orfeus had lost his restaurant job in Thessaloniki at the same time
as his marriage collapsed, along with the Greek economy. His wife
kicked him out, and for a while he slept on benches, rummaged in
bins, and woke with the gulls at dawn. He would watch them circle
over the White Tower of his city, whitewashed more than once of
its previous crimes. That was three years ago. Since then, he'd been
living here, in his friends' summer hut. In winter, the hut was buried
in snow. The waterfall froze, the dead-end road became impassable.
Inside the hut was a wood stove and a guitar. In summer, when
his friends came with their kids, he moved to another hut, with
mineral springs. And because the world is in *agonia*, he said, it's good
to be here. It's good to be forgotten. A garden, a few animals, water.
What more do you need? Orfeus smiled and his blue eyes tested
me gently.

Agonia: from the Greek *agon*, contest. The origin of agony is competition, struggle. To be in agony is to measure yourself against others,
a Sisyphean task. Perhaps agony is the very definition of being in the
world and playing by its rules.

★

Marta, Orfeus, and Achilles were opting out. Like Gergana the white-legged maiden, they were simply saying This is good enough. They'd built their hut on the invisible side of the river because they didn't want to depend on euros, Marta said, or people. Marta ran her own business. Her husband Achilles was a builder and maker of things. Others would join them by the waterfall, until there was a small community.

Perhaps all utopias begin like this. But utopias only fail because they end up imitating what they reject: agony. And the hut by the waterfall felt to me pretty close to ecstasy.

HOTEL ABOVE THE WORLD

The myth goes that Nessos the centaur worked as the river ferryman. He was a good ferryman, but after ferrying Deianeira across, he was seized with lust and tried to abduct her. To stop him, her husband Heracles shot him with a poisoned arrow from the other side, which was a bit rich because Heracles himself was a skirt-chaser and had once rather carelessly killed his own children. As he lay dying on the banks of his river, Nessos told Deianeira that his blood had magical properties and would ensure that Heracles was faithful to her for ever. She believed him and gave Heracles a robe anointed with the centaur's blood, which duly poisoned him. So this becomes a story of how the more you grab, the further it slips from you, a realistic story of everyday agonia. All the protagonists are left with less than what they had.

Named after the unfortunate centaur and overlooking the Nestos–Mesta River, the hotel sat above the world in the Rhodope hills. It was built in wealthier times from beautiful marble hacked from the mountains. Once you crossed onto this side of the river, that was it. The hotel was a portal to nowhere. Or rather, to where the canyon plunged deeper and the road began its climb to the border and the phantom village.

I had holed up here for a few days, in a room with a heart-stopping view over the valley and the hills beyond. After the freak-out with

Ziko, a curious sensation came over me. I had crossed a line within myself.

As if this was some kind of afterworld and I'd been reborn in a place where everything looked too beautiful, everything tasted too delicious, and I was stunned by the way the morning light seeped through the curtains.

In short, it was good to stay put and avoid sudden movements. I spent a lot of time sitting on my balcony staring into the plunging valley of vapours as if I'd find the answers to all my questions there.

But what I found below the hotel was a maximum-security refugee camp that glinted in the sun with its new wire, the same shiny wire that made the new wall between Greece and Turkey. The inmates were young men from Asia and the Middle East who had crossed the Evros River after their ferrymen, the traffickers in Turkey, had shown them a crossing point or just taken their money and pushed them in.

They had been definitively refused asylum, but Greece was not legally allowed to send them back. In the wasteland of days and nights that led absolutely nowhere, they kicked a ball and washed and dried their clothes on the barbed wire. If you stood by the giant rosemary bushes outside the hotel, which released their aroma in the afternoon, you heard an invisible man clear his throat and begin a low, mellow chant: *Allahu Akbar*, God is great. On Sunday, the church bells tolled loudly and often, a territorial sound that rang strangely hollow.

It was the hotel that fed the refugees, twice a day: croissants and milk for breakfast, and for dinner, cauldrons of spaghetti, soup, bean stew. It was tasty food and I ate what was left – because I was the only guest.

Actually, there were two others: a couple who never emerged from their room next to mine, and who didn't seem to eat, only smoke. They never made a sound and had the furtive air of runaway lovers too depressed even to make love. She spoke to me once, when we were on our balconies, but I never saw him. She was from a village over there, she pointed to the other side of the river valley, and though she lived in the coastal city full of traffic jams and heart attacks, she dreamt of returning to the valley.

Down in the marble lobby with packed bookshelves and crystal chandeliers that were never lit, the hotel owners and the cook sat in the gloom, smoked, and watched the news. The news was people falling out of boats on Greek islands.

Stefania sighed. Goran shook his head.

'We are the back door,' he said. 'The Germans give us money to feed them and keep them here. We feed them, and they wait. But there is nothing before them. The only way is back.'

'But they can't go back,' Stefania said.

'It's nice to cook for someone,' Eleni said matter-of-factly, 'but I want to feed a hotel full of guests, not refugees.'

Eleni the cook had worked in Germany for fifteen years, and although she loved it here, she was thinking of going back.

'Feel the air?' she said to me outside while picking rosemary from the giant bushes. 'Nice isn't it? But you can't live on air.'

Stefania and Goran were a local couple. I spent the evenings sitting with them in the crepuscular lounge, above the valley of vapours, as they received friends and discussed the future of Greece. From the panoramic terrace you could see how the village had sprung up around the railway, which had once carted tobacco leaves grown on these slopes. In the evenings, you could make out the blur of a small cargo train covered in colourful graffiti. It moved so slowly, you could hop on. But where would you go, and what did it carry now – hope, perhaps, naked hungry hope?

'A cartoonist was asked about the future of Greece,' Goran said and stubbed out his cigarette. 'And the cartoonist said: We have a great past. You can't ask for everything.'

Everybody laughed the way you laugh when it's not funny.

Goran had the air of a distracted intellectual. He would head to the bar to make an espresso but return without the espresso. He seemed perpetually caught out by reality. Nothing seemed to get done here, but then nothing seemed urgent. The hotel dwelled in a space halfway between despair and leisure.

Stefania had a mobile face. She made you feel as if you had always been part of the hotel and always would be, even though, she said, not looking at me, up here by the border, we feel very hurt about the Bulgarian occupation in the war.

'I'm truly sorry about that,' I said.

'And also about the Turks,' she added, but I didn't feel I could apologise on behalf of Turkey.

Stefania was the grandchild of refugees from Turkey. In the wake of the Greek–Turkish War, her grandparents – then children – were exiled with their large families from the fertile hills of Cappadocia, and joined one and a half million Anatolian Greeks on their journey west. Muslims from Greece travelled the other way. Greece simultaneously expelled half a million Bulgarian-speakers. It was harvest time. In Balkan tragedies, it is always harvest time.

Stefania's family abandoned houses, lands, animals, and sailed from Smyrna to Piraeus. But in the melee at Piraeus, officials didn't let all the families disembark and they sailed on to Thessaloniki. From there, they moved north and eventually settled in these border villages, newly vacated by the Bulgarians (including Pomaks fleeing to Turkey). Compared with Cappadocia, it was cold and poor here, and they were homesick for the rest of their lives. As she spoke, Stefania's face moved in a sudden way. Someone had brought back a handful of earth from the ground of their former church in Cappadocia, and Stefania had put the earth on her grandparents' graves.

'In the other world at least they'll be reunited with the land of their childhood.'

Night had fallen. The crickets were so loud in the rosemary bushes, I imagined them the size of horses. The lights in the refugee camp below were out; not a sound came from the cells.

Inside the camp, which had been a border army base for decades, Stefania's great-grandfather had a commemorative plaque. He'd been a teacher, and along with several other men in the family, ended up murdered by the occupying Bulgarians. Stefania's family had sailed to Europe only to walk into a deadly border conflict that wasn't theirs – for they were of Asia Minor, not of here. The occupying Bulgarians, many of whom were born in this region and expelled a generation before, at harvest time, had gone from victims to executioners. They had taken revenge on the wrong people. But that is the nature of revenge: somehow, it is always taken on the wrong people.

'That's why we don't like the Bulgarians,' Stefania concluded. 'And the Turks. Would you like another bowl of jam?'

'On the other hand, it would be nice to have our neighbours visit,' Goran said peaceably. 'Bulgarians, even Turks. But I suppose they have their own mountains.'

'The thing that bugs me,' Stefania put a bowl of plum jam before me, 'is that in 1923, they had to choose between faith and language. They chose faith.'

Her family had not been Greek-speakers. Theirs was a hybrid language called Karamanlithike: Turkish written in Greek characters, whose name came from the Anatolian dynasty of the Karamanids, overrun by the Seljuk Turks early on.

Perhaps her family could have chosen language over faith, converted to Islam, and kept their life there?

Stefania shook her head. 'The whole point was that their choice only looked like choice,' she said.

'Would you like another espresso?' Goran said amiably and rose from the couch, but by the time he got to the bar, he had forgotten.

★

When I asked Goran and Stefania about the monastery that Ziko had meant to show me, Goran looked mildly surprised. But he always looked mildly surprised.

'I've heard of it,' Stefania said. 'The old Bulgarian monastery. But I've never been there. Nobody's been there. The hillside is over-grown. You'd have to access it from the river, impossible.'

'But what about the monk?' I said. Stefania's face moved suddenly.

'There's no monk. Nobody has lived there since the Civil War.'

'On the other hand,' Goran said from his fog of smoke, 'if you haven't been there, you don't really know, do you?'

Others in the village had heard of the monastery, but when I asked around if someone could take me there, people looked at me as if to say: Aren't things hard enough already?

I sometimes imagine the ruined monastery with its undying monk and snow storms in midsummer where only Ziko knows the way, and where I'll never be ferried, or not on a return ticket. Because Hermes the *polytropos*, the many-shaped one, trickster god of borderlands, passage, communication, and miscommunication, is also the one who conveys you to the Underworld, when your time comes. That is why he wears his shoes backwards.

ursus arctos

In all my years as a mountain ranger, I've only seen a bear once, Ioanna said. Not even seen, heard. The bear was here, inside the ruin. For once, I was patrolling on my own because my colleague was off sick. I heard the bear on my way up the track and guessed it was a mature male. I turned and walked back to the Jeep, very quietly! The Jeep was a long way down so I kept reminding myself that bears don't want contact with humans, why would they?

The destruction of habitats has led to the extinction of the brown bear in most of Europe, with the exception of Scandinavia and the Balkans, Ioanna said. This part of the Rhodope range has the last of the *Ursus arctos*. On the Bulgarian side, the population is significant, but on the Greek side only a few hundred individuals remain and bear-hunting has been banned for twenty years now. Until the fifteenth century, the brown bear was common across the continent, except in Britain, where it was hunted to extinction by the tenth century. Although it was carnivorous at the time when the Romans used it for gladiatorial games, the disappearance of habitats forced it into vegetarianism, with the exception of the odd sheep and cow of course.

That's why, Ioanna said, when I say this mountain is dangerous, I don't mean the bears. I mean the humans.

GODDESS OF THE FOREST

Ioanna and I were sitting inside the ruined fortress of Kalyva, watching a hawk circle above. I had met Ioanna after I'd mentioned to Goran and Stefania that I was looking for a local guide with some English.

We sat with our backs to the so-called Priapus gate where a slab had been removed in the nick of time before treasure hunters got to it, with the carving of a hugely erect Priapus. The image of tumescence was meant by the ancients to either welcome or repel, depending on the visitor.

Ahead of us, the Nestos valley opened up like a dubious invitation. And all around was the oak forest, awakening from winter with its bears and beasties, its abandoned drove roads and initialled trees, its marked and unmarked graves. We had abandoned my car at the bottom of the hill where the old drove road couldn't go any further and you had to clamber up the stone steps still visible under the moss.

The fortress had been built on top of the original Thracian settlement dating back nine centuries BC, and had been one of seven strategic posts along these ridges, used for the control of troops and equipment from Macedonia in the west to Thrace and Constantinople in the east. They'd communicated with fires called *friktories*. It marked the time before the Via Egnatia ran to the south, the time when 'barbarian' Macedonia headed by Alexander the Great had passed along here on its way east to engulf the known world, all the way to the banks of the Indus. Inside the threshold of the gate, a pair of carved human footsteps could still be traced in the stone – they had been placed here as magical guardians against enemy breach. Clearly, their magic had run out when Macedonia was overrun by the Romans. Later, local Thracians and incoming Herulians sacked these forts, and that's the state they have been in since the third century AD.

Kalyva meant simply Forest Hut, a basic wooden shack with one or two rooms and sometimes a stove or fireplace, used for centuries by Balkan transhumant shepherds.

To get here from the winding, tar-sealed mountain road, we had followed the drove roads deep in the forest. They connected with the old stone bridges, of course, and according to Ioanna, they were the best because they followed the natural contours of the land. She had spent years walking, studying, and mapping out the existing trails in this part of the Rhodope.

'The forestry have done something terrible,' Ioanna said. 'They've turned these ancient roads into forestry dirt roads, wrecking the natural trails and erasing the living history of the land.'

My small Renault wasn't made for such roads.

'It's okay, I'll turn it into a Jeep,' Ioanna said as she took over the driving, and somehow she made her way many miles into the forest without getting stuck once.

Ioanna was born the same year as me. She had grown up in Athens and studied English and American literature in Belgrade until the USA bombed it during the Kosovo conflict. Like all foreign students, she went home, her degree unfinished. She then lived in Thessaloniki and worked as a teacher, until she found that teaching wasn't for her, and nor was the family life of Sunday lunches with the in-laws that loomed on the ever-shrinking horizon. Ioanna had been married to a city lawyer who liked it that the future was foretold.

'I was thirty, and suddenly I saw that I wasn't living my own life. I was living some generic life already lived by millions of women.'

While still married, Ioanna had decided to go against her husband's wishes and do a course in fitness training, until she discovered that the sender of hundreds of abusive messages she'd been receiving had been her own husband. She cut him out of her life and left the city for good.

'I won't speak of it again,' she said, 'because it's not important any more. I made my own way, and when I look back, I'd always made my own way.'

She was an only child of conservative parents.

'They don't get the mountains. But I was made for the mountains,' she said. 'I'd always lived by the sea, but the mountains were in my blood.'

Ioanna believed herself to be descended from the Peloponnesian general Kolokotronis who led the Greek War of Independence against the Ottomans, and this belief had given her the support from within that she lacked from without.

'So I came here to the end of the world and threw myself into the forest. Everybody said You can't do it!'

She laughed, ha-ha!, a laugh I recognised.

'I love it when people tell me I can't do something. You can't drive that Jeep! You can't chainsaw that tree! You can't walk all that distance!'

Personal power rarely comes to a woman without a battle, and you could see both the power and the embattlement in her. Ioanna turned up and possessed the moment. She made you feel that anything was possible. And of course it was, why wouldn't it be? Earlier when we walked through the village by the railway line, the men in the cafés looked at us in our mountain gear and boots as if we were aliens, although they knew her, she lived by the church.

'My living and my love are here in the Rhodope,' Ioanna said. 'But can you imagine being an unmarried woman in a small place like this?'

I could, because in the eyes of the café-dwelling local men, I saw that they couldn't place me: I was not a mother–wife and I was not a whore, so what was I?

'Exactly,' Ioanna said. 'You've summed up my life here.'

The isolated nature of the Nestos valley, with its inward-looking villages, had shaped the character of the people, she said. Until the late 1990s, the Greek border army was still stationed here – a punishment post for young soldiers – and identity checks were frequent. People have remained closed, suspicious of outsiders, and when the refugee camp opened inside the old army base, the locals reacted in an ugly way, she said: they protested. And the longer she lived here, the more disconnected she felt from people and the more connected with the forest and its animals.

Maybe it was a border syndrome, I said.

'If it is, then that's the price.'

She lived with her dog, a German Shepherd. Her boyfriend lived in a coastal city and was one of the country's pre-eminent climbers. The previous winter, he had suffered a massive heart attack while climbing.

'It was only then,' Ioanna said, 'when his life hung in the balance, that I realised we were dangerously addicted. You see, climbing mountains wasn't enough for me. Olympus wasn't enough. Musala in Bulgaria wasn't enough. If three thousand metres isn't enough, what next?'

Next, she started rock climbing, partnered by her boyfriend. He had already done the Himalayas.

'So many times,' Ioanna said, 'I have looked down from the rock face and thought, I'll never get down alive. And when you do, it's the most exhilarating feeling. But it only takes once not to make it.'

Ioanna had glanced at me from behind the wheel. She knew about my freak-out two days before and had told me I had been mad to go up that road.

'You must be careful not to get addicted to story hunting,' she said. 'Because it's like rock climbing. It only takes once.'

Ioanna had brought me on one of her forest patrols. What did she patrol for? I asked.

'Poachers, illegal loggers, drug-dealers, immigrants,' she said.

Once she found a guy with a rucksack. She should have taken him to the police, but he looked so gaunt, so hunted, that she couldn't bear to add to his troubles and drove him to the nearest village, where she left him to his fate. She didn't even ask his name.

Ioanna knew not to become too involved. I could take a leaf from her book.

'I never ever go into the forest on my own,' she said. 'It's too dangerous. You can break a leg and die before anyone finds you. Or be mauled by a boar. Or assaulted by dodgy guys. Or you get a flat tyre and by the time you change it, it's dark.'

Ioanna could change a tyre in fifteen minutes. She could skin a rabbit, find water, and give you first aid. And she always carried a chainsaw in the back, because in winter the drove roads became obstructed by trees and it was her job to hack through them.

Ioanna's job sounded pretty dangerous to me. She was required to stop trespassers but wasn't armed, there was no mobile coverage, and the forest was so vast that anyone caught doing anything they shouldn't could disappear within minutes.

The forestry ranger service was new to Greece, and so were the twenty-eight national parks. Ioanna hadn't been paid for a year and a half because of the austerity measures. Things got so desperate that she decided to finally give treasure hunting a go. After all, treasure hunters came to her with maps all the time, and she was only human. I was amazed she hadn't tried it earlier. So when she was given a map with irresistibly precise instructions, she went for it.

'With a female friend,' she said, 'because you never ever go into the forest alone, did I mention that?'

Throughout the 1940s, until they withdrew their support and left their Greek protégés to their sad fate, British pilots dropped money, guns, mines, and sometimes themselves into the border forest, in support of the leftist andartes. But the andartes of ELAS (Greek People's Liberation Army) were hopelessly outnumbered by the American-backed government army and were eventually betrayed by their faux friends Tito and Stalin. As the outcome of the Greek Civil War became clear, tens of thousands of guerrilla survivors crossed into Bulgaria and Albania, and from there to the rest of world. It was the first actual war of the Cold War.

Now, here's what happened in the forest to excite treasure hunters, Ioanna told me. When an andarte went looking for food and provisions from the nearest villages on either side of the border – including our Village Where You Lived For Ever – he or she would bury the payment under a stone and mark it. It was too risky to carry it on yourself all the way. Some of that money remained under the marked stones, as messengers died in the forest, or the procurers never found the money.

'So,' Ioanna said, 'we went to this spot in the forest, with the map.'

The instructions were: find the stone with the carved crown on it. They did. Walk seven metres east of the stone until you see a stone with an owl scratched on it. They did. Then you find the old Muslim graves, and that's where the buried treasure is. But it wasn't, Ioanna said. We looked for it all day. We never found the Muslim graves.

A few months later, when she was patrolling the area, she found that the stone with the carved crown had been removed and a big hole gaped underneath. Someone had come digging after her. They probably found something, she said, because every adult male in this area has hunted for treasure at least once in his life and some are successful. Very successful. When we went back down to the village, Ioanna pointed out a dashing guy in a leather hat sitting at a café, surrounded by other men. They call him Crocodile Dundee, he's a treasure hunter, she whispered to me, a successful one. Dundee waved to her and beckoned us to join them, but Ioanna politely declined with a wave. She preferred to keep her distance.

Meanwhile, back in the forest, we had come to a cave. It seemed to go deep inside the hill.

'Where are you going?' she called, but I was already inside the entrance which led into a tunnel. She laughed.

'Jesus! It's good to find someone as mad as me,' she said.

The man in the Crocodile Dundee hat had told his groupies in the café that this cave was the entrance to passages that went all the way to the port of Kavala.

'I came with a friend once,' Ioanna said as she caught up with me in the echoey first chamber of the cave. 'And we entered, with torches. I don't want to ruin the fantasy, but we didn't find those passages.'

The cave went on inside the hill then stopped, she said, and frankly she was relieved. She didn't fancy walking under ground all the way to the Aegean coast.

'But Dundee has definitely found something. It's just a matter of how far you're willing to go,' she said. 'I guess I'm not a treasure hunter at heart.'

We returned to the car and after a long, steep climb, we came to an alpine-style forest complex of wooden huts so high up, the air was thinner. It was a centre for marathon runners, cyclists, and outdoor buffs.

The manager was a retired colonel called Thanos, though he looked too much of the mountains to be of the army. Thanos was short and square-chested, with a lined face that looked carved out of stone. He didn't smile much, but these were not smiley happy mountains.

His friend made me a sandwich and when they found out what had brought us here, they made me another sandwich and refused payment.

'Borders are hungry places,' his friend chuckled. He was a short, ponytailed man with a battered face and a gnomic, toothless smile. They were both in their late fifties but had calves of iron.

The forest was called Haidou, meaning brigand. Good or bad brigand? I asked.

'Mixed,' Thanos said, 'just like the real story of the border. The one you don't find in history books. The one about real people.'

Thanos had spent his army career among these peaks as a communications officer.

'From there,' he pointed to a tower at the top of another hill, 'we could see into enemy territory.'

Until the 1970s, he said, the forest had looked different – much sparser, with birch trees only. The pines had been planted later. That meant that there had been higher visilibity in the most glacial years of the Cold War. He pointed to a rock face not dissimilar to the Judgement cliff.

'It's called Mavri Petra,' he said, 'Black Stone. It's the actual border, and people from both sides used to aim for it. You looked at the Black Stone so you didn't lose your way.'

Yes, he had seen escapees in the forest, people in a terrible state.

'It was hard for us here,' he added, 'but not as hard as for your side. At least we didn't have to kill people.'

What he and his friends were trying to do with the Haidou forest was restore the humanity to the mountain. Down below there were beautiful villages that had been decimated four times: by refugee outflows, World War II, the Civil War, and then the Cold War. In one village, the entire male population had been executed by firing squad by the occupying Bulgarians, in reprisals. Only two men had escaped – a burly giant in the rear line and his friend whom he had pushed into the wooded ravine behind them, then fallen in after him. The squad had not found them, they had rolled too far down. And along with the village men, Thanos said, the commander of the Bulgarian unit had been executed by his own soldiers for trying to prevent the massacre. Then the Civil War finished the villages off.

The only villages that still thrived were those of the Pomaks, who had clung on through it all.

'Because the Pomaks are the true people of this mountain,' Ioanna said.

'It's good all of that is behind us,' Thanos said, 'because the forest belongs to people. Not to governments.'

Thanos and his friend were planning a special run in the autumn. They opened up a map and showed us. Starting here, they would run and walk west, along the natural border through the Rhodope range, then cross into Bulgaria where, Thanos said, the real climbing would begin. They would climb the Rila range and their aim was the source of the Nestos–Mesta River, at 2,240 metres above sea level.

'I always wanted to do it before I die.' Thanos looked up at Mavri Petra. 'In the olds days, you couldn't. You could only look at it. Do you want to come?' He turned to me and Ioanna, but one of us didn't have calves of iron.

'Maybe we could walk it,' Ioanna said. She was serious.

'I'd love to,' I said, strangely moved. But we never did.

When we said goodbye, Thanos put a hand on his heart.

'There's something I want to show you,' Ioanna said. 'You'll like it. But we have to walk.'

An hour's walk inside the Haidou forest there was a mature beech wood where every other trunk was initialled and dated.

When I looked at the map, I saw that this was almost the mirror side of the Judgement, where the official road between the two countries was disconnected, where I had stood by pyramid number 47 with Hairi when he told me about the Czech couple. In the happy version of their story, the Czech couple would have ended up here, scratched their names, and Thanos would have seen them from his tower and made them a sandwich. And Todor, Grigor, and Ilcho? Their names weren't here either. They had been shot earlier on, at pyramid number 37.

'Look.' Ioanna stroked a tree that was dated 1949, but the scratched initials in Greek were so distorted by the expanded trunk of elapsed decades that we couldn't read them for certain.

It was hard to walk away from the initialled trees. They were like people. When you tuned in, you could almost hear them whispering. The most heavily carved decades were the 1940s, the decade of war and starvation for Greece, and the 1990s, the decade of paupery and starvation for Bulgaria. In between were the deadly 1950s, 1960s, 1970s, and 1980s of the Iron Curtain. Here were those who had made it or thought they had. One tree from 1997 had a name scratched in Cyrillic:

ЗОРА

Where was Zora now?

'I don't know. But I know that in thirty or forty years, you and I will be gone. And this tree will be slightly bigger.' Ioanna stroked Zora's tree. 'Which makes everything fall into place.'

tobacco

You plant it in May, Zora said. Bury it in June–July. Pick it in August–September. You pick it in four stages and at each stage you pick three or four leaves from each plant. You start from the bottom leaves, then move up with each stage as the leaves turn yellow and curly. The whole tobacco thing is a nuisance. These days, they grow broad-leaved sorts here like Virginia, not so much Oriental. Oriental is small-leaved and aromatic but Virginia's more addictive. Most brands are 85 per cent Virginia, for lightness, and the rest is Oriental, for flavour. Virginia grows huge. Then you dry it in oven-rooms for a week, until it comes out brown. Then it goes to Xanthi and from there, God knows.

It's all that grows here: tobacco and potatoes – their fields are the green squares you see on the hills. Zora lit another Marlboro and smiled tightly, in case that too was taken away from her.

THE WOMAN WHO
WALKED FOR A WEEK

Zora's short nails were done in white polish to cover the yellow tinge. She had a heart-shaped face, emerald-green eyes, and golden Virginia hair. Like her voice, her beauty had a huskiness. She moved with cautious confidence, like someone who had been given nothing for free in life except her looks.

I had found Zora, or 3OPA, through one of the freakish serendipities that seemed to shape this journey. Thanos had mentioned 'the woman who walked for a week', and when I arrived in her village, someone pointed out her street to me. It was the last, steep street that led out of the stony village into the tobacco and potato fields.

'I call it the Street of Widows,' Zora smiled. 'Every house belongs to a widow. All those twitching curtains.'

As we climbed up the stairs to her front door, women neighbours suddenly appeared with brooms in their hands. There was a stone water fountain at the top of the street, disconnected and dry. All that uranium in the water. Was it the uranium that killed off the men? I wondered, and she tilted her chin up, the Greek way of saying No or I don't know or God only knows.

Zora was forty-one, the same age as me and Ioanna.

'I became conscious at twenty, married at thirty, and was widowed before I was forty,' she said matter-of-factly.

When I asked about her husband, she closed the front door behind us, took off her shoes, and said:

'Eh. He was a good man.' She said it lightly but I saw her blinking away tears.

She was not accustomed to the luxury of reminiscence. All that she had lived through she held inside of her, as you do when there's nowhere else to put it. We were in a humble but immaculate kitchen. There was a framed photo of the couple in their happy days. He had been a bearish, relaxed-looking man, and had his arms around her.

Zora had been blacklisted by the Greek foreign office for many years, but you only find out you're blacklisted when you try to leave the country. Or re-enter it. When she crossed into Bulgaria to visit her parents for the first time since her illegal crossing many years before, the Greeks didn't let her back in. She was stuck.

'He came over the border. Every month for six months. In blizzards and ice. Ten hours of driving. Our winter of separation.'

Now she had the house and his three hunting guns. They were wrapped in blankets and laid out on a spare bed where herbs were drying, and the curtains were permanently drawn.

Zora was from a small town in the Balkan range. Her twenties had coincided with the country's darkest hour – the 1990s, known as the 'transition'. Hyperinflation and mega-unemployment brought the country to its knees. In Zora's bankrupted town, there was no work. Then-prosperous Greece was the most common destination for illegal migrants from its post-communist poor cousins Bulgaria, Romania, and Albania. They were like the Bangladeshis in Dubai, a modern slave force. Greece didn't want the poor cousins legally, only illegally: for menial work, care of the elderly, and prostitution. Zora was prepared to do two of the above.

In the space of two years, Zora made four attempts to cross the Greek border.

The first time, she was caught by a Greek border patrol.

The second time, she ended up in a tobacco warehouse in the Republic of Macedonia with other girls – and only a miracle saved us, she said. Actually, it was a guy who saved them. He came one night, unlocked the door, and told them to run. Zora and the other girls had been marked by sex traffickers.

The third time, she attempted the crossing in winter, sick with flu. She collapsed in the forest. The smuggler took pity on her and half-carried her on his back the way they'd come. He didn't charge her.

She remembered little about that smuggler except that he was blond and from a Pomak village.

'That's Ziko!' I said but she only smiled tightly. She wasn't easy to surprise.

The fourth time, she made it. But she walked for a week. I tried to imagine a week in the mountain of madness and couldn't.

'We got lost,' she said.

They had been half a dozen people, plus a smuggler who took $500 a head but didn't know the way. They had gone round in circles, moving only at night, hiding in caves during the day. The border army was pretty relaxed by then, but hunting dogs could give them away. It was September, the start of the hunting season.

'Eh,' she sighed in Greek, 'I don't remember eating, but I remember drinking rainwater from the hoofprints of cows,' she said. 'That was us. Poverty in action.'

Zora remembered only fragments, like flashes from a nightmare you want to forget, she said.

'I had this leather jacket.' She smiled tightly. 'My most prized possession. To protect it from the brambles, I wore it inside out. But the lining was ripped to shreds along with the leather. I arrived in Greece covered in rags.'

On the seventh day, they reached a waterfall. The waterfall where

Orfeus and Marta lived now. The smuggler left them there and vanished, along with their money.

'He was a wretched guy, like the rest of us. Frightened and lost. With just the shirt on his back.'

The bedraggled group reached the first village and dispersed. Zora slept in a tobacco field for a couple of nights.

'You'd think that after what we went through together, we'd stay in touch,' she said. 'But we didn't. We wanted to forget it as quickly as possible.'

Zora had spent the first couple of years doing odd jobs for cash in hand, living in fear of being reported and deported. Then she met her husband, a Greek whose family had come from Smyrna. I guess he'd understood exile.

'What are you going to do with his guns?' I asked. 'Do you hunt?'

'No, not me. Once you're hunted, you don't hunt. But I can't sell the guns, they're his.'

To own guns, you must sit a psychiatric test and become a Greek citizen.

'I passed the test. At least I know I'm not bonkers. But I don't want a Greek passport.'

In truth, she was too scared to go through the bureaucratic process again, scared that the ghost of her history would pop up in the files.

'It's not really about the passport,' she said, 'it's about holding on to something.'

Zora was free to travel now, but hardly ever went across the border. She felt out of place there, and here in the stony village she would always be the foreign woman.

'Eh, maybe I never did belong anywhere,' she said, but not with self-pity.

Her phone kept buzzing with messages and she kept smiling. She liked men and men liked her – it was on her face, and it was gratifying to think that Zora had a good love life, or at least better than most women after a certain age, so many of whom seem to give up loving or even liking men and settle for tolerating them instead.

In ancient Greece, there was a special category of woman: hetairas, educated courtesans. In a society where married women led immured lives no better than slaves, the hetairas enjoyed quasi-equal civic rights to men, on one condition: that they never married. In the classification of female archetypes by the Jungian analyst Toni Wolff, there are four: mother, Amazon, medial woman, hetaira. The mother is drawn to the needy. The Amazon fulfils a collective need for change. The medial woman bridges the material world with the spiritual. And the hetaira loves men. Arriving in Greece with her leather jacket in shreds, Zora had had three options on the black market: prostitution ('hetaira'), care of the elderly ('mother'), or manual labour. Many Bulgarian women who arrived illegally in Greece in the 1990s did something more subtle that combined the first two: they moved in with an elderly man and took care of all his needs. Or, just as often, an elderly woman. Pensioners in Greece enjoyed a very high standard of living and could afford such an arrangement. Sometimes, these relationships went on for a long time and the two parties became emotionally involved, and there were cases of carers inheriting the legacy of their well-to-do employer masters or mistresses. Because the hetaira, like the mother, is not free of slavery's shadow. Each of Toni Wolff's types, when it's out of balance, acquires a shadow side – the manipulative mother, the violent Amazon, the doomsday Cassandra, the femme fatale – and I wondered if Zora had a shadow side too. If, during that week of border crossing, she had shed one skin and grown another, in order to survive.

It was time for Zora to go to her allotment. She worked on other people's tobacco fields, but on her own allotment she grew what she liked – salad vegetables, tomatoes. And Bulgarian roses, her late husband's favourite flower. We stood on her balcony. The mountain loomed on all sides, showing the way to the border. She lived with this view: the view of her own escape. No wonder she couldn't forget it.

I asked her the question that had been on my mind all along. How come she hadn't given up after so many bruising attempts?

For once, she looked surprised.

'Because I wanted to live *here*. Not there. Freedom is the most basic human right. Isn't it?'

She and her husband hadn't had children. It would have been nice, but you can't force nature, and it's okay to pass through life without leaving a trace, she said, isn't it?

Except on her birch tree in the forest, I said. She smiled, tightly.

'Eh,' she said, 'that was from my first attempt. When I thought it was easy.'

The neighbour in black had come out again, to sweep her over-swept landing. She glanced up at us. I wondered if her husband had fancied Zora. I wondered if all the husbands in the street of widows had fancied her. Even I fancied her a little. I thought about the Cretan village widow in *Zorba the Greek*, the beautiful one who was knifed to death by the men who desired her, egged on by the pious village women who envied her; her lover, an intellectual, too gutless to save her.

But Zora knew how to save herself. She winked at me through a puff of Virginia leaf and her hard emerald eyes shone. Zora meant Dawn.

'Come and stay with me, next time,' she said. 'We'll have some fun. 'Cause it's not over yet, is it? It's not over till the fat widow sings!'

And her laughter rang down the stony street. The house walls threw it back but the marble mountain picked it up and magnified it, and it rang so that the neighbour in black dropped her broom and went inside.

PART FOUR

STARRY STRANDJA

*A wild and fabulous spirit overhung these waves, as though
this coast were still the end of the world, the forlorn ultimate
border of reality beyond which a cloud of legend, rumour and
surmise began.*

Patrick Leigh Fermor, *The Broken Road*

lodos

In Turkish and Greek, the southwesterly wind that travels across the Aegean. Sometimes it brings the dust of the Sahara to the plains of Thrace and all the way to the Black Sea. It's a warm, unrelenting wind that colours everything a whitish silver, the hue of remembered southern childhoods and civilisations. That's why in Bulgarian it's called 'white wind', *byal vyatar*, and why the Aegean is the White Sea.

The road that climbed down from the easternmost slopes of the Greek Rhodope into the open plains of Thrace ran parallel to the vanished Via Egnatia. Although the trees along the motorway stood freeze-painted in silver, my car was rocked by the wind of the coast where Alexandroupoli and Kavala marinated in Levantine memories. The motorway was many-laned and first class, but so eerily empty of traffic that I worried I'd taken a wrong turn. But there were no turns, it was a straight line to the Turkish border. A whirlwind of dust, pollen, and sea salt speed-tumbled like the ghosts of galloping horses.

Then, abruptly, it turned its back on the Aegean and went upstream along the border river Evros–Meriç. Halfway up the wide delta aflutter with long-legged birds, the road passed below the quilted roofs of Soufli. Established in the sixteenth century by Albanian tradesmen and probably named after a dervish monastery nearby, by the nineteenth

century Soufli, like Silk Town, was a hub of sericulture doing business with the world via the port of Kavala. It was also exempt from
taxes during the Ottoman era, which suggests a Muslim majority.
But Soufli, like the Nestos valley, like all once-disputed border areas,
is now promoted as 'a cradle of Hellenism'. Although the cultivation of mulberry trees, along with the market for silk, has declined
steadily since Soufli became Greek in 1923, today it is the only place
in Europe where silk is still made.

In a roadside silk shop, a tall dreamy woman with yellow hair made
me the coffee that is called Greek on this side of the river, and Turkish
on the other. We sat outside in the dust of passing lorries, and she said:
'Over the river is Turkey. Up the river is Bulgaria. No problem. In
Athens you can't sleep. Here you can sleep.'

Here, by the River Hebrus, romanised from the original Ebros, the
same Hebrus that was described by Ovid as the son of 'icy Rhodope
and Haemus with its shades'. Seven centuries before Ovid, a Greek
poet wrote: 'Ebros, you flow, the most beautiful of rivers, past Ainos
into the turbid sea, surging through the land of Thrake… and many
maidens visit you to bathe their lovely thighs.' How things have gone
downhill since then! Hebrus: where the might of the Greek and
Turkish armies was massed for decades, as their territorial tensions
spilled over from the Greek–Turkish War into the Cold War. And
lately, Hebrus of the illegal crossings. To the silk woman's surprise and
my own, I bought a bag of silk scarves. Maybe I needed to honour
something of beauty that had survived the civilisational destruction of
the old Levant.

The Greek–Turkish checkpoint came just after Kastanies, a little town
where the men propped up at café tables looked asleep, as if under

a spell. On the Greek side, officials waved me through with yawns, but the Turkish side greeted me fully awake with armed camouflaged soldiers. Customs officers dismantled my car. They even unscrewed a small whirling-dervish souvenir made of brass, which I'd bought in Edirne. 'Hashish? Cocaine?' the customs officer enquired, almost with hope, and I thought of *Midnight Express* and tried not to sweat. After studying my passport, he said: 'You entered Turkey through Bulgaria last month. Why?' I said I was writing a book. He banged the car boot shut and decided to let me off the hook, just this once. 'A love story?' he grinned. Yes, that's it, I said with relief. A love story.

Between Greece and Turkey was a long corridor with high walls of barbed wire, tight and one-directional like a birthing canal. Overhead, a single pink flamingo travelling east let out a hopeful caw. I pushed through and emerged on the other side, where I hit the cobblestoned road into once-Greek Karaağach (silent g), euphoric with relief. The stress of border crossings like this one is hard to convey; it is on a cellular level. Even with the right passport, in plain daylight, with nothing to declare.

I bumped over Edirne's humped stone bridges, past the Hilly Hotel with the shepherd and his three-legged dog, and after ninety minutes of empty south-east motorway, the *lodos* blew me into Kirklareli.

TO THE RIVER

Kirklareli was a thriving Thracian town and the only one of Turkey's eighty-one provinces that boasted a woman governor. There was a bronze statue in the centre, of a schoolgirl in a short skirt. Kirklareli was called Kirklisse (City of Forty Churches) in Greek and Lozengrad (City of Vines) in Bulgarian before the Christians were swapped for Muslims from the rest of the Balkans. Almost half the population had been Jewish; now, one Jewish family was left, owners of a petrol station. The handsome wooden houses and churches of the old Christian quarter Yayla stood crumbling on their hill. One of them, a former Greek dignitary's mansion, or *konak*, had been converted into a European-style restaurant called Gusto. Its owners were a dashing couple descended from Bosniaks and Bulgarian Muslims, and in Gusto you could degustate rich Thracian wines on the balcony and look across the lit-up panorama of what some say was the first inhabited town in Europe, so seductive is its climate, so conducive to growing crops of every edible and imbibable kind.

Here, you could look across this city of minarets, nod to the ghost of cosmopolitanism, and wonder: if the mixing of peoples was the order of empires and the 'unmixing of peoples' the order of nation-states, what's on the horizon? From the windy balcony of Gusto perched above the plains where East and West come together in a field of sunflowers, it seemed that what was on the horizon was a long column of refugees going east to west. Perhaps the insidious hybrid warfare of our times will have one upside: a new remixing of peoples. Or was the wine making me too optimistic?

On Kirklareli's outskirts, there were two roads. One went south to Istanbul and Asia. But if you had come this far, you had already taken the other road, because Kirklareli was a gateway to Strandja and Europe.

Kirklareli was also where Nevzat lived. He was the photographer I'd met at The Disco on the other side. It was great to see him again, and he and his wife Nursel welcomed me with hugs, like a long-lost relative.

'Where do you want to go?' Nevzat asked.

He had taken two days off work and I'd picked him up for an early start at the crossroads outside Kirklareli.

'To the river,' I said. 'The border river.'

'Good,' he smiled. 'It's where our family village is. Paspalovo.'

He handed me a freshly baked *simit*, the fragrant sesame-seed bread with a hole in it that you buy from bakers, and we set off for the Strandja hills.

Paspalovo? There was no such village on my map. Nevzat grinned.

'It's the old name,' he said.

Paspalovo had been swapped for Armutveren some time after the people of the village (Bulgarian Christians) had been swapped for Nevzat's people: Pomaks from a Rhodope village a few hours west of the Village Where You Lived For Ever. Nursel's family, Pomaks from the Drama region, were doubly unwanted by the Greek state for being Bulgarian-speakers *and* Muslims, but many Pomaks like them also fled from the occupying Bulgarian army in the Great War. And so the young grandparents of Nursel and Nevzat had travelled here along the equivalent of the road I had just covered. They had moved by foot and ox-driven carts, shaken by the white wind of the Aegean.

They say refugees of the Balkan Wars travelled by ox-driven carts because, unlike mules and horses, oxen didn't stop when faced with a steep hill, they continued on their knees.

When Nevzat's grandparents arrived in Turkish Strandja, there were plenty of empty houses, but everything was different: the air, the soil, the shape of the hills. Half of their family had stayed behind. Eaten away by homesickness, three years later Nevzat's people loaded up the carts again and travelled back, against the *lodos*. But their house in the Rhodope was occupied by others. So, for the third time, they made the long journey east, through the dark Rhodope passes once used by the Romans and across the Thracian plains, and this time the moist strangeness of Strandja enfolded them for good. One day, Nevzat's grandfather came back from grazing the animals and found his young wife crying in her garden in Paspalovo. Why are you crying?

Her youngest brother had been left behind in the Rhodope in the chaos of the last departure. The boy was herding in the highlands when the rest of the family had left. The parents were dead and he was alone with his goats. The husband saddled his horse again, kissed his wife goodbye, and for the fourth time crossed the border. He was helped by sympathetic (or bribe-friendly) soldiers on both sides. He rode to the Rhodope, a journey of perilous river crossings and brigand-dodging, found the boy, smuggled him back into Turkey, and adopted him.

Nevzat grew up with tales like this. The epic crossing took a central place in his mind, and the family's origin myth merged with the journeying myth. It was no longer the usual ancestral story of how things had begun and continued, but the story of a great interruption.

That was the story of the Rhodope Pomaks: for those who left, one mountain had to be swapped for another; and for those who stayed, one name had to be swapped for another. Nevzat carried all of this on his face. In the mysterious way families have of marking one among their many to make sense of the bigger picture, Nevzat had been marked. He was a down-to-earth family man whose day job was as head tailor at a boutique sewing factory. But every weekend he was on the roads of Strandja with his rucksack, recording its faces and silences on his camera. His portraits could see into people's souls.

Two years ago, he was granted a visa and went straight to his grand-parents' home village in the Rhodope. That's when I had met him.

'When I first saw the Rhodope, my heart started beating like mad.'

He was the first of his family to return since the exodus a hundred years ago. Turkey was a bottomless treasure trove for a photographer, he said. But instead, all he wanted was to go back to the Rhodope.

'Because there's something there,' he said. 'Something got left behind.'

Nursel and Nevzat married young in the border village that was once Paspalovo, and when their two children were past primary school, they decided to move to the city. They still lived in a comfort-able flat in Kirklareli, but now that their children were adults, Nursel was spending more and more time back in the village, tending her garden in summer.

'When we retire, we'll go back to live there,' Nevzat said, even if the village was down to a couple of dozen residents now.

Nevzat and I drove the empty roads of Strandja for several days, and went back to Kirklareli at night, where I stayed in a hotel despite their kind protestations, but ate at their place. Nursel, a woman with a face like her name – Stream of Light – always hugged me and said:

'Are you hungry? What a long drive!'

Yes, it was longer than the map could prepare you for. You can't prepare for Strandja. The rivers of Strandja watered Istanbul, though people said that south of the industrial town of Lüleburgaz they ran black with tar. For several months a year, Strandja shuddered with the northern wind which the Pomaks called *studenyak*, the coldie. Studenyak and lodos mingled here, and when you drove the forest hours that lengthened into days, you saw for yourself that Strandja had not had an ice age. The hushed forests felt untouched, untrodden, and unknown, despite the fact that the human story here was old. Uninterrupted oak woods were followed by giant-beech plantations, succeeded by an enchantment of sequoia and ash trees whose green light you could taste, and it tasted of chlorophyll.

At the end of a long forest road, left unsurfaced to keep it inaccessible, was an upmarket eco-farm that sold organic produce, and next to it was a gilded ghetto: holiday mansions for the millionaires of Istanbul. They were all empty and tended by gardeners, and each mansion was behind a gate with a personalised message in wrought iron. One of them said in English: Dare To Dream.

'Shouldn't be too hard to dare, with a few spare millions,' I said tartly, but Nevzat only smiled. He was not one for pointing out the obvious. He observed, photographed, and wished everybody well.

The one thing that upset him was the one thing you couldn't miss on the roads of Strandja: the monumental projects of the current government which had come at Strandja like a wrecking ball. Its pharaonic follies defaced the hills. Gigantic cement factories loomed on the horizon like dystopias, dynamite quarries blew up the hills, the mountain roads had been distended to accommodate lorries, a gold-mine was opening inside a hill, and a coastal nuclear plant squatted over Strandja's future.

Driving along, I had to close the car windows because the cement dust from the quarries covered everything with a fine grey film.

A nuclear plant?

'This is Turkey,' Nevzat said. 'An eco-farm next door to a nuclear plant.'

But the basin of the Black Sea is unstable and the coast sinks by a few millimetres every year! In the first half of the last century, eight hundred earthquakes had shaken these shores. Plus: the *longoz*, or lagoon wetland forest, of Turkish Strandja is unique in Europe! I ranted, and Nevzat nodded sadly.

'It's because Strandja is unknown to the world. They think they can do anything and get away with it.'

Not far from where the massive cement factory in the ancient town of Pinarhisar filled the lungs of locals with stuff that shortens lives was Coal Town, or Kömürköy. By the side of the road a family of three generations were building huge cones of twigs, and slow-smoking them into charcoal. These were the last traditional makers of *kömür* on the continent, a Strandja livelihood and technology that hadn't changed since antiquity. The chief coal maker had returned from a decade in Istanbul, and now he welcomed us with a smile made whiter by the sooty blackness of his face, and said:

'Every stone must have its place, and my place is here.'

His days were the colour of night, but he had the look of a man who liked being a coal maker in Coal Town, keeping a vigil through the night over his smoking cones, lovingly prodded and gently lit from within, a scene out of Bruegel.

'This too is Turkey,' Nevzat said. 'The *kömürdji* next door to the cement factory.'

The road through Strandja was pretty empty now, but it had been completely deserted until a few years ago, when a stupendous triple cave called Dupnitsa had been opened for tourists, and cars started turning up from Istanbul in the summer. The cave was in fact three caves on top of each other, dubbed Wet, Dry, and Maiden, each with distinct geomorphology. Some historians trace the vanished Paroria of Gregory of Sinai to this cave.

Back in the Middle Ages before the Turks turned up, traffic

through these hills must have been so scarce, roads so nonexistent, and the forests so impassable, that you wonder why the monks felt the need to go into the depths of a triple cave. Anywhere within Strandja would have been sufficiently godforsaken to seek communion with God. But even inside a triple cave, they were not safe. The Hesychasts were killed and dispersed by the Seljuks as they galloped across this doorstep of Europe. The destruction of Paroria was so complete that entire PhD dissertations have been penned on its possible location.

The remaining small roads were full of blind turns and punctuated by drinking fountains built by families in memory of soldier sons. Most deaths dated from the 1980s, a period of brutal clashes between the Turkish army and rebels in Kurdistan. The Pomaks had travelled all this way across mountains, only to see their grandsons die in a faraway conflict in Asia; it was no surprise that the Pomaks I met had no excess love for the Kurds. The policy was the same as in Greece: send young soldiers as far from home as possible. With Turkey's neighbours being what they are, army service has never been a laugh.

Those who could afford it bought off their sons' service. The current price was 18,000 liras (6,000 euros). Those who couldn't, waited and prayed. A few years before, one of Nevzat's brothers had welcomed his son back from military service, and had been so overwhelmed to see his son alive that at the welcoming-back party he'd had a massive heart attack.

'He died in our arms,' Nevzat said, 'at the festive table.'

At some of the old internal checkpoints, the road was still patrolled.

'Here, it was here,' Nevzat said quietly as we passed a checkpoint manned by two soldiers with automatic weapons who checked the car registration from behind dark glasses but didn't stop us.

When we were well past them, both of us exhaled with relief, the kind of relief that comes naturally to those who have grown up in a police state.

Nevzat was a teenager when he had been stopped by soldiers on his way home from herding goats, here at this checkpoint. He was with two horses and his grandfather – the same man who, sixty years before, had ridden west to find the lost Rhodope boy. It was 1981, the time of the junta, when this was a heavily militarised zone. As on the other side, you needed a special permit to visit Strandja, and if you were local, a special permit called *izin kağidi* to graze your animals, work in your allotment, and live here at all.

'Sounds familiar?' Nevzat smiled.

So familiar that you could almost imagine that the two enemy regimes on each side of the border had consulted each other on how best to terrorise their own people, and had come up with the same methods.

There were strict curfew hours.

'But it was after curfew that night, so they wouldn't let us pass.'

Nevzat's grandfather had stood his ground with the soldiers and things spiralled. A rifle was unslung from a shoulder, and for a bleak moment, Nevzat thought they would execute his grandfather on the spot.

They had turned back and spent hours groping about in the forest for a path that would take them back to the village before soldier patrols saw them again and shot them, because what business did they have roaming in the night? They had to abandon the horses and look for them later.

His grandmother had waited up all night – the same woman who, sixty years before, had waited for her man and her brother.

'We got off lightly,' Nevzat said. 'But that checkpoint stayed with me.'

For a century, the culture had been one where civilians were accountable to the army, and the army was accountable to no one.

The supremacy of the army was of course one of the tenets of Atatürk's Republic, and you could argue – many did, though not the Kurds or the families of dead soldiers fighting the Kurds – that it had achieved the most important thing, which was to keep Turkey together.

Even now, I frequently saw convoys of army trucks with shorn recruits in the back peering under the tarpaulin like stunned animals. In towns and between towns, we passed dozens of army bases with their red warning Army! *Asker!* signs. Some were still active, while others stood abandoned with their concrete blocks, rusty sports grounds, and Atatürk's slogan beaten in wrought iron: 'Proud is the one who can say I am a Turk!'

'Even on the beach, the *asker* has the best spot!' Nevzat said without malice – after all, he had been an asker too, on the Iraqi border, and seen with his own eyes the Kurdish victims of Saddam Hussein, their skin burnt by chemical weapons, all women and children, he said. And it was because of the junta that he'd missed out on a higher education. His parents hadn't let him study in the city, for fear of all the check-points along the way.

In the summer of 1970, a shepherd from their village had been watering his horse at the border river. He had seen a Bulgarian shep-herd on the other side, and shouted *Merhaba!* Hello! The man on the other side waved back.

A Turkish patrol overheard. The shepherd from the village was taken away in an army truck.

'Nobody dared ask where they'd taken him,' Nevzat said, 'but his horse knew. She stopped grazing and died in the winter.'

The shepherd was charged with espionage and given fourteen years in jail.

After a long, climbing gravel road interrupted only by a herd whose young shepherd was speaking on a mobile phone, we arrived in a high border village of a hundred souls so high up, it was called Bird of Prey. A friend of Nevzat's lived here with his wife, and theirs was the last house. Their surname was Karadeniz, meaning Black Sea.

From the top of their garden, you could supposedly see a Bulgarian village called Moryane over the hills. Mr Karadeniz's grandfather, Ismail, had been among the original people of Moryane who, a hundred years ago, were resettled here.

'Every time they looked over to their native Moryane in the distance, their wound reopened.'

Still, things were neighbourly between the two villages until the border hardened in 1945.

'Before the Cold War, people went down to the river to hear the women on the Bulgarian side sing in the fields,' Mr Karadeniz said. 'They were always singing.'

For centuries, *pehlivani*, or wrestlers, from both sides met at the river, where women would fire the kurban feast, the sound of bag-pipes and drums would echo from hill to hill, and potent home brews would be imbibed. One of the meeting places had been Valchan Bridge, the only bridge across the Rezovo River.

'The only problem back then were the *hajduks*.'

Hajduks: the brigands without borders who ran the show across Ottoman Europe. Around 1800, Valchan, or Wolf Man, was Strandja's foremost brigand whose 70-strong band, in the time-honoured manner of Robin Hood, plundered local grandees and caravans. Ambushed once next to the Rezovo River, he swore that in the event that his men escaped the sultan's soldiers, he would commission a bridge at that spot. They did escape (breathing under water through reeds), and the bridge was built, with Valchan himself disguised as an ordinary labourer, once again escaping the authorities, who resigned themselves to the fact that at least they were getting a public bridge for free; it became the main thoroughfare from Marina's pretty border town to today's Demirköy in the heart of Turkish Strandja, and onwards to Istanbul. Valchan enjoyed many more years of plunder, parties, and popularity.

Generations of treasure hunters have been removing stones from the bridge foundations for the treasure he supposedly buried there. In the 1940s, the Bulgarian side of the bridge was dynamited by the army.

A perfect symbol of the Cold War, the half-bridge stands to this day.

From the end of Mr Karadeniz's garden, I strained my eyes but couldn't see any of Moryane's houses in the distant forest.

'You can't,' my host agreed. 'The last houses were eaten up by forest.'

In 1948, when the border hardened and the army moved in, Moryane's people were removed to the Black Sea coast. Only one old man refused to leave his goats. He lived alongside the soldiers who turned the village school into their base. The old man provided them with milk, and they gave him a job: each evening, he had to turn on the lights in the empty houses, to show the Turkish enemy across the hills that populous Bulgaria was enjoying an electrical plenty.

'And our soldiers here,' Mr Karadeniz said, 'periodically fired their machine guns in the direction of Moryane. To show the enemy their might. Even though they had no shoes.'

The family lived in a military shadow that kept morphing but never went away. Until now – for next to his house was an expanse of dead grass where the remains of the last army base still stood.

'As a young man, every time I went for a coffee in the square, a soldier barred my way.'

You could see the square from the house.

Immediately after his grandparents Ismail and Ayshe arrived here from across the border, Greek soldiers rocked up in the village. The Greek–Turkish War had begun. As if either Greece or Turkey could afford another war. Eastern Thrace, already purged of its Bulgarian-speakers, was occupied by Greece, and between 1916 and 1922, the Greek army kept the newly resettled villages here in an iron fist.

In the house next door, there had been a young couple. The Greek soldiers so harassed the woman that one night, she just ran for the border. She spent five years in Moryane with old neighbours, until the war was over and the Greeks were gone. I wondered about the husband left alone here for five long years, with the soldiers next door and his wife gone.

Mr Karadeniz's father had been five years old when he'd thrown a stone at a pig requisitioned by Greek soldiers. Fearing a reprisal, Ayshe packed the boy up the same night and ran over the hills across to Moryane, where she'd grown up. Ayshe and her boy hid there with old Bulgarian neighbours for a year (the only difficulty during that time was her Bulgarian hosts' love of pork, Mr Karadeniz said). The old neighbours asked after her husband Ismail.

My Ismail never came back from Gallipoli, she said.

The old neighbours wept for Ismail. Many of their men hadn't returned from the front either. Just as the fire-walkers had predicted, looking at their blackest of black embers.

In 1922, as ceasefire loomed, the Greek soldiers evacuated the village and took the civilian population with them as hostages on a march to the Aegean coast. Bulgarian soldiers came across what must have been a very sorry procession of soldiers, peasants, and cattle, and offered the villagers refuge in their once-native Bulgaria. But it was too little, too late: the villagers were so traumatised, they trusted nobody in a uniform. None of them stepped across the line, and the march continued to Enez, a journey of 240 kilometres. Children and old people died en route. The rest eventually made it back here and started again.

Among the survivors was Mr Karadeniz's father, the five-year-old who'd thrown a stone at the pig.

'But he always said Be ready, kids! We might be on the road again.'

Into the old Greek garrison next door moved the Turkish army. Mr Karadeniz sighed.

'We have suffered far more from our own army than from any other. With the exception of the Greeks. You know the Turkish expression *yunan giaour*?'

Nevzat laughed. Originally meaning 'Greek infidel', it was now widely applied to mean all manner of untrustworthy bastards. We sat in the summer kitchen for a meal of the buttery white 'Paspalovo beans', young garlic, yogurt, and heavenly home-made bread baked in a clay dish by Mrs Karadeniz.

Mr Karadeniz thanked and praised his wife for the food and she smiled, but didn't eat with us, she just sat on the side watching us contentedly, as was the custom in village households.

Afterwards, the village mayor gave us tea in the square.

'The army is gone, at last,' Mr Karadeniz said, 'but now it's the refugees. They walk through town. Seeing them like this, walking across the hills with nothing left in the world, we understand what our ancestors went through. And you wonder: when will it end?'

The local authority instructed villagers to drive the refugees to Kirklareli, but when Mr Karadeniz did this, together with the village mayor, the police arrested them en route.

'Saying we were helping the refugees escape to Bulgaria!' the mayor said and shook his head. 'Even though we were taking them south, not north!'

The mayor was a large, awkward man with a good-natured face. We swapped ritual tobacco, and he asked Nevzat how come his wife allowed him to travel with another woman.

'Because my wife supports what I do,' Nevzat said simply, and the mayor looked embarrassed, and quite possibly envious. 'Of course, of course!' he said.

Everybody said that European Turkey is more liberal than the Asian side (where I have never been), but Turkish Thrace felt pretty conformist. True, there was tradition. The family unit was the only approved unit, and while bachelors of all ages were the norm in the depopulated village square, a solo woman was not only anomalous but associated with either immorality or disease. The women looked uniform under their flowery scarves and in baggy clothes designed to unshape their bodies, their plain faces bored and motherly. A very different look lurked in the eyes of Bulgarian provincial women: the sorrow of unmet expectation, of unfulfilled dreams. The Turkish man of Thrace was resigned, guarded, with sadness in the eyes. His Bulgarian counterpart was suspicious, aggressive, and alcoholic. If you had any doubt whether you'd crossed the Strandja border – after all, it was the same mountain, the same food, the same dental devastation – all you had to do was look into people's eyes. The state of the provincial nation was there.

But there was also something organised about this conformity, something Big Brotherish. Every day in the villages and towns of Turkey, a public megaphone announced events, sales, points of interest to the citizens, like being back at school. But people rarely opened their houses to strangers. In Bulgaria, nobody gave a toss, and the private merged with the public. In Turkey, you had a nanny state with a pious, paternalistic façade behind which all manner of excesses raged. In Bulgaria, the excesses of the kleptocracy were hanging out for all to see – a long-standing tradition. In Turkey, the state supported and smothered you. In Bulgaria, you were abandoned to your misfortunes, but you could buy vodka and skinny-dip without being arrested.

You could say that once-capitalist Turkey and once-communist Bulgaria had swapped boots, as true neighbours do. Or you could say that two former police states, regardless of their ideological stripes,

were already wearing the same boots anyway. After all, the same curse
had fallen on both sides during the Cold War. Earlier, I had visited
two mirror villages on the border, cut off from the world for fifty years
– Slivarovo (population: 7) and Karacadağ (population: 13) – whose
welcoming mayors, the Bulgarian one a woman, bore a painful hope
on their faces: that somewhere in time there is a future for their village
with its fragrant apple trees, its empty houses, its vistas across the river
valley, its disused observation towers and soldier barracks full of weeds
where something new could grow, if only the people would return.

'This border takes a toll on people,' Mr Karadeniz said.

'It's not for everyone,' Nevzat agreed, but I could see that he loved
these villages. He and Mr Karadeniz resonated with the ruinous beauty
of this landscape. Because they were its children.

'We love it here, we can't help ourselves,' the mayor said with a
fatalistic smile. 'There is nothing that won't grow in this soil.'

'There was a man of ninety,' Mr Karadeniz said, 'turned up in the
village one day and moved into an abandoned house. He'd been one
year old when his family emigrated to America. But he wanted to die
here.'

'That'll be me in Paspalovo, one day,' Nevzat grinned.

And me in Bulgaria, I thought. If you can't live there, at least you
can die there.

Back in their house, Mr and Mrs Karadeniz gave me a wreath of
garlic, to plant in Scotland.

'So you don't forget the taste of Strandja,' they said, and hugged
me so much that I nearly burst into tears.

'The mountain gives birth to people, the plain gives birth to pumpkins.' Is that how it went? A bit harsh on the people of the plains,
but it's true that the people of the Rhodope and the Strandja had a
special quality.

We might call it the paradox of mountains, perhaps a universal one: the rougher the history, the tougher the terrain, the more exceptional the people. They seem to know what others don't: kindness is the one thing that matters in the end. All over Strandja, villagers pulled their resources together from the ruins. Literal ruins, ancestral ruins, linguistic ruins.

With Nevzat in the passenger seat, we passed through villages of dingy, inscrutable beauty. Old men sat on chairs, looking at something that can't be seen. We climbed to a high village that some still called by its old Greek name, even though its new Turkish name is in honour of the Turkish *bey*, or governor, who had brought peace to the area by purging it of hairy brigands like Valchan. Half of the houses had stood in ruins for a hundred years now. The walls of the biggest ruin bore the pencil calculations of the Greek shop owner who had noted the names of his debtors, and the amounts. These uncollected debts of history had not been whitewashed by the locals, out of respect. And out of respect, the merchant's house stood at the heart of the village like an open-air museum to what should never happen again, but did – in the Yugoslav wars of the 1990s.

The mayor was a blue-eyed man who looked like Paul Newman after twenty years of chain-smoking, tall and proud in his wellies; the water supply had broken down and the men were all mobilised to fix it. His pet name for his village was Little Paris, and it's true – Kuçuk Paris was so beautiful that when you reached the top of the road and looked down, the uninterrupted view of green hills snatched your breath away and you had to sit down and have a glass of tea with two lumps of sugar.

The people of the village were descendants of Bosniak refugees, Bosnian Muslims, with fair skin and light-coloured eyes. The men drank tea in the square like spectators in an amphitheatre, watching the daily show of hills multiplying to eternity.

The mayor ran the only shop. In the evening, a few of the men got quietly wasted in the penumbra of the shop.

'I'm a Bosniak and a Turk. But above all, I'm a European,' the mayor said when I asked how he defined himself. He spoke an old remnant of what people here called the 'Bosniak' language.

Unlike the rest of his siblings, who had made their lives in the city, the mayor had drifted back here, drawn by his mother's tears, he said. Ah, the clingy mother, a Balkan predicament, I said, and he laughed heartily. His sunburn made his light-coloured eyes stand out more brightly, but I saw within them the ancestral blues I also saw in Nevzat and in many of the Pomaks here. The kind of blues you inherit.

Many in the village still had family in Bosnia, but it was a long way and few made the trip, what with the visas.

What did you do during the war in Bosnia? I asked the mayor.

'What could we do? We stayed here, played Bosnian music and cried,' he said. In fact, someone was playing Bosnian music next door at that very moment.

While we had tea in the square, two Greek cars arrived. The visitors got out and looked around, dazed. They were from Kavala, come to see their grandparents' houses. This was the ancestral pilgrimage of Thrace: every summer, cars and busloads arrived from Greece and Bulgaria. It was harder for a Turk to travel to Europe than vice versa, so the locals went through all the emotions with the visitors as if they were their own. Because they were.

The mayor shook hands with the visitors solemnly and took them to the upper parts of the village where the ruined Greek houses stood. A while later, the visitors came back, their faces hard. The mayor asked them to stay on, have tea, but they were off down the hill, back into the white Aegean wind.

'We have no guesthouse yet,' the mayor said, a bit crestfallen. 'But I'm working on it. A guesthouse that will offer Bosniak pies, my grandmother's recipe. So that people can stay longer and remember their visit fondly.'

Then he was off to fix the water supply, striding in the dust on his long legs. Like many of the men, he was married with a family, but where were the women of the village? The women were at home, milking the animals, sleeping, gossiping over sweet cups of coffee. With the hospitable but hard-faced women of a three-generational family in Little Paris I had an exchange in Turko-Bosniak.

Eldest woman: Man?

Me: Home.

Younger woman: Children?

Me: No.

Younger woman: Parents?

Me: In New Zealand.

Eldest woman, looking around worriedly: Doctor!

The youngest was a girl who said nothing. Her T-shirt said 'I Love Paris' and she grinned at me, her face lit up with possibilities. I couldn't see her staying here, once she'd grown up and been educated in the city.

Tucked under the wipers of my car was an anonymous note: 'Don't forget Little Paris.'

Our last destination that day was Paspalovo. In a bend of the river, we stopped for a snack on the remains of a mill. The water was cold and emerald green.

'I love this river,' Nevzat shouted over the rush, and I understood. I was even a little jealous. True, I'd had a first-class education in Sofia, but there had been no river in my childhood. Even in this arrested forest, Nevzat and his brothers had spent the summers grazing animals, sleeping under the stars around a fire that had to be kept going all night, to ward off wolves. They had the kind of freedom that a city kid can only read about in books.

'You can swim across the Veleka River now, even the Rezovo River, and no one will shoot at you,' Nevzat said over his sandwich. 'Though they will check your papers.'

'What happened to the shepherd who shouted hello to the other side and was jailed for fourteen years?' I asked.

In 1974, four years after he was jailed, there was a change of government and he was released in a general amnesty. But when he returned home, his wife and son were gone. She had despaired of seeing him again and remarried in another village. And since he had also lost his flock, he joined another shepherd and spent the next decade in the hills above the village that was once Paspalovo.

My sandwich began to taste like a last meal. The tug of the border was powerful among the river dragonflies, like a gravitational force. Whichever way you turned, something was behind you and nothing ahead of you. Perhaps that's what history is.

'As a kid, I took lunch to the two shepherds in the hills. One winter—' Nevzat looked at me, 'I'm sorry, this is a sad story. One winter, when I took the lunch up, I found only one shepherd. His friend, the man with the horse, had hanged himself.'

We drank from the river. How many times, in his prison cell and later in the hills, had the shepherd gone through that moment by the river when life had been good, and he'd raised his hand to wave, and in a fraction of a second decided to shout a greeting too? The days and nights of bewilderment, the 'what ifs', the unbearable regret festering over four long years.

Or perhaps not. Perhaps, like Felix S., he had no regrets, because he had done the right thing, the thing you must do in order to be young before being old.

Nevzat's parents were sitting on the steps of their house. They had been weeding and watering. Their one-storey house was dark and lined with kilims, with no furniture except the beds and the TV. This is where Nevzat had grown up. The summers were long and glorious and the winters were deadly. Nevzat kissed his parents' hands and touched them to his forehead.

His father enquired gently after our journey, and his mother rolled a cigarette from the tobacco I had brought from Drama. She didn't smoke, but if it was from Drama…

They had been married for sixty years, raised seven children, lost one, and to see them sitting together in the cherry dusk of this crumbling village, where they had created a world – through exile, military rule, border terror, poverty, and hard physical toil – well, it left me speechless.

'Come on, ask them your questions,' Nevzat encouraged me, and held the camera up to film us. But my mind had gone blank.

They were dressed in sleeveless woollen cardigans, baggy trousers, and rubber galoshes. I felt it like a presence: the spirit of the Balkans was here, in this garden thick with greenery. The true spirit of the Balkans that hangs on, no matter how renamed and resettled, imagined and invented. Our bitter beloved borderless Balkans.

Nevzat's father patted my hand and smiled. His mother, tiny and almost blind behind thick glasses, felt my face with cracked hands, as if she was washing it. She had the hands you get after seventy years of working the land. Two months later, she would be gone and her husband would refuse to leave the garden even for a day. He'd keep it weeded and watered, then at the end of the day he would sit on the steps, watch the sky redden as the muezzin called the ghosts to prayer, and wait.

kaynarca

From the Turkish for spring, *kaynac*. In Kaynarca, a village of springs
between Kirklareli and the Black Sea, there is a tea house with the
following story. For a hundred years, an old shepherd's crook, or *gega*,
hung over the door. It had popped out of the spring one day, and
they said it belonged to a shepherd in Romania. Angry with a sheep,
he had thrown the crook at it, which had fallen into the Danube.
He'd been distraught. But that's a long way, you say, and the Danube
flows into the Black Sea, and anyway how do you know it's the same
crook? Easy: one day a stranger walked into the tea house, picked up
the gega, and unscrewed its top. Yep, he said, it's the one. Inside the
handle were forty gold coins, a fortune. No wonder the shepherd had
been distraught. The stranger replaced the gega over the door. It is not
said whether he took the coins.

The village had grown around the spring, which had only recently
been built into a stone fountain. I stopped here on my way to the
coast, to fill my bottle. I know it's the way of springs, but it struck
me as miraculous that the water hadn't run out since the days when
wealthy Thracians enjoyed ablutive holidays. When the Persian king
Darius paused on his way to war against the Scythians on the northern
side of the Danube, he drank from the spring and declared: 'The
world belongs to me, and the best water belongs to Kaynarca.' He

was right about one of these. In the fifteenth century, Sultan Mehmet, another man who thought the world belonged to him, paid tribute to the spring's mysteries. When his servants threw straw and coal into the Danube, he marvelled, it came out in Kaynarca!

All over Strandja, the bubbling springs narrate: what goes in pops out, what goes in pops out, even a hundred years later. And what is a hundred years to a spring?

THE MONK OF HAPPINESS

'A hundred years is nothing to a spring,' Tako said, 'but thirty years is half my bleeding life. Excuse the language.'

He was careful not to swear in polite company, and that's why he was called Tako: as a child, when he felt like cursing his elders, he'd shout instead 'Tako tako tako tako', a stream of nonsense. The name stuck.

'Famous Tako' was famous to those who knew him because he volunteered to sit in a plastic chair at the entrance to a sixth-century rock monastery called Saint Nicholas. Caves, springs, rock sanctuaries: the Thracians had passed them on to the Byzantines. Saint Nicholas was one of several rock monasteries and hermitages in the area, built during the reign of Emperor Justinian, though built isn't the word: it was hewn into the hill.

'Why do you do it?' I asked Tako.

''Cause I grew up here.' Tako pushed back his sunglasses over his black hair.

Tako was short and stocky, with a lined mahogany face, and he avoided smiling with his mouth open. Despite the cracked leather sandals, he wore a smart white shirt and greeted visitors with a dignified nod. He lived on meagre donations, because Tako's guardianship of the monastery was unofficial. Although he had a shack with his wife on the outskirts of town, he had built himself a small shelter here under a fig tree, where he slept on a wicker bed, drank with friends at night, and played melancholy or upbeat tunes on his brass trumpet, depending on his mood. And kept an eye on the cave all year round. What about winter, when the broken stone arches joined up with icy stalactites?

'Yep,' he said, 'I'm here in winter. But I sleep inside 'cause it has a permanent temperature. Sometimes, when it's really cold, I light myself a fire over there.'

'Over there' was one of the several entrances to the monastery, all dating from different centuries. Though they all looked indistinguishably crumbled. This was a historically and topographically charged spot, once impregnable except by river or sea. A section of the Byzantine fortress wall still stood, and the town was still inside the gated walls. Time and salt had turned everything a faded pink, and when you walked down the steps to the harbour, as ancient holidaymakers had done, the centuries-old name of the town still rang beautiful and true: Midye. In 1960, the government decided that Midye sounded too un-Turkish, and renamed it to Kiyiköy: Village of the Shores.

Tako, Nevzat, and I stood only a few hundred metres from the estuary of a river that emptied into a golden-sanded beach. Another river touched the sea further south, and on the small peninsula between the rivers was the Village of the Shores. That's where Tako lived when he wasn't at the rock monastery.

With the golden sands under your feet, the fragrant forest in your lungs, and the merging of fresh and salty waters, you could see why this place had been enjoyed by leisured folk since the days when it was called Salmydessus (Place by the Salty Water). Thracian aristocracy built holiday villas here, and by the time of Emperor Nero, it was established as a favourite summer resort. Although the Pontic Greeks controlled coastal towns, they didn't settle here. Perhaps it was the forbidding hinterland that put them off, a land that somehow looked inwards and not out to sea, like all of Strandja. Inwards, the hills were white and vertiginous with karst cliffs, and inside those cliffs were dozens of rock-hewn monasteries like this one, though none of them was accessible.

It was here that the army of the Persian king Darius landed, before it entered the Balkans en route to crushing the Scythians. Why none of the Thracian tribes fought Darius, with the exception of the fierce Getae, not even Herodotus explained. But common sense comes to mind: the Thracians were too fond of their leisure and their gold, and the Persian army was the largest in the known world. The Getae at the mouth of the Danube, unfortunately for them, 'offered fierce resistance and were at once reduced to slavery', Herodotus notes, before they were forced to join the war march to the north. Perhaps Darius visited the sanctuary of what is now Saint Nicholas, and washed in its icy spring where Thracians worshipped the cave–womb of their Mother Goddess, where pagan locals would be forcibly christened (ironic, when you learn of the high number of local Christians who were horribly martyred by the Romans), and where Tako chilled his bottles of cheap wine. It's also where tourists fell in the water now, because the local authorities had stopped Tako from building a railing.

Tako, who hadn't studied any of this, understood the grandeur of his surroundings in his way: he guarded it with his body.

'How come you never leave your post?' I asked him.

''Cause if I leave, this place'll go the same way as Asmakaya,' Tako said.

On the way to the formerly Byzantine ecclesiastical hub of Vize, past a quarry that sliced the hill like bread, inside the karst ridges was a place you couldn't find unless you knew it was there: Asmakaya. It meant Hanging Rock, and Nevzat knew that you reached it via a steep goat path that at any moment might hurl you into the gorge. There, a ninth-century niche monastery stared at you with white sockets. But there was no Tako to protect it from treasure hunters, who had dug holes in the floor, the walls, even the ceiling. On the other side of the gorge, only crossable by a thin rope bridge, was an eerie sight: a twentieth-century decoy village scattered over the scrubby hill, with a mosque and hollow roofless houses, observation towers, and barbed wire.

'A target Kurdish village,' Nevzat said. 'For anti-terrorist practice.'

This open-air military training ground had gone out of use only a few years ago. Before then, even the local road was off limits to civilians, and the monastery at Asmakaya was used by soldiers and shepherds. Above the animal droppings, on the fume-darkened walls of the monks' cells, generations of Cold War soldiers had carved terse messages. Some were done in huge letters, like silent cries for help:

KERIM, 69/3, 561

'Kerim was born in March 1969 and had 561 days of service left,' Nevzat deciphered. He too had written graffitti like this on the walls of abandoned buildings, near the border with Iraq. To pass the time and make you feel better, he said.

What was it like, to spend two years of your life in this gorge, looking at the minareted basilicas of Vize in the evening haze, balancing on the rope bridge between the abandoned rock monastery and the fake Kurdish village, a chasm of time below you?

'What happened to Asmakaya is what I don't want to happen here,' Tako said.

Tako had spent thirty years at Saint Nicholas. I was unable to find out whether the site had been deliberately concealed by the military detritus of Kemalist Turkification or naturally concealed by alluvial drifts, or both, but in the 1950s the wake of a massive river flood revealed the astonishing sight of the monastery. Inside it were carved animals both 'zoological and mythical, cryptic Byzantine symbols, crosses, elaborate carved ceilings, and the icy-cold spring that gurgled somewhere in the hill and served as a bottle-chiller now.

Tako had pinned up some newspaper articles about the place, handy since the official sign was illegible with rust and random English, and he'd made a small tourist display of brochures on the plastic table before him. But most people gave nothing. Some gave nothing plus their arrogance, like an Istanbul lawyer who said to Tako: Sod off, people like me can't give money to the likes of you. Because Tako was a Gypsy.

Still, he persevered. His latest effort was a newly built toilet in the woods, so that visitors came to a civilised place, he said, and didn't have to go off into the woods, which weren't safe. Especially not for women.

Once, he'd made a poster too: Welcome to Saint Nicholas! But the police came and tore it up on one of their visits. At one point, a previous mayor had forced Tako to leave.

'That was a terrible time,' Tako said. 'I knew the place would be wrecked.'

He was right. After three months, treasure hunters had dug up the clay floor, drunk hunting parties had turned the monastery into a rubbish dump, empty bottles and cigarette butts filled the tombs and alcoves. People stopped visiting.

Grumblingly, the mayor called on Tako to resume his unpaid duties. Tako cleaned up the mess, patched up the floor, and sat in his plastic chair again.

'Next time they'll have to remove me with a crane,' he said.

Tako, a Muslim, was in awe of the carvings, the arches, the votive chambers, the tomb niches, and the silent mangrove of the estuary where he could lie in the peppermint bushes with a cigarette, listen to the sea waves, and be the happiest man on earth.

'Church or mosque, it's all the same,' he said. 'A place of God and silence. You have to treat it with respect.'

His family, originally from Salonica, had washed up here with other Greek Muslims in 1923. Arriving in Midye, they found a ghost town vacated by its Christians. Tako's family had continued their traditional trades: fishing, building, field labour. His brother took tourists upstream where languid forests closed over the river, in a boat called *Tako*.

'And my nephew is leaving for the Syrian border today,' Tako said. 'Thank god I have daughters.'

The way Tako and the monastery have been treated by the authorities has something to do with two types of cultural barbarity, which in the end come down to one. The Gypsies enjoy a less dehumanised status here than in the rest of the Balkans, but they remain pariahs. Since the eleventh century, the Roma have been in every Balkan village and town: they are the woodcutters, labourers, cleaners, coppersmiths, shoe shiners, bear trainers, horse traders, fortune tellers, and, of course, musicians that the Balkans couldn't do without, though they won't admit it. There is hardly a public event without a Gypsy accordionist, trumpeter, drummer, or fiddler. Even in Ottoman population registers, 'musician' was the most common Gypsy occupation.

'But why?' I asked Tako again. 'Thirty years is a long time to work without pay, recognition, or a kind word.'

Jobs are not plentiful in the village of the salty water where fishing is seasonal, and this was a way to get a few liras here and there, plus the odd gift of clothes and food, Nevzat explained. Nevzat had known Tako since they were teenagers.

Just then, a wedding party pulled up by the river. It was the latest fashion: brides photographed by the rock monastery. Though Tako was never in the picture.

'This is why.' He nodded at the groom and bride. 'Because it gives me pleasure to see people here. And I can't abandon it now. I took on a responsibility and must see it through. Come.'

He got up from the plastic chair and led me and Nevzat inside.

It was warm and humid. The slimy, moss-green walls bore the insignia of two main eras – medieval and the late 1900s – in which the three main visiting nationalities had wanted to keep up with history by signing their names in Latin, Greek, and Cyrillic.

'Look at this!' he said and waved his arms to take it all in. 'Isn't it something?'

He showed us the ossuary, the cells, the carved snakes with heads lopped off by treasure hunters. He showed us the stone steps that led down to the reservoir at the back. It was flooded and filled with stones and debris. Tako had started cleaning up the reservoir, but the stones were too many. They had been dumped deliberately, to block off a tunnel.

'The tunnel starts here.' Tako pointed at a submerged sea-facing wall.

When he was a kid, the access was open. He and his friends had entered the tunnel and walked it, until they encountered a blockage. The tunnel was said to cut through the hill and lead all the way to the sea, where it popped out at a large standing rock that looked to some like a nun. You could see the rock from the beach, but not the entrance into the hill.

'They say that back in the day, when this entrance touched the river, there were only two ways to reach it. By boat, and through the sea tunnel.'

This is how the monks smuggled people in when the going was tough.

'Stand here,' Tako instructed me. I stood on the step he indicated, just under a carved ceiling dome. It was warm like a sauna.

'Now go down one step,' Tako said.

One step down, it was freezing like a cellar. Tako grinned.

'Can you explain it? Neither can I.'

It was like this all year round.

'You'd have to pay me to spend the night in here,' I said and Tako humoured me by smiling. He'd done it for free for thirty years.

But he had experienced things at night, things he couldn't explain.

'The first time I heard it,' he said, 'my blood froze. Bloody hell! Pardon my language. It was a child crying. And a woman saying something. She was dumping the child. I heard a sad song too, like a lullaby.'

Always at night, the child's crying came from somewhere in the hill above the cave. But when he moved closer, the sound moved away. Now it came from the hill, now it came from the river.

'Some things don't go away,' he shrugged. 'I guess a woman had given birth to an unwanted child.'

I shuddered, but Tako wasn't scared of the dead, only of the living.

Tako was the opposite of the nomad whose wandering image had fuelled the settled peasant's fear and loathing of the Gypsies since their arrival in the Balkans. A sixteenth-century sultan's decree begins like this:

'Groups of Gypsies ride fine horses. They do not stay in the same place but move from town to town.'

And ends like this:

'They have to renounce their nomadic way of life, to settle down and to take up farming. The Gypsies must from now on be forced to sell their horses, and if anyone objects they must be punished with a prison sentence.'

Settle down – the eternal instruction given by the unfree to the free, adults to kids, patriarchs to reprobates, people to dogs. In that decree, even Gypsy acrobats were banned from using horses. But behind this equestrian phobia was something mundane: taxes. It was difficult to collect taxes from a community on the move. Either way, it didn't work; Anatolia was the only place in the empire where the Gypsy community 'settled down'. The Gypsies could not be separated from their horses and libertine ways, and they always paid a price for their freedom, with the double tax of money and stigma. When a Gypsy community took Islam, its members still paid taxes comparable to those paid by the Christian *raya,* or infidels; they had no relief. Gypsy women who took multiple lovers ('unlawful activities'), even when it was more for pleasure than for money, paid the heaviest taxes to the sultan – which is odd, seeing that the sultan was doing the same.

Here is a description of Balkan Gypsies by the seventeenth-century English traveller Henry Blount:

'They prophesy your future in the same deceptive way as our Gypsies do, and are, too, satisfied with very little. They are used mostly for dirty work. They happily clothe themselves in rags, and live in shacks and small houses in the outskirts, surrounded by contempt.'

By 'dirty work' understand the usual, plus executioners, undertakers, and frontline fodder in the Ottoman army. Gypsy soldiers were the principal defenders at major battles against the Austrian Empire, like Kosovo Polje in the 1700s. But nobody thanked a Gypsy. The Gypsies can be Muslims, Christians, or neither. They can dress in rags or cover themselves in gold. They can live in a mansion with a goat. And no matter what they do, they remain incorrigibly themselves: borderless. Self-chained to the monastery, Tako was the most settled person I'd met, yet he was still, somehow, a free man.

When I produced a bottle of premium Bulgarian grape raki, Tako's face cracked into a grin for the first time. He immediately went to the nave in the back and placed it in the water, to chill for later that night.

'You asked me why I guard the monastery,' he said just before we left.

When he was a child he was convinced that the secrets of life were inside the niches and tunnels. The Gypsy community came and camped by the river in the May fest of Hidrellez, Saint George's Day. They hung swings from the still-standing wooden columns of the monastery façade and swung until they were dizzy, no doubt contributing to the demise of the columns. When he was a teenager, he brought his first girl here. He still remembered that first kiss. And the taste of his first cigarette.

'Maybe it's my own memories I'm guarding,' he said. 'My own happiness.'

We said goodbye. Other tourists were arriving. The slow sound of Tako's trumpet simultaneously greeted them and sent us off, a one-man band. In the car, Nevzat said what I was thinking:

'When Tako goes one day, happiness will go with him.'

But Nevzat was an optimist. Turkey had its first-ever Gypsy MP: a man from a nomadic horse-trading background. Who knows, maybe one day the authorities will wake up and put Tako on the state payroll?

In the village centre, by the nibbled pink ruins, a different kind of send-off party was taking place. A band of musicians played a cheerful tune and a group danced *kuchek* around a young Gypsy guy with a red Turkish neck-scarf. Soon, he was bundled into a car, and to the festive beat of hooting and drumming, he was driven away like a groom to his bride. But this wasn't a wedding.

This was Tako's nephew, off to do army service. The family were clapping to give him courage, but when I looked more closely at the women's faces, I saw the tear stains on their smiles. And still the band played on.

eternal return

According to the philosopher Mircea Eliade, 'the myth of the eternal return' is the idea that by performing divinely inspired rites, 'prehistoric man' feels connected to a mythical dimension outside linear time and therefore history. That's what the nestinari are about.

I'm not prehistoric man, yet something about the Black Sea coast gives me a sense of eternal return in my own small mythical way. Right now, I stood on a needle-like clifftop. The Black Sea ahead and Strandja behind, two different wildernesses overseen by the same light. Huddled in the shelter of the pointed promontory is the sleepy village of Iğneada, Needle Point.

Along the coast between the Bosphorus and the border, half a dozen tranquil fishing villages like Iğneada and Midye dwell in silence all year, and are briefly startled into wakefulness by holidaymakers in summer. The last village before the border is Beğendik, and there, Turkish fishermen swap gossip with their Bulgarian arkadashes in Rezovo, across an invisible line in the sea that used to mean a lot more, because the border river empties there. Things are friendly now, but the two countries waged a petty piscine dispute in the last decade of the Cold War. Each side built up the estuary by dumping soil in it, to claim more territorial sea waters and more turbot. The turbot started dying in protest.

★

From Needle Point, you can almost see the invisible sea border, but then you're never sure what it is you glimpse in the sea mist; everything looks as if it might be a memory in the making. This place felt to me less like a place and more like a continuing moment in time, a single perfect Pontic note. Lashed by the lodos from the south and Siberian currents from the north, you stand in a portal. Now you're mortal, now you're not. Now it's you, now it's everyone who passed here before you.

If I stood here long enough, I might just fall out of linear time and begin to see a ghostly glow from the depths. Because this coast is a submerged world of wrecks. The name of Cape Oil, north of Tsarevo (Michurin) in Bulgaria, is a memento of the untold quantities of olive oil that infused the sea during wreckages. They say when things got rough, a siren would appear out of the waves with a torch and lead you on to some point of eternal return or other.

THE GOOD SIREN

Turkey's coast had 482 lighthouses, but only five of those were still manned, I'd heard, and one of them was here, on the needle-like promontory: the sole lighthouse between the Bosphorus and the border.

High on the cliffs, Limanköy Feneri cut a lonely white figure. Its north–south needle quivered in the breeze. This needle had been hand-greased by generations of keepers, who climbed onto the dome from the little balcony. Until twenty years ago, the lamp had run on gas oil.

People still called it the French Lighthouse, because it was a French merchant-navy officer who had constructed it. A veteran of the Messageries Maritimes line that sailed between Marseilles and the Near East, Captain Marius Michel began to think of how to modernise coastal signalling after surviving a sea wreck near Alexandria. By the time he submitted his proposal to Napoleon, who referred it to his ally, Sultan Abdülmecid, the Crimean War was raging, much of it at sea. The British and the French were Ottoman allies against imperial Russia, and seeing the strategic need for coastal safety, the sultan bought the French captain's idea outright. Between 1855 and 1866, under the directorship of Marius Michel, the new venture, called the Administration des Phares de l'Empire Ottoman, built 111 lighthouses.

Handcrafted in France to the latest technology using lantern lenses, the lighthouses stand to this day, some in Bulgarian territory. A small workshop on the shores of the Bosphorus painstakingly repairs the antiquated parts in the rare event that they break down. After completing his commission, Michel was honoured with an Ottoman title and went down in history as Michel Pasha. Already wealthy, he became fabulously wealthy from the hefty fees imposed on passing vessels for lighthouse services. The revenue was shared with the Ottoman state until its final dissolution in the Balkan Wars of 1912–13. A passionate orientalist (not surprisingly, seeing how well the Orient had done for him), Michel Pasha returned to France and recreated a Victorian Constantinople in his home town on the Riviera. That is where this charmed man died of old age, in the same mental waters where he had sailed: somewhere between East and West.

When the lighthouse keeper brought me to the white lighthouse on the cliffs, he pointed out two motionless cargo ships on the horizon.

Across the dark sea, so dark you could believe 90 per cent of it was hydrogen sulphide, the rust-coloured ships looked like revenants of a purely Pontic dimension.

The signal can be seen as far as twenty miles out at sea, and many anchor out there, to rest and refuel, the keeper explained. After all, this is one of the busiest and most treacherous maritime routes in the world.

'And unlike anchorage on the Bosphorus, it's free,' he smiled, though he wasn't a smiley man.

Each lighthouse has its unique signal frequency. When ships see a yellow light every three seconds, they know it's Limanköy Feneri.

'It must be comforting to see a familiar signal on land when you're far from home,' I said to the keeper, and he nodded, pleased.

'The signal has never failed,' he said with quiet pride.

He was a tall, bald man of fifty with watery blue eyes and a soft body that had caved in, as if from a blow. I wondered whether it was his nature or recent events that had caused this slump.

Because he was an *ex*-keeper. Although it had been his brother, the eldest of six siblings, who had inherited the title, the whole family considered themselves lighthouse keepers. It was a badge of honour. A couple of years ago, the government had ended not just the keeper's contract, but the post altogether. The family had been forced to hand over the big key of the round tower to the new owners: the naval forces. Never again would a keeper live at the bottom of the spiral stairs that led to the glass dome of light.

The keeper was put on a pension, and the house was put up for auction. The four sisters and two brothers had fought a long battle to buy the house, pleaded with the government, offered more money than it was worth. But it went to a hotelier from Istanbul who was now converting it into a café.

'This is where I was born.' The keeper opened a door to a modest room. It had been stripped of its furniture like the other two rooms. 'We were all born here, and my mother was born here too. We were married off here and sent away. All of us.'

He tried the door to the stairwell but it was locked, the key in some regional office of the navy. They were married off here but none of the six children had left the vicinity. They all stayed close to the lighthouse.

'We had to keep an eye on it,' he said. 'What if it went out, who would go up the stairs and fix it?'

No, they couldn't leave it.

'We had a curtain that we pulled round the tower in the morning, to protect the lamp crystals from daylight, but I see they've removed it.'

His earliest memory was of going up the spiral stairs to watch his mother pull the curtain open and light the lamp. It was in the days of gas, and the signal needed 'feeding' every two hours. The family had a nightly roster, and in the absence of alarm clocks, they had a system consisting of the gas tin which was attached to the rotating lamp. When two hours were up, the empty tin would fall and wake them up with a bang. Nobody ever missed a shift.

'Here was the kitchen.'

The fire oven was still there, and the well for collecting rainwater. It was a shock for the keeper to see the rooms stripped of life. We stepped out into the small courtyard at the back of the house to get some air.

'When we were young, my dad would lock the gate. But we'd jump over the wall and go to the village anyway.'

Limanköy, Village of the Harbour, hadn't existed until after the lighthouse was built. This was a wild coast, unsafe for habitation because of pirates on the sea and bandits on the land.

One day, a Pomak family from central Bulgaria found itself on the road of exile. They crossed the border and stopped in the first village on the Turkish side: Beğendik. This was in the wake of the ever-present Lausanne Treaty of 1923, when the heroine of this story was five years old. Her name was Selvet.

In due course Selvet was married off to the son of the lighthouse keepers, and this is how she ended up living here on the edge between a wild sea and a wild land as a young bride. First with her in-laws, then without them, and eventually without her husband, because World War II was upon them and he was off to the Bosphorus.

By then, Selvet had three small daughters. There were still no other houses, no electricity, not even a track on land. Rare provisions, and most importantly gas tins for the lighthouse, were brought to the cliff by boat and pulled up. Every two hours, Selvet rose from her bed to climb the stairs and light the lamp. She locked the flimsy door at night, against brigands of all stripes who roamed the land on horseback.

She was acutely alone with the three toddlers and acutely close to a disputed border.

After six years, Selvet accepted that her man would never return. For fourteen years, she ran the lighthouse alone, worked the land behind the house and watched her daughters grow. There were perks to the job too: the lighthouse was a symbol of modernity, and Selvet was the proud owner of the first radio in the area, the first TV, and the first pieces of European-style furniture. Girls from the village came up to visit her daughters and gather in the walled courtyard to gossip, listen to music and the news, and wait for the young soldiers from the nearby border barracks to come and flirt with them from beyond the lighthouse walls.

Selvet was the keeper's grandmother.

In the 1960s, the baton was passed on to her eldest daughter, who became our keeper's mother. The more I asked, the less talkative the keeper became, not meeting my eyes as if he was trying not to show me his pain; not because so much had happened here, but because it was over. It wasn't just the family history that was over, but also that chapter in the human history of Black Sea lighthouses, and with it a certain harsh poetry had ended in favour of mundane mechanics that would never make a story.

He slumped with the weight of it, as if only the need to prop up the lighthouse had kept him upright.

We took a walk inland. Between the lighthouse and the village, along a still-unpaved dirt road, was the cemetery, where two marble slabs marked the graves of the keeper's parents. Engraved above their names was a single word:

FENERCI

Lighthouse Keeper. A profession, a mission, a way of life, an identity.

The keeper's father had been a lover of books and printed media, and insisted on educating his brood. Every day, he had taken his six children to school, three kilometres down the road, on foot.

Today, the clifftop village is dwarfed by palatial holiday villas. The fishing harbour of Limanköy has been marked by the cement-extracting companies hacking into Strandja to expand it into an industrial port that would ship the shattered hills away.

I asked him what he misses most from the lighthouse.

He looked at me, a rare moment of eye contact, and I regretted asking, because we both knew the answer.

'This place contains my life,' he said. 'I can't single out one thing. But it's okay. Because we're still here. We've never left.'

The evening wind rose and the breaking waves below grew bigger and whiter. It was only August, what about the winter? The keeper's face relished the memory.

'That's why it's called the Black Sea,' he said.

Winter storms were so ferocious, sometimes the house rattled and salt spray came through the windows. The roar was deafening. The sea could take them any moment without leaving a trace.

'It was a lonely life. The sea before you and nothing behind you. No neighbours. The village miles away. And yet.'

The keeper had heard stories of pirates from grandmother Selvet, passed on to her by the old keepers. They had seen the last of the pirates, and the last of those unsung Pontic heroes who moved between forest and sea, sea and forest: the *gemidji*, boatmen who shipped the logs and charcoal of Strandja to Constantinople and beyond, braving storms, dubious sirens, and fickle markets.

Before we left the deserted site, the keeper pointed at two houses beyond the lighthouse, the only ones close by. They belonged to his sisters.

'You see,' he straightened up, 'we haven't abandoned it. We're still keeping an eye.'

The cargo ships on the horizon hadn't moved.

When I looked up at the glass dome, a last ray of sun caught in the halogen lamp and made me blink, and in that blink I saw Selvet, with her girls asleep in the room below, climbing the spiral stairs every two hours of the black night to refuel the lamp. Her man was somewhere out there, she didn't know where. The wind howled, the sea raged, the war had gone on too long. Wrapped in a blanket, she climbed, heavy with sleep and misgiving, to guide *gemidji* and warships alike, as if all was well on the Pontus.

And if you were a passing ship, all you'd know of it is the yellow light that still flashes every three seconds in the night. Without fail.

muhhabet

In archaic Turkish: 1. conversation; 2. love. *Muhhabet* is free, but it is
also a luxury, because it takes more than one to have it. The word, if
not the practice, has gone out of use in modern Turkish, but survives
among older people and country folk in the Balkans: a faraway Arabic
word that lives on in Europe's mouths.

I was on the road for the last time with Nevzat. A song came on the
folkloric radio station that pierced you with its lament. It was called
'Bir Firtina Tuttu Bizi' ('We Were Caught in a Storm'), requested by
a shepherd in the hills of Cappadocia, the radio host said, in tribute
to his family, who came as refugees from Thessaloniki. It was a song,
Nevzat said, in which the beloved is the homeland, and the homeland
is Rumelia.

Rumelia: the Ottoman designation for the land of Romans, that is
Byzantines, that is Christians, that is Europeans. Rumelia was the
once-Ottoman Balkans, or 'Turkey in Europe', a vanished world. I
thought of Stefania who ran the Hotel Above the World, and how her
family had sailed the other way, blown by the same storm and singing
the same song but about Anatolia.

★

We were caught in a storm. Dragged and scattered to the sea.
Our reunion is postponed to the day after we die.
I grew old with waiting. My eyes faded, my flesh fell away.
Our reunion is postponed to the day after we die.

There was no muhhabet in the hills of Cappadocia, but at least that
shepherd had a radio.

THE LAST SHEPHERD

It was raining when we reached the last village of Strandja, and wrapped in an oilskin jacket, Mustafa was sheltering with a cigarette under the roof of an abandoned house. His sheep and goats were scattered motionless over the hill. A small transistor radio sat in the broken window next to him.

He was so startled to see visitors that the cigarette fell out of his mouth. He stepped into the rain to greet us and his face lit up.

'Come, come,' he said, 'Feride will be so happy to see you.'

He picked up his shepherd's crook and led the way, taking huge strides. He was immense and powerful in a way men aren't any more, only biblical kings. The lambing season has just been, he said, and he had one hundred new lambs. One hundred beautiful new lambs.

'Do you want to see them?'

'Yes, but let's see Feride first,' Nevzat said.

Their house was on a hill with sweeping views. Feride came out of the house, her hands covered in flour from bread-making. She was a small woman with an open, unlined face under the loose headscarf. Next to Mustafa, she looked like a child. We sat at the outside table under an apple tree for an exchange of rolling tobacco.

'We have everything here, look,' Mustafa gestured over the village below.

'Everything except people,' Feride smiled.

All the houses were abandoned. They lived in the last standing house. It had belonged to Mustafa's parents. The village was called, oddly, Darkness, but the sky over the hills shifted with many-coloured lights, like in a fairy tale. Sunrays had broken through the rain cloud and the rich grass was heating up again.

'We have three types of water,' Mustafa said, and pointed at the spring gushing just outside the house.

'That one's good for tea,' he said. 'The one up the hill is good for washing. And this one,' he pointed at another spring just beside the table, 'is good for drinking.'

'Everything except muhhabet,' Feride said.

Like Nursel and Nevzat, they had a flat in Kirklareli but didn't love the city, they loved it here where they had grown up.

Beside the house was their absent son's car, the bonnet sprayed with an eye and a motto recognisable in the whole of Turkey:

'Doing army service. Don't look for me.'

He was in the last months of a posting on the border with Syria and his parents waited and prayed, prayed and waited. They showed me a photo of him and his fiancée. They would get married as soon as he was back, and Mustafa would raise the wedding money by selling some of his flock.

'I wanted to prove it was possible,' Mustafa said, 'to live from shepherding. To live a free life. Like people used to.'

I suddenly recalled a simple song that my grandfather, a city accountant for most of his adult life, liked to sing off-key, when he felt happy and carefree:

> 'When I was a little shepherd,
> up in the hills with my flock
> I had nothing, I was poor
> yet happy with my lot.'

Everyone in the Balkans comes from a village if you go back far enough, but my grandfather's generation was the last to grow up close to animals, before collectivisation arrived. Strandja in particular was always an Arcadia, the ultimate land of humans and sheep. Twenty-seven centuries after Arcadia was mentioned in ancient texts, this 'blind district', or *kyor kaz*, of the Ottoman Empire had the highest number of sheep per head in the world, bar Australia. Nothing had interrupted animal husbandry, not even the plague, until now. What will remain in Strandja of the early twenty-first century, other than the rust of army bases and hills eviscerated of their riches?

Mustafa with his flock was going against the flow of history.

Feride looked after the house, milked the animals, and talked to herself on those long days when Mustafa was gone in the hills with his radio. And because they couldn't abandon the animals in winter, they stayed here all year, even when the snow went halfway up the house and the three types of water froze. The road became impassable.

At one point, the electricity was cut.

'I said to the Mayor, come on arkadash, put the electricity back on. And he said, Slaughter me a lamb and I'll give you electricity. I slaughtered him two lambs.'

They had electricity now, but no street lights. At night, the only light for miles around came from their windows.

The reason why once-thriving Darkness had become a phantom village was the same as with all the others along the border: the junta had frightened the locals away.

'All we need is another family,' Feride said.

'See the house by that pear tree?' Mustafa pointed to the hill opposite. It was a long-abandoned house that had belonged to a Bulgarian family who fled across the border with all the rest. Afterwards, the neighbour had dug up the pear tree and found treasure. He built his sons houses in the city with the money.

'But what was under the tree didn't belong to him.' Mustafa shook his head.

The fleeing family had buried their money under the pear tree, hoping they would return one day. Their descendants were the men and women I'd met on the other side: the shopkeepers and forestry workers, border guards and honey-makers, factory labourers and fire-walkers, drunks and émigrés blown by the winds of fortune.

The pear tree still bears fruit.

'Maybe they'll return one day?' Feride said but she didn't believe it. It had been a hundred years.

Two summers ago, Mustafa said, four black horses appeared on the hill.

'Like a sign from above,' he grinned. 'Black horses without riders.'

The horses had escaped and crossed the border. Mustafa and the owner spoke on the phone. They tried their best from each side of the Rezovo River, but there was no convincing the horses. They were a valuable breed, Mustafa said, worth 5,000 US dollars each, but in the end, the owner accepted that his horses had gone wild. Now he visited them once a year, and that meant muhhabet under the apple tree.

'I saw them on the other side!' I said. 'Going south. Two summers ago!'

'Nothing goes away in Strandja,' Nevzat smiled, unsurprised.

'But the horses won't help Feride when I'm in the hills,' Mustafa said, 'if somebody comes to the house.'

There were two types of unwanted visitor: refugees and the army. The army came to question the couple about the refugees. The sight of trucks disgorging people within view of their house had become a frequent distress. Once, a group of Syrian women and children came to the door. It was the middle of winter. Some were in sandals.

'Sandals in the snow,' Mustafa said and his chin shook.

'We were not prepared,' Feride said.

Traffickers brought people from Istanbul and Edirne and dumped them here, literally in the Darkness.

'And they come running to me,' Mustafa said. 'Bulgaria? Bulgaria? And my heart sinks when I say No, Turkey, Turkey. Sure, I can show them the way over the hills, across the river, but do you know what those hills are like?'

'Not even boar can pass through that forest,' Feride said.

'And yet,' Mustafa said, 'it would take just one family to bring life back to the village. We have motorbikes. I'm not managing on my own. I need another pair of hands. Why is it so difficult?'

The mayor, I was told later, was deliberately keeping the village empty, that's why he'd disconnected the power.

But Mustafa and Feride never complained. They had too little favour, and too much to lose. What was at stake was their livelihood and their dream. Few people are so lucky as to have the two converge.

'Do you want to see the lambs?' Mustafa said and his face lit up.

We said goodbye to Feride and went to see the lambs. They were inside the dark pen, one hundred of them, white and trembling with youth. Mustafa fed them milk from bottles. He beckoned us across the muddy courtyard, where our feet sank into dung.

'My beautiful babies,' he said, and stroked them one after the other with his huge hands. And though Nevzat wanted a portrait of him, Mustafa kept placing the lambs in front of him to be photographed. One after the other.

On the way back, Nevzat pointed at something and I braked. We sat and watched them graze on a meadow of late-summer grass: four black horses.

It was my last day in Turkey. We drove south in the shadow of Mahya, the highest peak of Strandja. It has buzzed with military

secrets since Turkey joined NATO. I wondered if the army knew
the truth about the vanished Paroria of the Hesychasts – because one
theory puts it here on Mahya, where civilian access has been barred
since 1952.

I dropped Nevzat off at our habitual place of meeting and parting:
the crossroads at the end of Kirklareli among the fields of sunflowers.
Dear Nevzat produced a present from his rucksack: woollen socks
hand-knitted by Nursel, to see me through the Scottish winter.

'Well, say hello to the other Strandja for me,' he said. His old visa
for Bulgaria had expired and he had been refused a new one.

We hugged and I climbed into my car. It was the border that had
brought us together and opened up a whole new world for me, but
now that I was about to cross it again, I felt a terrible wrenching, a
sense of impending loss so great and so out of joint with the present
that it had to be from the past.

Turkey felt to me like a home long lost somewhere in time,
perhaps in the same way that Bulgaria felt to Nevzat.

Nevzat stood at the crossroads and waved, and in his gesture I
glimpsed a distant scene from our childhood. Not the childhood we'd
had, but a slightly different one.

Summer 1984. Across the border river, I saw a dark-haired boy
with horses, waving. In my beach bag was *The Call of the Wild*. The
river was free of soldiers and wire, just a brilliance of green rushing
water and dragonflies. Soon it would be September and storks would
darken our Pontic sky. Soon we would grow up and this would be a
memory.

I waved back.

uroki

The evil eye, in Bulgarian. When you have strange dreams or phantom pains, when you can't sleep, or when unholy suffering grips you, you know it's *uroki*. Along the border live healers who perform exorcism against spells and unease. This one was recorded in the nineteenth century:

> *Sleep with God, rise with God,*
> *he will heed, he will field*
> *seventy-seven badnesses*
> *if they cross me in my sleep,*
> *on the road, on the crossroad,*
> *on the fire, on the bonfire,*
> *if they cross me, if they strike me,*
> *seventy-seven badnesses.*

Two years on from the Village in the Valley, I had come to a 'crossroad'. I knew I needed to take the road leading away, not the one that would take me round and round in an endless cycle. Several of the farewells I'd had with people had been at crossroads – and in the mythical mind, crossroads are ritual sites of transformation. Strandja people traditionally used crossroads to cure the ill, send off the spirits of the dead, and induce fertility in seeds. There are only two journeys that can't be crossed: a wedding and a funeral, and the fire-walkers too never cross each other's way across the embers. But me?

My heart was heavy with gifts and my head full of voices. I had to go home and lay them down, and home meant Scotland, in one temporal dimension. But there was another dimension, where a sense of unfinished business held me back.

Since leaving the Village in the Valley two years before, I had revisited it many times, in my dreams. Again and again, my subconscious took me down into the moist valley of warm, familiar faces, where the door of an old house creaked open to reveal something rich and vital that I couldn't do without. The eyes of jackals lined the fringes of the forest like lanterns, then I would wake up. By coming to Strandja, I had opened some kind of Pandora's Box in my own psyche. Strandja was now holding me in. There was a powerful gravitational pull in these ranges. What if some voodoo had been put on me two years ago, in the Village in the Valley? Back then, I hadn't believed in uroki, in mountains that didn't let you in or out, or in springs whose cold water drew you back. Now I wasn't so sure about the things I didn't believe in.

For the last time, I crossed the border. From Kirklareli an empty new motorway ran all the way to the checkpoint where, this time, the Turkish side waved me through with apathy, but the Bulgarian side welcomed me energetically with a car search, during which the unfortunate whirling dervish was once again parted from his feet.

HOW TO LIFT A SPELL

The healer appraised me over her glasses. She was a retired nurse with a bird-like face, bony fingers, and a chirpy manner, and she lived at the top of a steep street from which the roofs of the pretty border town looked like pebbles in the dark cup of the hills.

Her courtyard was aromatic with geraniums and her house breathed with heavy old-fashioned furniture. Marina had brought me here because the healer had helped with her insomnia. Marina, who wasn't one to say 'I told you so!' even though she *had* told me so, saw nothing strange in my condition.

'The mountain has let you in.' Her smile quivered. 'Now it won't let you out.'

I was anxious to have the healer's assessment. But she took her time. She put a box of chocolates on the table and twittered about her grandson without looking at me directly. Her incontinent chatter contrasted with Marina's silences.

I was getting lulled by her stream of consciousness when she said:

'Yes, I've had a career in conventional medicine, spent my life with doctors, pharmacists and patients, and the roots of human illness are a mystery, probably all illness has spiritual causes, medicine loathes to admit how powerless it is, oh yes.'

I woke up. She gave me a piercing look as if to say 'If you think I'm just a dotty old woman, you've got another think coming.'

Two generations of border army personnel had passed through this living room, including generals, along with the entire staff of the regional hospital, including chief surgeons (she liked to mention high ranks), and hundreds of locals. People brought her gifts or cash as they saw fit, but the service was offered for free – because it was a vocation, passed down from woman to woman in the family. Her mother had been a healer, and in her last years, blind from diabetes, she had used her daughter's eyes when performing rites, but didn't reveal the words until just before her death.

The most common of the rituals was called Melt the Bullet. The healer left the room and brought back an old hunting knife with a blackened blade, and a tin dish. These were the tools for Melt the Bullet.

The other rituals were Lift the Spell and Reverse the Footprint.

For Melt the Bullet, you need a bullet that has been used to kill a wild animal. You, the afflicted soul, rub your head, chest, and legs with the bullet, and sleep with it under your pillow. Then you come to her with it; if you can't come in person, you send a T-shirt worn by you and touched by the bullet. She melts the bullet and pours it into the water in her dish, until the lead assembles again. In the shape of the molten lead, she sees things about your current state and about your past.

As she pours the lead, she mumbles the special formula three times.

'A colonel came to me once with insomnia. He couldn't talk about it but I saw it in his lead. A figure with a gun. There had been an incident on the border.'

Read between the lines: she healed killers of their guilt.

Eventually, the lead had to come together again into one piece, so the person's 'burst' heart would 'collect'.

'To be fair, some people's hearts are so burst that it takes many attempts,' said the healer. 'Like the colonel's – his lead kept breaking down until it was porridge. You can't make a bullet from porridge. It took many attempts.'

Then the healer hands you back your healed bullet–heart, strains the water in which your bullet has 'collected', and pours a bit of it over your head, heart, and legs. Or you can drink it. If a garment has been used, you throw it into a clean stream to wash away the suffering after forty days.

Why forty days?

Forty days: a symbolic number in the spiritual world. When someone dies in Bulgaria or Turkey, mourning is strictly observed for forty days, and after forty days, a ceremony honours the passing of their soul with offerings of food and prayer. In Tibetan Buddhism, the number of days is forty-nine, and it is believed that the spirit of the dead person remains in the interim realm called the 'bardo of becoming' for that length of time, after which it looks for a channel – usually a human womb – through which to be reborn, and restart the cycle of *samsara*, suffering. Unless a transformation of the spirit occurs in the interim and healing results. It's never too late in Buddhism, but in Christianity it is always too late. Suffering is the order of the day. Thank God for pagan healers.

If we consider the evil eye or any other spiritual affliction to be a state between life and death, then the healer was a mediator between realms. That's why there was a personal risk to the healer, Marina said.

'All the bad energy she took from me went into her.'

The healer shrugged. 'You take on people's darkness when you lift it from them. It has to go somewhere. Then I perform rituals to cleanse myself. But that's nobody else's business.'

Marina's sleep had been fine ever since her bullet–heart 'collected'. Melt the Bullet was performed for people who'd had a fright, a trauma, a bereavement, or some other emotional disturbance that was manifested psychosomatically.

Uroki was a different matter. Victims experienced a rupture in their life-flow. It was a form of energetic malevolence that could take hold of you for a long time. It could even kill you.

'Sometimes a child can fall down stricken,' the healer said, 'and if you don't have the words against uroki to hand, the child can waste away.'

I must have looked dubious because she went on:

'Just imagine,' she said, 'if you had the evil eye and came here, and saw my grandson, and said Why, what a lovely boy! Next thing, he falls down stricken.'

Perhaps that's why she kept the poor henpecked grandson in a separate room where he munched snacks and watched TV all day, forbidden from going out in the street alone, although he was ten years old and huge. Still, the question remained: what if the evil eye really exists? After all, my old certain self had weakened. Something *had* changed in me.

On the Turkish side, the belief in the evil eye, or *nazar*, was alive and well too, and nazar is the familiar round blue eye talisman. The Koran speaks of this too, and even the Prophet Mohammed says, 'The influence of the evil eye is a fact.' The evil eye is also 'a fact' in the Old Testament, and you might say that one of the Ten Commandments deals with just that: Do not covet what belongs to your neighbour. Nevzat's friend Mr Karadeniz had told me how his own uncle had had an evil eye he couldn't control.

'It was enough for him to sit down with a glass of tea, look at a passing cow, and say *Mashallah!*, what a lovely cow, for the cow to collapse. They had to call in a *hodja* to say a prayer for the cow.'

The hodjas are religious scholars and teachers, but also popular healers. The healing chants in the Muslim tradition are verses from the Koran sometimes mixed up with some form of numerological calculation, while in the 'Christian' tradition they feature animals, spirits, and body parts, and all mentions of God seem incidental. Somehow, across a chasm of time, the chants have survived monotheism, modernity, and censorship. Perhaps their endurance is down to the absence of organised witch-hunting in the Balkans. In Western Europe and North America the Inquisition, the Reformation, Puritanism, and later industrialisation crushed centuries-old native customs, but in Oriental Europe where Islam and Judaeo-Christianity cohabited for centuries, it is another story: natural and supernatural healing methods, herbs and potions, chants and incantations remained an integral part of life. For example, what is the best way to cure a woman or a man lusting after a dragon–lover? A potion of gentian and wormwood, of course, accompanied by a purifying night-time ritual involving a fire and a (naked, I believe) female healer. True, church murals in Bulgaria depict scenes where those who have taken cures from beautiful orisnitsi, or witches, are subjected to eccentric punishments in hell, such as having the Devil himself defecate on them, continuously. But to its credit, the Eastern Orthodox Church only condemned pagan practices in principle, not in practice.

Marina's explanation was simpler: oral knowledge is more enduring than the written word. What you pass on from mouth to mouth is hard to destroy, and like folk melodies, fire worship, wine libations, and the honouring of curative springs, the evil eye has been with us since antiquity.

Although the healer insisted that it was pointless to apply psychological interpretations, the Arabic for evil eye translates as 'eye of the envious', which strikes me as *quite* psychological. After all, if you like the plump child or milky cow so much that they fall to the ground, surely you have a little problem? But in the times before psychology, these matters were addressed by a priest, hodja, rabbi, or shaman, and this grassroots psychotherapy clearly works if you're open to it. I asked the healer if she was religious.

'Well…' she trailed off. 'Who has the time?'

Then she told me that the only person she ever refused to heal was an Orthodox priest.

'He was so obsessed with the evil eye, he saw it everywhere and I feared I'd never be rid of him.'

Marina belonged to the small Roman Catholic community, but her true passion was with the elemental world of seasons and energies, where anything was possible.

'The people of Strandja are believers,' she said, 'not Christians.'

And what was I, if I was neither, yet I was looking for something?

'You're a pilgrim in the footsteps of Boreas,' Marina said, typically cryptic.

'Anyway, you don't have uroki,' the healer concluded. 'Neither do you have any condition that benefits from Melt the Bullet.'

It's good to be healthy, but I felt disappointed.

'Just accept it,' Marina came to my help. 'It's the way of Strandja.'

'Hmm,' the healer smiled, sceptical. She was a pragmatic nurse, after all, I thought, and she had other gifts, but lacked Marina's gift for metaphor.

'I've seen many cases of incomers that the mountain doesn't let out,' Marina went on.

There was the Russian woman from Israel who came every summer, and every time her car broke down on the day she tried to leave. The scholar from Sofia who became ill if she didn't get her dose of Strandja. The Polish academic who came for the annual hiking pilgrimage and felt negative energies in his tent, always in the same spot, on the edge of a particular village.

'The Horned One was raging last night, he'd say in the morning.' Marina smiled.

Nobody can figure out Strandja, I thought. Perhaps it isn't a place for humans.

'Strandja is empty of people but it's busy in other ways,' the healer said, as if reading my thoughts. 'Do you know that you can channel energies if you want to? And sometimes if you don't want to.'

I gaped at her.

'I'll Reverse your Footprint. Because you've picked up a lot along the way. It's here with you, in the room. Come,' she said and got up.

She led me to the garden and Marina sat under the vine to wait for us. Knife in hand, the healer led me to the abandoned house next door with an overgrown courtyard. It had to be untrodden soil, energetically calm. She instructed me to place my foot on the ground, toes pointing east. Why east?

The musicians and nestinari before the fire rite face east, she said. The feet of the dead point east. The sun rises in the east. With the knife, she outlined my foot three times anticlockwise, and muttered an incantation three times that I couldn't hear. Then I removed my foot from the spot, and with the knife she cut out and overturned the soil in my footprint.

She straightened up.

'All bad energy stays here. All that you don't need. You are free.'

Amen. I wanted to believe it, or else I would be scared. She touched my arm.

'One more thing,' she said. 'Go wash in Saint Marina.'

Marina and I walked down the scenic broken street. The empty square slumbered in greenery and afternoon heat. The big old houses were shuttered. A lone rooster crowed on the other side of the valley.

Marina had returned to live in her native border town because of aged parents. They were among the oldest clans, not refugees from Turkey but indigenous, here since the early days of settlement, and now dying out in this ghost town. I had known Marina for two years but she remained an enigma. She never spoke about herself. She now ran a children's day-centre where the few remaining kids of the town came to paint, read, dry herbs, and be healed from family life and things like cutting trees in the forest with an axe, because some kids were from Gypsy woodcutter families. The children adored her and I adored her too. In this plundered place, she cared about everything, from small people to big trees.

Marina sighed and lit another cigarette.

'Living here,' she said, 'I've learnt the futility of planning for the future. You are glad if the present still exists.'

Marina frequented hidden places in the hills. One of them was The Stone, an ancient cult site where you feel heat through the stone, as with the standing stones of Orkney.

'Have you been back to the Village in the Valley?' Marina asked.

'No, not yet. Who's Boreas?'

She smiled, in that shaky noncommittal way she had.

'The northern wind. Moves anticlockwise. But even Boreas must stop.'

It was time to say goodbye. Marina looked at me without making eye contact.

'We are not saying goodbye,' she said, turned on her heel, and walked away under the lime trees that cast thick shadows in the empty square.

I returned to the Village in the Valley. The corkscrew road had been fixed, and at first I was glad to see positive change. But it was fixed only for the lorries that continued to carry away the riverbed, of which less and less remained, until one day it would be a river without a bed.

What is a river without a bed? It is like a village without people.

The new threat people discussed in hushed tones was not just to the river, but to the whole of the Strandja national park: that it might become a super-dump, the backdoor garbage pit of newly planned resorts on the already overbuilt Black Sea coast. The stranglehold of big business and state interests tightened its grip over Strandja, and on both sides of the border, big business and state interests seemed fused solid.

What remains sacred if a sacred mountain becomes a super-dump? I felt strongly that within my lifetime, we may all become exiles. That we may all be robbed by devouring daemons disguised as policy and industry, that we may all walk down some road carrying in plastic bags our memories of forests and mountains, clean rivers and village lanes.

In fact, refugees were coming down the hills from Turkey in great numbers now. The locals were baffled; some went and bought food to distribute, others sat on benches and stared curiously at the strangers; yet others went home and closed the door, just in case. A woodcutter couple had not returned home one night, and when their family went looking for them, they found them tied to a tree. The Syrian men who had done this were determined not to be handed to border patrols again.

Blago and Minka hadn't moved from their seats at The Disco and welcomed me warmly but without fuss, as if they'd last seen me just a week before.

Ivo the herbalist stood at the corner, dignified with his white moustache, discussing his latest recipe with the Polish émigré S., who recognised me and shook my hand with emotion. He was pleased to see the ranks of returning émigrés expand, even if only for a few days.

Local Gypsy workers stripped to the waist were painting the mayory a glamorous dusky pink, and children shrieked in the new playground. D. the honey-maker and a few other men were now growing corn in the river meanders, and sprinklers livened up the path that led to

Kreynero fountain. A couple of babies had been born. Hope surged in my heart.

'Don't get too rose-tinted,' the mayor said, lighting a cigarette in the square with grease-covered hands after fixing a van. 'This is peak time. Nothing has changed. I lie awake at night and wonder how to raise the dead.' The school was key, the handsome yellow school which continued to gape with its broken windows, while chickens pecked at an old mattress discarded in the courtyard. The swimming pool was full of weeds. For the school to reopen, enough children had to be born and raised here, and for that to happen, the parents had to have a livelihood away from the city, and not everyone is cut out for border policing or forestry.

Big Stamen and his brother worked for the sand-extracting company at the river, because there was no other work. This conflict had driven a silent wedge in the community, like another axe-blow from some deranged god who doesn't know when to stop. The river was so churned up, you couldn't swim in it.

Otherwise, it was the rakia-brewing season, and the small village brewery was busy round the clock, as each household took its barrel of sugar-fermented fruit to the bubbling giant cauldrons, tasting and double-tasting. It was a matter of pride how your home brew turned out. Everybody had a rosy flush, and the village was infused with a sweet alcoholic vapour so potent you felt tipsy just breathing it in.

Nedko's mother had died and he lived alone in the big panoramic house at the top of the lane. One evening, he cooked a rich bean and pork stew on his outside stove, and the beautiful Russian and I joined him under the vines, whispering about strange dreams and signs while Nedko picked peaches for us from his garden trees, to wash down with rakia. As soon as we stopped talking, the silence of the mountain rushed in like a fourth presence. I could almost touch it next to me at the table, the humanless, ancient silence of Strandja. In the moonlight the bulk of the nearby hills loomed as alien as ever, and I couldn't help but feel that somehow, we shouldn't be here at all, that no human truly belonged in starry Strandja, that we were all just passing through on our way elsewhere.

I slept in a house owned by an absent English couple, sat eating goat's yogurt on the outside steps, and at The Disco, Minka placed fried liver before me.

'Enjoy.'

And together, we sat gazing at the hills that rise and fall, rise and fall like an old dream from which you can't wake up. Until I saw another possible life for myself reflected in the disturbed river.

A crossroads appears twice in the mythical mind: when you travel and when you die. In both cases, you must make a choice that shapes your next destination. In Strandja folklore, the left-hand road leads to darkness (Chaos), and the right-hand road leads to light (Cosmos).

I saw myself move into one of the old Greek houses with a curious removable tile in the roof. I'd take a job marking trees in the forest and earn just enough to buy logs for winter. In winter, my bones would feel old and I'd count the months to spring. In spring, the fire-walkers would trample the embers to the belly-sound of bagpipe and drum. In summer, the border guards would fire salvoes, the Wee One would open his accordion, yesterday's killers would offer me home brews, and the mothers would cackle with missing teeth. In autumn, I'd watch the falcons hang in the rain like omens. A creaky door would open into the old house with an iron-frame bed, blackened pots left behind by the Greeks, abandoned photographs of children, faded faces from some unmournable past that lives under the skin. As if the border itself was the collective skin. As if, by staying in the Village in the Valley for ever, I'd be reunited with something. All the roads and crossroads of my adulthood, all the arrivals and departures, all the cities and faces vanished when I was in the Village in the Valley, like mist over the hills. All I had to do was drink from the River Lethe. What is more atavistically pleasing than the end of the road?

I was an animal that wanted to drag itself to its original drinking hole. Back to that red Riviera beach, to a borderline state where innocence meets transgression.

The border forest is where destiny becomes manifest, if we linger too long. No wonder it repels and attracts like a karmic magnet. In the border forest, we condemn and absolve ourselves, again and again. There is death foretold in that, and there is immense compulsion.

Then one day Marina's voice came to me: *We are not saying goodbye.* And I woke up and looked away from the river. I packed my bags. I packed Galen's geranium root from the Bears' Cave, Mr and Mrs Karadeniz's garlic wreath, Nursel's knitted socks, Ventsi's pigeons. Autumn was already gilding the days and hornets had stung the grapes black. Without saying goodbye to anyone, I drove to the border river, abandoned the car inside a grove, and took a churned-up track that can't be driven, only walked. You fall down and get up again, on your knees if you have to, like the oxen.

To the forest where the bones are yet to be named and the ghosts are so many we must thank them for making room for us, the living.

To the cave worshipped by mists, animists and monotheists, the poor and the lost, the wise and the insane.

The border was a few hundred metres away, and the cave of Saint Marina was above the river, reached along a steep path. The forest was rich with birdsong and imminent autumn. The river glinted with gold. Snakes waited under stones.

Melted candles, damp photographs, and votive carvings sat in the entrance, inviting a miracle. Miniature people, organs to be cured, hands that held nothing, calls from the voiceless. I took off my T-shirt, tore it into strips and looked for somewhere to hang them. Then I crawled into the cave. We arrive naked and depart with empty hands. It's good to practise lest we forget.

I lay under the dripping rock which is really – when you look up – a mountain of living stone, and washed my changing face in the water that doesn't change, crazy with love for this earth where everything begins with a spring.

ACKNOWLEDGEMENTS
AND SOURCES

I would like to thank Creative Scotland for the grant which supported the production of this book. My gratitude equally goes to the Society of Authors for their Authors' Foundation grant.

Sarah Chalfant was instrumental in the early shaping and encouragement of these narratives and has my deep appreciation.

Laura Barber of Granta believed in the border project early on, which helped me continue. I thank her also for her astute and sensitive editing, as ever.

Thank you to Nedret Benzet and Sasha Kartchev, who selflessly acted as translators on my travels. Special thanks to Maria Dimieva, Diana Stoyanova, Hairi Milezimov, Orlin Sabev, Dimana Trankova, and Chris Fenton-Thomas of Wild Thyme Organic Farm.

Border is also the title of a Bulgarian feature film (*Granitza*, 1994, written and directed by I. Simeonov and C. Nochev). An early feature I wrote on Strandja appeared in *1843* magazine (then *Intelligent Life*) – thanks to Samantha Weinberg.

Dagmar Gaster in Berlin first wrote about the artist Felix S., not his real name. Stephan Appelius is the expert on Cold War German escapes at the Bulgarian border and holds the case histories, some of which are available through the Konrad Adenauer Foundation. Versions of some of these, including Thomas von Grumbkow, Grigor Vassilev, Todor Georgiev, Ilcho Haralampiev, Brigitte von Kistowski, and Klaus

Prautzsch are featured in the German TV documentaries *Die Verges-senen: Tod wo andere Urlaub machen* ('The Forgotten: To Die Where Others Holiday', 2011, directed by Freya Klier and Andreas Kuno Richter) and *Fatal Flight* (2014, directed by Paul Tutsek and Dieter Roser). Kirsten Ghodsee used the term 'red Riviera' in her epony-mous book, where I first came across it. Mary Neuburger's *Balkan Smoke* is the source on matters of Oriental tobacco. 'In the Footsteps of the Nestinari from Madzhura to UNESCO' by T. Gondov puts forward the thesis that the Hesychasts may be the original *anastenarides*. These books were useful in my research: *Stasiland* by Anna Funder, *Black Sea* by Neal Ascherson, *Gypsies in the Ottoman Empire* by Elena Marushiakova and Veselin Popov, *Levant* by Philip Mansel, *A Short History of Byzantium* by John Julius Norwich. On the subject of Bulgar-ian Muslims and the Ottoman legacy, *The Turks of Bulgaria* by Anthony Georgieff et al. and *The Orient Within* by Mary Neuburger were val-uable sources; the feature film *Stolen Eyes* (2005, directed by Radoslav Spasov) is a powerful rendition of the events of summer 1989. *A Guide to Thracian Bulgaria* by Dimana Trankova et al and *Tamara Shishman and Murad I* by Anna Buxton were helpful resources. The two photo-graphs described in 'Girl Between Languages' are from *Göçün orta yeri hüzün* ('Migrant Sorrow'), a photographic book by Behiç Günalan. *You Believe: Eight Views on the Holocaust in the Balkans* by Lea Cohen presents lesser known aspects of Jewish history.

The Esma Redžepova quote is from *Princes Among Men* by Garth Cartwright. Georgi Markov's *The Women of Warsaw*, quoted on page 5, is a novella set in Strandja. The quotation from Ryszard Kapuściński in the chapter 'The Chicken Shack' is from his *Travels with Herodotus*. The 'Hymn to Hermes' quotation is from *The Homeric Hymns* (Pen-guin Classics), translated by Jules Cashford. The *tarikh* by Evliya Çelebi is my rendition from the Bulgarian translation of the Turkish origi-nal, as it appeared in *Svilengrad: From Antiquity to Modernity*, edited by

Kalina Peeva and Elena Miteva. All other Evliya Çelebi quotations are from *An Ottoman Traveller*, edited by Robert Dankoff and Sooyong Kim. The incantation against *uroki*, in my translation, is from Странджа ('Strandja') by Stoyan Raichevski, an ethnographic study where the symbolism of liminal landmarks is seen through the folkloric imagination. I have borrowed the comparison of Bulgarian-style communist totalitarianism with feudalism from two other writers: Georgi Markov in 'Bulgarian Reportages in Absentia' (published in English, after his assassination, as *The Truth That Killed*) and Misha Glenny in *The Rebirth of History*. The documentary film *Goryani* (2011, written and directed by Atanas Kirjakov) is a rare source on Bulgaria's early anti-Soviet resistance movement.

This book touches on many complex areas of specialism. I have no scholarly claims, though I have striven to the best of my ability for truthfulness and accuracy where events are related by me, rather than related to me by others or through secondary and tertiary sources.

My incalculable love goes to TD (everything begins with a spring) who not only endured my border obsession for three years, but helped me find my way through it.

But above all, I want to thank with all my heart the people of the border who let me in, both the living and the dead. You were not vehicles for the story of the border – you are the story.

Keep in touch with
Granta Books:

Visit grantabooks.com to discover more.

GRANTA

TWELVE MINUTES OF LOVE

A Tango Story

Kapka Kassabova

'A sharp, clever and engaging tale of obsession' *Independent on Sunday*

From downtown Buenos Aires to the banks of the Seine, Kapka
Kassabova has danced the tango. But tango is never just about the dance,
and here she takes us on an exhilarating journey across the globe in search
of music, adventure, love and belonging.

'A mesmeric memoir of love, lust and tango' *Marie Claire*

'This is more than a book about dancing. It is about people, places,
movement, love, trouble, a journey. I was gripped' Monique Roffey

'This mix of travel writing, personal experience and history is
something that Kassabova is frankly brilliant at… a wonderful mix of
self-deprecating humour and genuine insight' *Independent on Sunday*

'Travel writing is dead. Long live great travel writing' GQ

'Hilarious and moving, poignant and occasionally sublime' *Big Issue*

'Warm, witty and deftly written' *Time Out* ★★★★

'A captivating and elegant meditation on love, longing, travel
and the art of the tango. Kassabova is a powerful new voice
whose writing demonstrates, in every sentence, that non-fiction
can be every bit as creative as fiction' Aminatta Forna

STREET WITHOUT A NAME

Childhood and Other Misadventures in Bulgaria

Kapka Kassabova

'A fascinating book, at once evocative, disturbing,
and chock-a-block full of charm' Jan Morris

Born on the muddy outskirts of Sofia, Kapka Kassabova grew up under
Communism in the 1980s, got away as soon as she could, and has loved
and hated her homeland in equal measure ever since. When Bulgaria
officially joins the EU club, Kapka revisits the country and her own
muddled relationship to it to discover just how much it – and she – has
changed. With the irreverence of an expat and the curiosity of a visitor,
Kapka travels back to the surreal scenes of her childhood when the shops
were empty and the walls had ears; samples its bizarre tourist sites and
rough-hewn hospitality industry; and uncovers its centuries-old history
of bloodshed and blurred borders.

'In the mosaic of books about the bad old days, this book is the piece
that was always missing. Now we have it, and it shines' Clive James

'Poignant and sometimes extremely funny, she has painted a rich
but honest picture of a small, very beautiful and endlessly fascinating
country. A very fine piece of writing' Misha Glenny, *Guardian*

'Not many books on the travel shelves have the force of revelation,
but this one does. Kassabova leads us into her country with an elegant
assurance, an acid wit and a heart-rending precision that can make you
see the world quite differently. This book is a treasure' Pico Iyer

'Sharply observed and poignant, this is a skilful, highly
readable memoir and travelogue' Vesna Goldsworthy